D0016033

ALSO BY CHARLES J. GIVENS

Wealth Without Risk
Financial Self-Defense
More Wealth Without Risk

SuperSelf

Doubling Your Personal Effectiveness

Charles J. Givens

Simon & Schuster
New York London Toronto Sydney Tokyo Singapore

SIMON & SCHUSTER
Rockefeller Center
1230 Avenue of the Americas
New York, New York 10020

Designed by Irving Perkins Associates
Manufactured in the United States of America

1 3 5 7 9 10 8 6 4 2

Library of Congress Cataloging-in-Publication Data
Givens, Charles J.
SuperSelf: doubling your personal effectiveness / Charles J. Givens.
p. cm.
1. Career development. 2. Self-realization. 3. Success. I. Title.
HF5381.G554 1993
158—dc20 93-36548
CIP
ISBN: 0-671-70097-9

This book is based on the author's practical personal experience and does not purport to provide psychological counseling.

To

Chuck and

Rob,

my sons,

and

Adena, my wife,

my greatest supporters

Contents

Contents

PART III
Doubling Your Personal Effectiveness

SuperSelf

is the operations
manual for creating
your life.

Preface

There's a You inside of you that you may not have discovered or experienced yet—at least not on a continuous basis. It's the You able to achieve more than you ever imagined. It's the You able to make a personal or business plan and stick to it, bringing it in on time and on budget with no need for praise or accolades from anyone, just the satisfaction of knowing that once you think it, you can do it. It's the You who welcomes new challenges with zest instead of trepidation; who deals with the inevitable loss of a job, money, or someone close as a natural part of life instead of as a devastating problem or some kind of punishment. It is You in control of your life instead of being controlled by circumstances, events, children, bosses, parents, and plain old fear.

That You is someone you already are, and someone you can begin to experience immediately, if you develop a set of personal abilities that few know about and even fewer apply. That You is your SuperSelf, and my job in this book is to help you bring it out.

Preface

Although most people associate my name with powerful, unique financial strategies, I long ago discovered there is more to life than winning with money. Of course, having the money to take care of yourself and your family so you can live out your dreams is not just an individual objective, it's universal. All too often that goal seems beyond reach. But what if every area of your life—from career and finances to all your relationships and personal goals and accomplishments—worked just the way you would design it if you were in complete and total control? And what if there was still time left over to travel, relax, and do everything else you've ever wanted to do—all with minimum stress? You would be operating at maximum effectiveness. You would be experiencing your SuperSelf.

"Well, you can't have it all," I hear you saying. I'm here to tell you that you can. You can design your life so that it's full of rewarding accomplishments and positive emotions, with a minimum of the frustration, fear, anger, resentment, boredom, loneliness, and other negative emotions that can deprive you of even the smallest crumb of excitement and vitality. But it won't happen by accident.

You can have it all only by learning to bring out that someone you already are—your SuperSelf.

Just as there is a set of financial strategies that enables you to win constantly with your money—the subject of my three number-one best-selling books—there is also a definitive set of concrete strategies that enables you to win in every aspect of your life. I call them my Success Strategies. During the time you and I spend together through the pages of this book, you will discover these strategies, and in the process you will become equipped to apply them, one by one, to your life.

Real wealth

Monetary wealth is only one piece of the puzzle of life. Real or total wealth is determined by the level of your ability to live out your dreams and achieve your goals, regardless of whether others consider them practical or outrageous. Real wealth is measured by your ability to enjoy every moment of the experience of accomplishing those dreams and goals. My Success Strategies will help you acquire this ability. In this book, I will share them with you in clear-cut terms so that little is left to chance and so that the possibility of failure is eliminated. Put quite simply, my Success Strategies will enable you to master the art of successful living by creating a blueprint for realizing your dreams and goals and by doubling your personal effectiveness as you work to achieve them.

These strategies are based on my own personal experience of what works and what doesn't. I don't have a corner on truth, but I'm certain that it's the application of these strategies, far more than my financial strategies, that is responsible for creating the incredible wealth, success, and happiness I have enjoyed for the past twenty years. I discovered these strategies primarily through trial and error, and although some of them may sound familiar to you, for the first time you will both understand and learn to apply them as a complete system with no missing pieces. Taken all together, these strategies represent a brand-new results-producing approach to life and how to live it to the max.

The Success Strategies

A strategy is a formula for action. It tells you what to do, when to do it, and how to get it done. The formula contained in each strategy produces a positive, desired, predictable result.

To qualify as a strategy, a formula must work, work every

time, and work for everyone. That's a tall order, and that's why this book was almost fifteen years in the making. I knew the strategies, all right, inside and out, almost all of them discovered and proven from my own life experience and the rest from my direct observation of the experiences of others. The question became, How do you teach the all-important but virtually undiscovered strategies of successful living with clarity of meaning and motivation through a mere hundred thousand or so words in a book?

That level of precision took me fifteen years to master, and its success has already been demonstrated in the financial lives of millions—yes, millions—of people who have read my books or attended any of the three thousand lectures and workshops the Charles J. Givens Organization conducts each year throughout the world. That's some kind of track record, but it's exactly the kind of record you should demand from someone who is confident enough to claim that through the pages of a book he can immediately and positively affect your future, empowering you to run your life in the direction and at a speed chosen by you.

Best of all, in this process you are no guinea pig. Teaching these strategies and observing the results are not new to me. I first began teaching them in 1975, when I created the Awareness Motivation Institute, which in 1980 became the Charles J. Givens Foundation, which in turn grew into the Charles J. Givens Organization. From the beginning, I have watched many people who attended my programs achieve incredible results in planning and controlling their own futures, and enjoying the rewards of personal effectiveness beyond their wildest imaginings.

The ability to plan your own future and to double your level of personal effectiveness is precisely what's in store for you when you incorporate my Success Strategies into your daily life. My Success Strategies are formulas for personal action designed to produce positive, predictable results. Science is also based on discovering formulas for predictable results. If you throw a rubber ball up against a concrete wall, the result is predictable and mathematically definable. The ball will bounce back—every time. The same result will occur no matter how many times you throw the ball against the wall. If you throw it up against the wall one hundred times, the ball will bounce back a hundred times. There are no exceptions. My Success Strategies have the same predictability. They are carefully crafted and consciously chosen actions that will give you optimum control over your life in the present and in the future.

It took me many years to identify, quantify, and catalogue this set of strategies. I have clearly defined and explained them in the pages of this book. The prime responsibility for applying these strategies, however, is yours. That is something I cannot do for you. Along the path from where you are now to becoming your SuperSelf, you will battle old, ingrained habits and responses that have been responsible for many of the failures and disappointments you have experienced in your life. That fight is worth winning because the victory will allow you to master life instead of being manipulated by life. No one who has the determination and desire to win that battle has ever lost it for any other reason.

Your objective is to transform my Success Strategies into new habits that will guarantee success, not failure—a process that requires constant, conscious repetition. Once you master these strategies, they will enable you to create your own blueprint for life and automatically compress time, allowing you to accomplish twice as much in an hour, day, month, or year as you turn that blueprint into concrete reality. In other words, you will experience your SuperSelf in every area of your life.

People who have spent time around me and my family invariably ask us the same five questions:

1. Why are you always happy, excited, and full of energy?
2. Why don't you ever get angry or yell?

3. How can you run a huge, successful business conglomerate and yet find the time to spend three months every year traveling and exploring the world, never allowing anyone to call you about business?
4. How did you get to the point where you are always ahead of schedule instead of being controlled by schedules?
5. What's the reason why you always seem to come out a winner, no matter what the adversity?

The answer to all five questions is the same. Every day of my life my family and I live and apply the strategies I am about to share with you.

How my Success Strategies will change your life

There is no standing still in life for those who have discovered and applied my Success Strategies. What once seemed like major barriers become minor obstacles. Dreams and goals which may have seemed unreachable become a reality. You will find yourself in control of your time, your direction, and your life. When the world seems to be collapsing around you, you will remain solid as a rock, able to take on willingly whatever life throws your way. You will find yourself confident, courageous, and able to make the right decisions and take the right actions. When everything around you is in an uproar, you will remain mentally and emotionally balanced.

That is the experience of your SuperSelf, the ability to plan and control your future, to increase your personal effectiveness, and to get what you want done when you want it done. Your SuperSelf knows no limitations and does not recognize your age, sex, color, education, level of wealth, or past as a handicap.

Preface

Once you learn to apply my Success Strategies, life becomes much simpler. You know what you want and how to get it, what to do and when to do it, and what to say and when to say it. This doesn't mean that you will no longer face adversity or problems. It does mean you will have a set of tools for dealing effectively with whatever comes up. You will find yourself equipped to handle problems and stumbling blocks quickly and effectively, with a minimum of wasted motion and emotion.

Winners in life understand that walls are for bouncing balls, while losers are constantly attempting to walk through those same walls, bumping their heads and complaining of the frustration and pain. Much of the difficulty in dealing with and controlling life, including designing and controlling your future, is the result of attempting to walk through walls instead of accepting the reality that walls don't work that way. A wall itself is neutral. It's not out to get you. It's not bad luck that you bruised your head and it is not someone else's fault. The reality is that if your head and the wall attempt to occupy the same space at the same time, you will end up with a headache. My Success Strategies will save you a countless number of those headaches.

My interest in maximum effectiveness was first piqued in 1957 when I was a sophomore at Decatur High School. Although I considered myself shy and not very good at being myself, I had no problem acting like other people. As a result, I landed the lead in the high school play that year, much to the chagrin of the older students. The play was *Cheaper by the Dozen,* a comedy about the life of Frank Bunker Gilbreth, an industrial engineer who invented the science of time-and-motion study. I played Gilbreth, who, as the patriarch of a family of a dozen children, continually attempted to apply his time-and-motion concepts to the operation of every aspect of his family's life, including how to take a bath.

In one of the most humorous scenes in the play, Gilbreth gathers his wife and all twelve children in the parlor to demonstrate the proper way to take a bath and dry off by moving both the soap and the towel over the entire body in one continuous motion, without wasting time and energy by backtracking. Although the scene generated great laughs, to this day I still take a shower and dry off in slightly less than six minutes using those same procedures.

During my first year of college, I chose courses in time-and-motion study, which seemed both practical and useful to me no matter what career track I would eventually follow. After college, it soon became apparent to me that whatever the situation, every plan, decision, and action could be made more effective, and that the ability to effectively plan and manage your life was a major factor in the process of creating surefire success. Over the years I expanded the basic concepts of effective planning and management until I had developed a dynamic, powerful, and practical system that anyone can employ in every aspect of life. In the following pages, I have broken down this system into a series of Success Strategies that will take you step by step toward the realization of your fullest potential: the you that you have always wanted to be —your SuperSelf.

To Your Success,

Charles J. Givens

Introduction

Doing more of what doesn't work won't make it work any better.

Jobs are lost, relationships are destroyed, emotions run out of control, and huge sums of money are frittered away all for the same reason: attempting to do more of what didn't work in the first place, using what we were taught about life and how it "should" work instead of doing what does work. You and I didn't learn how to use the tools, techniques, and strategies necessary for effectively dealing with life from our parents, our friends, our teachers, or anyone else because, unfortunately, they didn't know them either. It wasn't that they were selfish and wouldn't let us in on their secrets. They just plain didn't know. And we had to learn the hard way—from our own experience.

Success Strategy No. 1:

Learn from the experiences of others, rather than your own.

You can cut the learning curve by up to 90 percent in anything you set out to accomplish through the application of this simple strategy. You become truly wise not when you get a college degree, but when you learn to learn from both the positive and negative experiences of others so that you don't have to repeat their mistakes and travel all of the dead-end roads yourself.

As a child I heard over and over that experience is the best teacher. That piece of parental wisdom is a myth. Learning from your own experience requires a conscious choice. First of all, it does not happen by chance. Otherwise there would not be so many divorces, and surely no one would ever get more than one speeding ticket before figuring out that the only sure way to beat the system is by not speeding. I once had a seventy-year-old man in one of my SuperSelf classes who had been married four times—to the same woman—and he was currently contemplating divorce again. So much for learning from your own experience.

Secondly, not only is your own experience often not the best teacher, it is generally the most time-consuming and painful teacher. But much of the time and pain can be eliminated by learning to learn from the experiences of others rather than your own. Mimic the actions of those you know or read about who continuously produce success and constantly overcome adversity. Avoid the actions of those who seem to produce and perpetuate problems. Or better still, follow the strategies outlined in this book, and you can quickly accomplish what might have taken months or years of observation and evaluation to figure out.

Live your life as most people do and you will be forced to settle for what most people settle for.

In life, most people become masters of mediocrity, spending more time just dreaming about living than they spend living out their dreams.

Let me ask you this: If you made a list of all your dreams and goals and were then given the tools to propel yourself toward their accomplishment twice as fast and with twice the level of confidence and happiness, would you then be open to some powerful, positive changes? Making changes is the only way to accelerate your ability to accomplish what you want in life.

If you have dreams, I will show you how to make them come true, beginning from where you are right now. I can't supply your dreams, but I know all the changes you will have to make in your life to reach them in the minimum time. You may feel stuck where you are, but you do have the power to change. My Success Strategies will give you that power.

By now you may be asking yourself, Okay, exactly what's involved here? What's in it for me? That's simple. My Success Strategies will enable you to:

- Double your personal effectiveness
- Make things happen . . . instead of waiting for things to happen
- Control your own mind . . . instead of being controlled by others
- Control your emotions . . . instead of allowing your emotions to control you
- Double your creative power
- Create happiness, joy, and aliveness . . . instead of waiting or wishing for them to happen

- Produce results . . . instead of becoming trapped along the way
- Eliminate fear, anger, guilt, and worry . . . instead of allowing these emotions to cripple you
- Build positive, powerful synergistic relationships . . . instead of having to "work at" relationships

Sound too good to be true? Believe me, it's all possible if you follow my Success Strategies. Here's how they work:

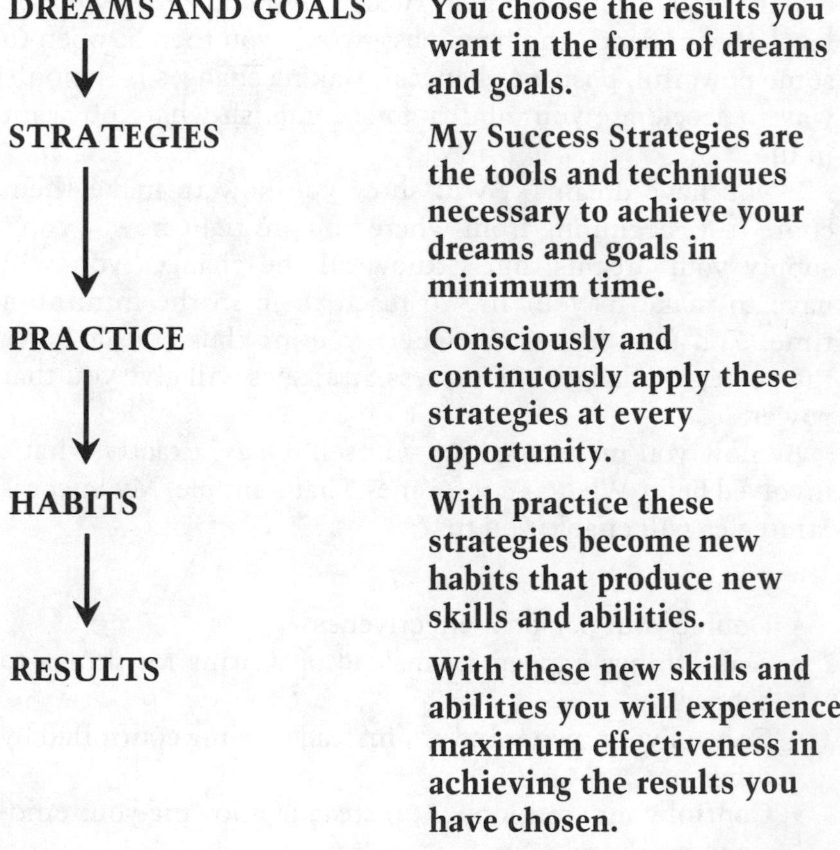

As you can see, it's an easy, practical, and powerful step-by-step process. And the results are guaranteed. So let's get started.

PART I

Experiencing Your SuperSelf

CHAPTER 1

Where You Is, Is Where You Is

Life is like an ice cream cone, you have to lick it one day at a time.

—Charlie Brown

The world, your world and my world, is composed of only three time zones—the past, the present, and the future. Focusing your mind exclusively on the past or the future will get you into trouble and render you ineffective while you are in the present. All of your power to accomplish, your ability to be effective, make decisions, be happy, and to exert maximum personal control over your life, lies only in each succession of present moments.

Your only point of power is in the present moment.

Think about it. If you want to move the chair you're sitting on, you can only do it in the present. Even your physical power is limited to the now. You cannot move the chair in either the past or the future. You can wish you had moved the chair yesterday, or last week, you can think about moving it sometime in the future, but neither your wishes nor your thoughts are of any consequence.

You have no power to change your past physically. However, you do have the power in the present moment to change your thoughts, feelings, and attitude about bygone events. After all, it is your mind, your emotions, and your attitude, and in any single present moment no one has power over them except you—unless you give that power to other people or to past events by the way you choose to think about them.

In effect, you can choose either to react or to respond to your past. *Reacting* to your past is the process of allowing your thoughts to trigger and stir up the same negative emotions about past events you didn't like when you experienced them the first time. *Responding* to your past is the process of accepting where you are in the present as an okay place to be, and then dealing with your past as nothing more than a stream of already lived events that have no direct power over your present other than that which you give it. Mentally accept where you are and move on from there.

All too often when you dredge up unpleasant memories, you trigger the negative emotions of guilt or self-criticism characterized by self-flagellating thoughts of what should have, could have, or ought to have been. Or you center the blame on people, events, or bad luck, and end up experiencing in the present the negative emotions of anger, hate, self-pity, jealousy, revenge, and resentment. Yet you have changed nothing. You have punished no one—except yourself. All you have done is render yourself ineffective and emotionally out of balance, leaving yourself powerless in the present. Which is the easiest way to run a hundred yards: pulling a wagon loaded with two hundred pounds of bricks, or totally unimpeded by anything dragging along behind you?

Success Strategy No. 2:

To design and control your future effectively, you must first let go of your past.

The more you dwell on the past, the more the past limits and controls your future. In taking control of your life you must begin with a clean slate. That means dumping the garbage of the past and its hold on you.

It is all too easy to get caught up and trapped in the magnitude of what happened to you in the past, whether in your childhood or the day before yesterday. In reality, whatever negative experiences have happened to you will often seem gargantuan, simply because they were your experiences. You can even begin to feel as if you're the only one who ever had to go through such trauma.

You may be surprised at what other people around you have also gone through that they don't often talk about. Over the past eighteen years in the two-day SuperSelf seminars I've conducted, people have voluntarily shared their most devastating, emotionally traumatic past experiences. To help you put the baggage from your past in perspective, I want you to know that I've heard and seen it all.

- Hundreds of descriptions of child abuse, with crippling memories and emotions carried forward into adulthood and parenthood
- Couples who have lost a child to murder, auto accidents, and war
- Physically and emotionally abused women and men
- People destroyed financially by loss of a job, a business, a lawsuit, even the IRS

This is not a list from the waiting room of a psychotherapist's office. These are the past experiences of individuals and couples I've met personally, successful and supersuccessful included. Traumatic memories of past events cross all socioeconomic lines, races, sexes, and neighborhoods. You are not alone. Almost without exception, people everywhere are unconsciously held prisoners of their past. It is difficult to be alive without having gone through many traumatic experiences. But your past, no matter what it contained, can be either a quagmire of negative emotions to drag into your future or a solid platform of opportunities for future accomplishments.

Success Strategy No. 3:

To get where you want to go, first firmly plant your feet on the ground where you are.

The rapid accomplishment of your dreams and goals requires acknowledging and accepting where you are, what you are, who you are, and what you have done in life, for the indisputable universal truth remains: Where you is, is where you is. Mentally accept that where you are now is an okay place to be, at least temporarily, regardless of what has happened to you in the distant or recent past. Given the opportunity, your past can stay around to haunt you. Don't give it that opportunity. You simply cannot afford the extra baggage.

Accept Yourself Exactly Where You Are No Matter What Your Circumstances

If I'm in an unfulfilling job I despise . . .
If I'm in a fat body . . .
If I'm in a lousy relationship . . .
If I'm in a wheelchair . . .
If my spouse dumped me for another man (woman) . . .
If I'm broke and deep in debt . . .
If my children don't understand me . . .
If my parents don't understand me . . .
If I'm continually frustrated and depressed . . .
If I'm lonely and bored . . .
If I feel unloved, unattractive, and unappreciated . . .
If I've lost my job . . .
If I've lost my confidence . . .
If I've lost everything I had . . .

Where I Is, Is Where I Is— But Where I'm Going Is Up to Me

Imagine yourself standing on the bank of a fast-flowing river. The only safe way across is a series of slippery, moss-covered rocks protruding only slightly above the rushing water. As you start across, it becomes obvious that the best way to step onto the next rock is to first firmly plant both feet on the slippery rock beneath you. With both feet firmly planted, you have created maximum balance and stability with which to make your next move. Your only point of balance lies on the rock beneath you. At that moment you have no choice or chance of being somewhere else. Complaining about the circumstances that got you there will only distract your focus from the task at hand—to get to safety on the other side of the river. Feeling and thinking like a victim—"Why me, what did I ever do to deserve this?"—will only contribute to your ending up in the water, almost as a way of proving to yourself that you truly are a victim and worthy of sympathy.

Take your attention away from where you are and you dramatically increase your chances of missing your mark, of ending up in the very circumstances you sought to avoid. Attempt to leap quickly from slippery rock to slippery rock and you will, more than likely, end up in the water, wet and struggling. But if you keep your focus on exactly where you are and stop to regain your balance after every step, slowly, consistently, and persistently, you can make your way from rock to rock no matter how slippery the path.

In life, gaining a firm foothold comes from accepting yourself and your present circumstances, no matter how much you wish you were someone or somewhere else. The refusal to accept leads to frustration with your current circumstances, anger about past events and the actions of other people, guilt and anguish about your own behavior, and loss of courage and confidence in your ability to handle what is going on around you. Acknowledging and accepting where you are does not mean giving up or taking your vision off your desired future. It does not mean you have become satisfied or complacent. On the contrary, accepting where you are puts you in a position to exert maximum control and influence over your future, because you are operating from your only point of power—the present moment.

Your strategy is to keep your focus on the present. From now on, whenever you find yourself caught up in the emotions of the past, including anger, guilt, and self-doubt, say to yourself or even out loud, "Where I is, is where I is." I've done just exactly that thousands of times over the last twenty-five years. Every time you catch yourself caught in the negative events of the past, use that statement to get back to business in the present—time and time again, until it happens almost automatically. At that point you will find that your past is losing its emotional grip on you. Eventually, through constant repetition of this process you will lose all emotional attachment to the past—no matter what and how much happened to you.

Remember, the past is no longer real. Your only reality is the present moment. Your past is only a set of thoughts that could just as easily have come from a movie as from your own experiences. That stream of thoughts cannot possibly control your life or your future—unless you allow it to occupy your mind and divert your attention from the task at hand. Anytime that happens, take back control of your own mind by refocusing on the present.

I didn't learn what I know about the importance of dumping your past from any high school or college psychology textbook. In my life a tough childhood wasn't theory. It was for real, and what I was forced to learn from my own experience I've shared with thousands of people, who have been able to use the same techniques and strategies to release the hold the past has had over them.

My father and mother married in 1937 in Chicago. A couple of years later they moved 180 miles away to the small town of Decatur, Illinois, where my father used his skills as a salesman to start a home-remodeling business, which specialized in roofing, siding, and eventually a new product called Perma Stone. He knew how to run a successful business and gather the right people around him, and before long the tiny C. J. Company, which had been started on a shoestring, became supersuccessful by small-town standards. Soon my parents belonged to all the right clubs, became part of the Decatur elite, and bought a lovely three-story, three-bedroom house in the fashionable west end of town. During this time, the 1940s, my brother and I were born and were brought up with all the amenities: maids, nannies, two new cars, the right school, and incredible vacations lasting weeks, sometimes months.

To all appearances, my parents had everything a couple could want. But as well as they knew how to handle their business and social lives, it became obvious that no one had ever taught them how to live their personal lives. With each new business success they grew more and more apart, my mother spending every day at the South Side Country Club losing large sums of money in the quarter slot machines, and my father spending more and more time away from home—some said with his parade of girlfriends, others said on hunting trips, and in truth a combination of the two. The arguments grew fiercer and fiercer as both began drinking heavily. My mother would call the police at least once a week to have my father arrested, but the chief of police was his buddy and partner in several gambling ventures, so he never stayed downtown long, which made my mother even more furious. Because of their personal problems, and because my father was spending more time drinking with his key people than selling, the business began to decline rapidly.

Then one night, after the fight to end all fights, which culminated with my father putting his hand through a glass door and bleeding profusely all over the carpet, he left. We hardly saw him more than once a year after that, usually at Thanksgiving and sometimes at Christmas when my mother would allow him to come over to see his kids, but only for a couple of hours.

Their nasty divorce was finalized in 1953, and in the settlement my father gave the business to my mother and told her he expected to see her out on the street. In those days, men and certainly construction crews did not take orders well from a woman, especially one who could be as demanding and bossy as my mother. Within a year the business was bankrupt. To try to save it, my parents had already spent all the money they had put aside to send me and my brother to college. As things got worse, my mother spent the money that should have been withheld for the employees' payroll taxes. When the IRS finally found out, it pulled the plug.

My first encounter with the IRS was when people showed up at our house on South Westlawn with a moving van and took everything we owned, including our furniture, my mother's expensive clothes, my electric train set, and even my piano. The only things they missed were our bicycles, which were stored in a room under the house. Everything was sold at a public auction and my mother never recovered from the humiliation and embarrassment. When the house was also sold, the money was taken by the courts to pay the debts and my mother, brother, and I were forced to move into an old, run-down, damp clapboard house that was sold later at an auction for only two thousand dollars.

My mother, in her inability to deal with the losses in her life, became an alcoholic. For the next twenty years, until she died from alcohol abuse at a relatively young age, she drank an entire quart of liquor every night. Still, she was able to sober up in the morning and finally got a job as a low-paid bookkeeper, with half of her salary going for liquor and cigarettes. Even though our rent for the dump we lived in was only sixty dollars a month, there was not much left for food.

Alcohol brought out the pent-up anger, hate, and violence in my mother. She hated the world, her life, her ex-husband, and whenever she was drunk she also hated the sight of me because, she would scream, "You remind me of your S.O.B. father. You're just like him!" She yelled at the top of her lungs for two hours every night until she passed out and all would be quiet again until the next night. My brother and I were never allowed to mention her drinking. We had lost our possessions, our father, and now our mother, and had nowhere to turn.

Within two years, my mother's nightly verbal attacks took on the extra dimension of physical violence, and soon everything in the house that was breakable was broken. When my brother and I locked ourselves in our room to get away from her, she would take a butcher knife and stab at the door until it was in splinters. As a young teenager, I found that the best way to avoid the violence was to stay out at night in the local pool hall or wherever else I could stay for a few hours. When I came home, as punishment for leaving I would find all my possessions, from clothes to schoolbooks, in the front yard. If it was raining they would be covered with mud. There was no escape. At thirteen, with $6.50 in my pocket to buy a train ticket, I ran away to Chicago to my aunt's. She sent me home. No one would listen. No one wanted to deal with the situation. At least two or three nights a week, one or more of the neighbors would call the police, but they seemed powerless to do anything except file another disturbance-of-the-peace complaint. Our family was the neighborhood joke.

As time went on it only got worse. In a rage one night, my mother was in the kitchen and while my back was turned she flung a two-pound meat cleaver at me. I felt the wind as it barely missed my head and buried itself an inch into the wall. She was furious because my brother and I had poured her liquor down the drain in a vain effort to stop her drinking. We never did it again. We had just one television set in the living room, and if I wanted to watch it I had to sit within two or three feet of the screen so I could hear above my mother's screams, a habit I continued until I was forty years old. To this day no one understands why I listen to the television with the volume turned up so loud.

I learned to keep quiet through all the constant nightly yelling, since anything I said only made it worse. But by the time I was fifteen I could no longer stay home at night at all. My mother had gotten in the habit of throwing whatever she could get her hands on from her seat on the couch ten feet or so from where I usually sat. I had bruises on my head and face, and even my glasses had been broken a couple of times when I turned my head at the wrong time. One of our next-door neighbors was a policeman. He and his wife suggested that my mother should be committed to an institution as a way of helping her. But when I went to the courthouse to inquire about the procedure, I just couldn't go through with it. What if it was a mistake—what if it was the wrong thing to do—how would I live with the guilt?

When my mother found out what I had done, she got even worse. There were nights when my brother and I, now older and bigger, had to carry her into her bedroom and tie her down in her own bed with ropes to keep her from hurting herself and us, and further destroying the house. Still everyone turned their backs—our relatives, all of whom lived out of town; our father, who had become a broken alcoholic himself; and even the school guidance counselor I once tried to talk to. The response was always the same: "Just mind your parents and everything will be all right."

Because I was not able to do my homework, and often stayed out so late that I got little sleep, my grades over the years had dropped like a ten-pound weight. Nothing in my life seemed to be working. I was bitter, angry, and full of blame, but at the same time I wondered if somehow this life was partly my responsibility. I fought that traumatic situation by becoming emotionally sterile, not caring, not reacting, not feeling.

That's the past I started with, one that could have left me emotionally scarred had I continued to dwell on it for the rest of my life. I could have used my early life as an excuse for failure. But by the time I was out of high school and away from home, I had already figured out that my past had no control over me other than that which I gave it by mentally reliving again and again all the horrid events that had lasted for years. I realized that I could use what I had been through to toughen me up instead of crippling me.

I am thankful I had such a tough childhood, because what I learned from it helped give me both the inspiration and the strength to build the incredible life that I have now. And you can do the same, no matter where you find yourself at any point in life. Drop the emotional baggage of the past. When you do, the actions you take and the decisions you make will be conscious choices, stemming not from where you were in the past but from where you are in the present and where you want to be in the future.

Success Strategy No. 4:

Use the losses and failures of the past as a reason for action, not inaction.

Action is always in order when you have experienced a loss or failure of any kind in your life. But when action is needed the most, that's the time when your tendency might be to slow down or even quit. To move on toward success, you must do the opposite of what you might first feel, even the opposite of what those around you might expect.

Once you are down, how you got there is no longer relevant. But dwell on it, and I guarantee that you will remain stuck there, wallowing in your own self-created emotional misery. It is your choice, and you must make the changes that will be to your benefit and not to your detriment. Affirm to yourself over and over, "Where I is, is where I is." Then go into action to get where you want to be.

If your business has failed, or if you've lost a job, or a loved one, or your possessions, stop allowing your mind to relive the past. There is nothing you can do to change or modify what has already happened. But you can change the way you think about it. So let the past go and get on with the present. It's your choice, victim or victor—victim of your past or victor over your future. You can choose either, but if success is your goal, letting go of the past is your only alternative.

"Where I is, is where I is, and that's okay . . . but where I'm going is up to me."

CHAPTER **2**

Playing to Win: The Ballpark Principle

Before you have an argument with your boss, take a good look at both sides—his side and the outside.

—ANONYMOUS

It's no news that you often find yourself forced to play by rules that others have made. Much of your life has been and will continue to be spent playing in someone else's ballpark, operating under conditions that often produce frustration and stress. To achieve your dreams and goals, you must learn to work and operate effectively under those conditions.

Some ballparks are easy to function in, particularly when the rules, values, and environment are similar to those you would have chosen yourself. More often, however, you will find yourself operating under undesirable conditions, conditions you would not have chosen for yourself. You are playing in someone else's ballpark when you:

- Work for a boss you don't get along with even though you like the job and the company

- Have a relationship in which you demand more than the other person is willing to give, and you don't want to give up the relationship
- Pay Social Security taxes even when you feel socially secure
- Are forced to deal with regulators like:
  —zoning boards
  —the IRS
  —the FTC
  —labor boards
- Belong to a club or group that you enjoy, but that is run by overbearing officers
- Spend time with a group of friends that you like, but that is dominated by someone you would prefer not to be around
- Are in a successful business partnership where the partners constantly argue
- Attend a school or university that has rules that seem archaic to you
- Live with your parents
- Live with your children
- Live in a rented house or apartment

Sound familiar? Every day you find yourself in environments controlled by others. Attempting to change or fudge on the rules will always cause you to lose, even when you think you're right. Drive 15 mph over the speed limit constantly and you may get away with it 99 percent of the time. But that one time out of a hundred you will get a ticket, because speed limits are set by someone other than you. You can get angry or complain about the unfairness of the system, but in the end you lose. You pay the ticket and suffer the corresponding loss of time and money.

Eventually, if you keep fighting any system controlled by someone else, you will lose—count on it.

Success Strategy No. 5:

To win in other people's ballparks, play by their rules.

How do you know you're losing when you're playing in someone else's ballpark? If you hear yourself thinking or saying:

It's not fair . . .
Nobody can make me do that . . .
You can't talk to me that way . . .
What did I do to deserve this . . .

You set yourself up to lose anytime you're playing in somebody else's ballpark and you break or attempt to change the rules without the agreement of the rule maker. If your goal is to gain control of your own mind, your own life, and your own future, how can you possibly operate effectively when it appears that you have little or no say-so—no control? The answer is simple: Play by the rules even if you're not the one who makes them.

If we define winning as maximizing your progress toward your dreams and goals, then the more time and energy you have available for that purpose, the sooner you can expect to accomplish what you are after. You're wasting time and energy when you fight the system. It may be a natural tendency to want to buck the system, and you may succeed, but only in the short term. In the long term you will lose. You will lose credibility, authority, money, "face," even a job or a relationship. You're playing a losing game any time you fight a system which you have no power to change or control. If you choose to stay in other people's ballparks, you can only win by playing by their rules, like them or not.

Being right is often in conflict with winning.

When you work for someone else and want to succeed in your job and experience the satisfaction of raises and advancement, your only possible strategy is to play by the company's or the boss's rules. Whether your way is right or better is irrelevant. Your objective is to win. And if to you winning is defined as getting promotions, raises, developing credibility, and gaining the confidence of the "bigger" shots, you will have to follow rules you didn't make. You can choose to prove you are right or you can choose to win, but usually not both at the same time.

I'll bet you've had the same thoughts I did when I was in the corporate world: the belief that, in general, you know better than those you work for. From 1965 to 1971 I was employed by a company called Genesco, which at the time was the world's largest manufacturer of apparel—a billion-dollar-a-year company. I worked in the division that designed computer systems, and I always thought I knew better than top management. Today, as an employer of more than five hundred people, I know that everyone who has ever worked for someone else has had the same thoughts, and often they are correct. I figured if they made me president of Genesco the next day, that was the smartest move the company could make. I'd straighten everything out for them pronto. My biggest problem came from the fact that I let people know how I felt. In the corporate world, that does not necessarily endear you to the higher-ups.

I became known as a corporate maverick. I was able to keep my job because I was good at it, but I was passed over for promotions and other perks that normally come with the package—typical of what happens when you make up your own rules. If management said, "We're all going to look like IBM-ers and wear white shirts," I'd wear pastel shirts just to prove that it was a ridiculous rule. When the rules said "No sideburns allowed" (remember how everyone wore sideburns in the sixties?), naturally I let my sideburns grow.

I believed they couldn't afford to fire me. And they didn't. So I got to be right—I could do it my way—but I was losing and I couldn't figure out why. I knew I had the talent and at that age I thought talent was all that was supposed to matter. That, however, is not the way life works. Finally, my boss's boss put it to me this way: "Chuck, we have a credibility gap with you."

I knew then what the general corporate attitude toward me was, loud and clear. I had become a necessary nuisance, not one of the gang. I was proving I could bend the rules, but in the process that attitude was costing me the things I wanted most. If I wanted to win the game, I had to play by their rules, like it or not. It became painfully clear that it was not within my power to change the rules. My only alternatives were to accept the situation the way it was or leave the company.

Attempting to change the rules in someone else's environment is a game that cannot be won, and each time you attempt it you will pay a price. The price may be anger, frustration, or even depression, or it could be worse. It might cost you time, money, credibility, or even your job. I had to learn to make the rules work for me, instead of against me.

Of course, you still have choice when you're playing in someone else's ballpark. You can pick up your ball and glove and go home. If you don't like the boss, you can either quit or ask for a transfer. If the negatives of a relationship outweigh the positives, you can get out of the relationship. If you don't like the speed limits, you can stop driving those roads or stop driving altogether. The point is, even when you're in other people's ballparks you are still in control. You can choose to be there or you can choose to leave.

Success Strategy No. 6:
Accept the rules or change ballparks.

I made the choice to accept my job and the rules as they were, instead of how I wanted them to be. I said to myself, Okay, my salary is $40,000 a year [in today's dollars]; therefore from now on I'm going to view my job this way. I get paid $10,000 of the $40,000 a year for what I know and do, and the balance of $30,000 for putting up with all the crap. Once I adopted that attitude, accepting the fact that the company was going to run the way it wanted to run whether I knew better or not, my association with Genesco began to improve, and over the next couple of years my fortunes also improved. I doubled my salary in less than four years; after almost losing my job two years earlier, I worked my way up from the first-floor computer room to the bottom rungs of top-floor executive management in the division by the time I was thirty.

Learn this lesson well if you value winning as much as I do: Become a team player or get off the team. Your objective is to win, and you win by doing anything that moves you quickly toward your dreams and goals. However, you can later make a choice to change ballparks. It was 1971 when I finally decided I didn't want to play the corporate game anymore. I wanted to start my own companies and begin to run things my own way. In other words, I built my own ballpark and hired my own players, who now play by my rules.

Accept or change, those are the only two winning strategies. Period. And as you incorporate this Success Strategy into your daily activities, you will find your life changing in simple but important ways.

For instance, you:

- won't exceed the speed limit, not even by 5 mph.
- will get to work on time, every time.
- will stop complaining about your boss and/or upper management.
- won't park in no parking zones, hoping you will leave before you get a ticket.
- won't purposely underpay your taxes by understating income or overstating expenses.
- won't betray a friend or coworker.
- won't drink and drive.
- won't drive if your license has expired.
- won't borrow things without returning them.
- won't write a check if there's no money in your account, thinking your next deposit will beat your check to the bank.
- will pay your bills on time, every time.
- won't put off filling your gas tank until it's almost empty.
- will stop complaining about how things are done in the groups you belong to. If you want to make a change, you will first get yourself in a position to make changes.

Attempting to beat the system by making up your own rules will cause you to lose hundreds of hours and thousands and thousands of dollars during your lifetime. Why set yourself up for even one of those unnecessary losses? When you play by the rules, you don't have to look over your shoulder to see if something is about to get you from behind. It's a waste of time and your only reward will be a crick in your neck.

CHAPTER 3

Trying Is Lying

Those who say winning isn't everything have probably never won anything.

—ANONYMOUS

In order to recognize success, it is first necessary to define failure.

Failure is the refusal to establish a plan and work toward its accomplishment regardless of the obstacles.

Most of us were never taught that failure is a matter of choice, just as success is a matter of choice. Failure is not, as many people believe, the result of lack of talent, money, time, or other resources. Failure is simply the refusal to establish goals or objectives in your life and to work toward their achievement. Talk to people who have neither goals nor the motivation to succeed and you'll find that their lives have no excitement, no purpose. They feel like failures.

The fact that you started a business and it went broke does not mean you failed. In my early twenties, nine businesses that I started eventually ended up going broke. Did I fail in those nine businesses? Absolutely not. I simply found nine ways that a business wouldn't work, and once you discover them all, it is difficult not to succeed the next time. At any point along the way, I could have quit. I could have said I don't have the talent for business, and at that point I would have failed. I would have refused to continue, regardless of the obstacles. Instead, I knew there was a brass ring out there somewhere, and if I stayed with it long enough, I'd learn everything I needed to know to create a successful business.

To succeed, you will constantly find yourself sailing uncharted waters, doing things you have never done before, but if you want any more from life than mediocrity, that's where you'll have to go. Any time you break new ground, you are taking a risk. You neither know exactly what's ahead, nor how you're going to handle it. The only alternative is not to go anywhere.

When striving to achieve your goals, there is no such thing as trying.

You read it right! We've all been told from the time we were children that it doesn't matter if we win or not, just as long as we try hard. That is one of the greatest lies you can tell yourself or your children. "Trying" is a word meant to rationalize failure. It's an excuse. In truth, when reaching for any objective, short term or long term, you either succeed or you don't. There is no in-between. Trying, therefore, is a nonreality.

Lack of immediate success, however, is not failure. It is nothing more than the feedback you may need to modify your target date and even your plan for reaching your goal. "I tried" is a quitter's statement. It says you have either given up or decided that not reaching your goals is an okay way to continue to live your life. Both attitudes, and they are only attitudes, are devastating to your personal effectiveness. Drop them. Drop the "I tried." When you run head-on into a brick wall, simply get yourself back in the race with a new plan for winning.

Success Strategy No. 7:

Use near misses as a sign that you're off course, not a sign that you have failed.

It's not how many times you fall down that determines whether you will eventually reach the top of the mountain. It's how many times you get up and get moving again. Implanting the word "try" in your mind (or your children's) is an acknowledgment that it is okay to give up instead of get up. Failure occurs only when you quit or make excuses for your inability to succeed.

Skeptical? Put a pen down on a table in front of you within easy reach. Now, *try* to pick it up. There are only two possibilities. The pen either came off the table or it didn't. If the pen came off the table, you didn't try to pick it up, you *did* pick it up. If your fingers gripped the pen but it did not come off the table, you simply didn't pick up the pen. There is no in-between. You either did or you didn't. There is, as you can now see, no such thing as trying. Trying is, therefore, lying—lying to yourself about what you're really doing. Here's a story from my own experience that demonstrates the point.

In 1964, a week after my son Rob was born in Decatur, Illinois, I drove my wife Bonnie, my son Chuck, who was eighteen months old, and Rob to Tulsa to stay with Bonnie's parents while I ventured to Nashville, Tennessee, to seek fame and fortune in the music business. Each weekend for the next three months, I made the eight-hour drive from Nashville to Decatur to play rock and roll with my Decatur band at Paul Wax's Corner Lodge for a hundred dollars a weekend. This was my only source of income, and even after three months I neither had the time nor had saved enough money to get to Tulsa to see my family. Then inspiration struck. I had been taking flying lessons in Decatur prior to moving to Nashville and still had a charge account at the airport. Why not rent a plane on credit as a student pilot and fly to Tulsa and back?

There was only one problem: I had just seven hours of total flying instruction and had never soloed out of sight of the Decatur airport. In short, I had no experience in flying. But inspiration and desperation overcame hesitation. Standing in front of the counter at the flight instruction office, I matter-of-factly stated, "My flying instructor told me I should do my cross-country solo today," knowing full well that my instructor was nowhere to be found. Without checking, they assigned me a plane—a Cessna Cherokee B, a small, low-winged, single-engine aircraft.

With my limited instruction and experience, I had no idea how the instruments or the radio worked. All I knew was how to get a plane up in the air. To figure out how to work the "Omni," the only radio-controlled direction-finding equipment that existed in those days, I circled around the Decatur airport for fifteen minutes turning and twisting knobs until I could locate a signal. Finally, I homed in on the St. Louis tower a hundred miles away as my immediate destination. But just to be sure on this beautifully clear day, I decided to fly along the railroad tracks until I reached St. Louis, following the train route I had traveled so many times as a kid. Can't get too lost, I thought, St. Louis is slightly southwest and with the tracks and the compass—no problem.

The weather remained clear all the way to St. Louis. As I

watched the Omni needle switch from "to" to "from," indicating that I had just flown over the St. Louis radio tower, I said to myself, This is easy! I banked the plane south while searching for another Omni radio frequency, but within a few minutes my life began to change. As I crossed into an incoming weather front, the small plane started to toss and buck violently, and suddenly I was reminded of how much I didn't know about flying. A quick call to the St. Louis tower revealed that I was headed directly into severe thunderstorms, a message backed up by the lightning flashes I began to spot around me. How much can this baby take? I thought as I noticed my sweaty palms and tighter grip on the wheel. The thunderstorms were directly south of St. Louis, so I decided to fly west across the state of Missouri to Kansas City. I could then circumnavigate the storms by approaching Tulsa from the north. Sounded logical to me, but then what did I know?

All the way to Kansas City I watched the dark clouds building to my left, and thanked my lucky stars that I was not caught in them. At Kansas City I landed the small plane almost effortlessly—that is, after some confusion about what the numbers painted on the runway really meant. I paced the pilot's lounge while the plane was being refueled, wanting to get moving again. The clouds had come in low but seemed to be lifting. Although my calls to the tower indicated that the airspace between Kansas City and Tulsa was marginal at best, I was determined to be in Tulsa that night to see my family, and a few clouds were not going to stop me.

The fuel tanks were full as I lifted off from the Kansas City airport and headed south toward Tulsa. In less than ten minutes I leveled off at an altitude of 7,000 feet and soon found myself in a cloudy sea of light with no visibility whatsoever. The clouds became so thick that the windshield looked as if it were pushing its way through a box of cotton balls. I could hear the whine of the engine but couldn't even see the nose of the plane.

I began to fumble with the charts stretched across my lap. I didn't need to worry about looking where I was going because there was nothing to see. What if there's another plane up here? I thought. He can't see me either, at least not until we are windshield to windshield. As I became engrossed in the charts, attempting to figure out where I was, the plane slowly tilted and began to plummet. The wings were almost perpendicular to the ground, losing lift. But since I couldn't see, I couldn't tell.

I'd fallen several hundred feet before I glanced at the instruments and realized that the plane was almost in a free fall. The altimeter was spinning rapidly counterclockwise, showing that the ground was rising like a fast-moving elevator. A dozen scenes of disaster danced through my mind as I gripped the wheel tighter and tighter, attempting to level out the plane without popping the wings off. It worked, but I realized flying blind reeked of dangerous downsides.

By the time I'd climbed back to 5,000 feet, the instruments indicated all was well again, although I still couldn't see a thing. It didn't help my confidence that I hadn't seen the ground or the sky for over an hour and a half. I knew I needed a mental break from this mess. Why not see if I could get above it? I climbed to 8,000, 9,000, 10,000 feet. The clouds were still as thick and creamy as clam chowder when the numbers on the altimeter reached double digits. At 12,000 feet, the stories I had heard about the lack of oxygen above that altitude began to haunt my mind. As I topped 14,000 feet, I remembered my flight instructor saying, "Only a few minutes above 12,000 feet and then your mind begins to play tricks on you. You think you're awake and alert, but you have so little oxygen that you often don't know what you're doing. You can become giddy and disoriented and even pass out. Without extra oxygen you're in a heap of trouble."

By this time I was wondering if the air was thick enough to hold up the plane. As I passed 15,200 feet, I found the sky but had lost most of the oxygen. My breathing was labored as I monitored my mind to see if it was still functioning. The relief of seeing the familiar sky above had been enough to outweigh the danger. But I knew I couldn't stay up there long. My lungs were already hurting. Gritting my teeth and gasping for air, I pushed the stick forward and dove back into the clouds, dropping at over a thousand feet a minute. Ten thousand feet and safe, I thought, as I switched from the empty right fuel tank to the full left. The minutes went by like hours. Nothing to see but pure white, nothing to hear but the monotonous droning of the engine. The left fuel tank, which contained the only remaining fuel, had now gotten frighteningly low—down to a quarter tank as I crossed into Oklahoma.

The only way I could locate my position precisely was to fly across the Tulsa International Airport and watch the Omni needle flip from a heading of "to" to "from," indicating directly over the airport tower. Putting down at the big jetport was not a possibility. I would have to find the Tulsa North Airport, where I had planned to land, but Tulsa North had no radio homing equipment.

When the Omni needle flipped over Tulsa International, I said to myself, I'll just dip down through the clouds and get reacquainted with the ground. As I broke through the lower layers of white, I could see the big jets lined up, ready to take off in the light rain like missiles launched from the barrel of a cannon right into the area where I was now flying.

Suddenly someone in the control tower yelled over the radio, "Who is that idiot up there?!"

"Whoops," I said aloud, realizing he was talking about me. I pulled back on the wheel and quickly slipped up into the clouds before the controller could get a chance to spot my tail number and have me grounded for two lifetimes.

As I headed for North Tulsa Airport, I tuned to its radio voice channel and after a few harrowing minutes finally managed to get someone away from his cup of coffee.

"Where are you?" I asked.

"More importantly, where are you?" came the reply.

"Well, all I know is that I'm somewhere near Tulsa International," I said softly, as if someone might be listening.

"Well, it's a good thing you called now, because we were just getting ready to go home. Nobody's dumb enough to fly around up there today!"

Obviously *one* person is, I thought.

"What should I do?" I asked, being the least knowledgeable of the bunch.

"Well, I'll give you some compass headings," replied the voice over the radio, "and you fly back and forth until we hear your engine. We'll know it's you. There's no one else."

"Well, I'm real low on fuel," I said, watching the needle push toward the red empty mark.

Back and forth I flew, as the engine sucked the last few gallons. Finally I just had to see ground again and dipped below the 400-feet mark. When I came out of the clouds, the wheels seemed to virtually skim the trees on top of a hill. With a gasp, I leaned back and headed into cloud country one more time.

"I think I hear you," a voice came over the radio. "You're over by the baseball field. By the way, you'll have to fly between two 1,000-foot radio towers on either side of the airport as you come in. We'll *try* to talk you between them."

That was the first time in my life I fully understood the inadequacy of the word "try."

"Okay. Come on down," said the voice on the radio, and I dropped through the clouds with the airport off to the right but definitely in sight. I banked with a silent cheer as I lined up the wings parallel to the runway and between the two towers. I was so happy to be there I didn't even review the landing procedure card. As my wheels touched the runway I knew something wasn't right. The air speed indicator showed 140 knots. Landing speed was only 80 knots.

I'd forgotten to put down my flaps!

At that speed, not only did the brakes refuse to work at all but the plane didn't even want to be on the ground. The fence and telephone wires at the end of the runway were rapidly closing in and I realized there was no way I could stop the plane in time.

If I couldn't go through it, I had to get over it. Now within fifty feet of the fence, I jammed the throttle into the dash, pulled back as hard as I could on the wheel, and closed my eyes, hoping I didn't stall the plane and drop to the ground. I began counting. I figured if I could just get to six, I was still alive. Four, five, six—I opened my eyes just as the wheels barely cleared the telephone wires above the fence. Somehow I'd made it. But did I have the gas to go around again?

When I came in again on a short approach, flaps down this time, the engine began to sputter. My heart was racing as the plane touched down and I braked it to a halt.

Three guys came running to the plane as I taxied in. "Hey, kid, how long have you been flying?" asked one with a sneer.

"I don't know," I replied. "What time is it?" I had just spent more than half my total flying career flying blind and baffled.

I was thankful to be alive. But one thing in particular stuck in my mind. The crew at Tulsa North Airport had said they would "try" to direct me between the two thousand-foot towers in zero visibility. Either they were going to get me through or they weren't. So what if they meant well? If my plane ended up looking like a wart on an Erector set, do you think it would have made any difference to me that they'd tried?

"I tried" is not an acceptable excuse. In fact, no excuses are necessary for success. Tried is an excuse for failure. Using the word "try" creates an illusion in your mind that your effort produced an "almost win" and stops you from moving on. Accept failure as an alternative and, consciously or unconsciously, it will diminish your effectiveness and power to achieve your goals.

You never fail until you quit, make excuses, or die.

If you're tuning in a radio station and you turn the dial too far and hear static, have you failed? Do you switch off the radio whimpering, "Well, I tried"? Of course not. The static gives you invaluable feedback that you have not yet arrived at the correct frequency. Your alternative in this case is obvious. You continue to adjust the dial until you find the station.

When you get feedback that you're not making progress, instead of quitting or making the excuse "I tried," ask yourself, What are my current alternatives? What is my next step? Then choose the best alternative and keep moving. All life is choice, and you can be stopped only if you choose to allow it to happen. "Trying" is nothing more than pinning a mental medal on your chest for having been delayed or stopped along the way to achieving your goals.

Success Strategy No. 8:

Use negative feedback to make positive course corrections.

You win by doing, not by trying. When NASA scientists send a rocket into space and it goes off course, they don't get discouraged and say, "Well, we tried," and go home, leaving astronauts to float off into oblivion. They make in-flight corrections to get the rocket back on course. The rocket reaches its destination not by trying, but through continual course corrections made along the way. Working toward achieving your goals is no different than launching and navigating a rocket. The launch occurs with the first step you take, no matter what it is. As long as you keep moving and use negative feedback to make positive course corrections, you cannot be stopped.

Traumas, problems, bad situations, stumbling blocks, and disappointments need not be negative cripplers. Instead, they can be used as positive input that course corrections are immediately warranted. The more distant your objective, the more times you can expect to stub your toe along the way, and the more course corrections you can anticipate. Don't take it personally. That's just the way life works. No, you won't always get the job, the raise, the loan, the guy or girl, or, for that matter, even your own way. Just chart a new destination and effect a new course correction. If you take enough shots at the target, you will eventually hit the bull's-eye. Dozens of misses will be forgotten once you score only one hit.

Someone once said to me, "You only have to be right 51 percent of the time to be rich." He was correct. I became rich even with the endless, unintentional financial errors I made all along the way. Whenever I've financed new businesses over the past ten years, I didn't demand that they all work—only that more worked than didn't. That philosophy has made me millions of dollars of profits and taught me one of life's most important lessons:

Cut your losses short and run your wins long.

That means knowing when to regroup, change direction, or even pull the plug when something isn't working. When you've got that winning attitude, you build on it to achieve success, making the losses you encounter insignificant by comparison.

If your child is playing baseball and strikes out, don't say, "It's okay, sweetheart, you tried." It's not okay, and your child knows it. Teach your child to shake off failure without self-criticism and get on with determining what will make a difference the next time at bat. If you get a pat on the back for being unsuccessful, what's the point of doing any better?

To okay a "strikeout" in life is to acknowledge that temporary failure is an excuse to quit. How long do you keep swinging? Until you hit the ball consistently. Remember, professional baseball's greatest hitters only hit the ball one out of three times, but a batting average of .333 instead of .260 can earn a player an extra $500,000 or more per year. Players only get paid for hits, not for misses.

There is no reward in life for trying, only for doing. Don't forget it.

PART II

Planning and Controlling Your Future

CHAPTER 4

Developing Your Blueprint

Your level of success in life is directly proportional to your level of planning and control.

Most people spend more time every year planning a two-week vacation than they spend planning their lives. And yet, the key ingredients that separate those who live out their dreams from those who only dream about living can be encapsulated in just two words: planning and control. Planning is the process of putting together a blueprint for your life, both personal and business. That blueprint forms the framework for the life experiences you have chosen for yourself and is comprised of five key elements: Dreams, Goals, Values, Action Plans, and Daily Activities. You are in control of your life when you incorporate these key elements in your blueprint. With planning and control comes automatic success.

Living your life without a plan is like attempting to build a house without a blueprint. You might put the doors in the wrong place so you couldn't easily get in or out. The roof might leak and the elements would eventually destroy your house. Windows might be in the wrong place and there would be no fresh air or daylight. With an improperly built foundation, the house would collapse. By the same token, without a detailed blueprint, your life will become riddled with structural defects. However, if you follow the strategies I am about to teach you for developing your life's blueprint, you will place your future on a rock-solid foundation and build the structure of your life in your way and on your own timetable.

Without planning, the future you want may never materialize. Without control, you'll find your life full of frustration, disappointment, anger, feelings of inadequacy, failure, and lack of confidence—the list of negative emotions and experiences goes on and on. No one, you and I included, would purposely incorporate into our lives any of these negative emotions or experiences, but life seems to be full of them. You may have lived with a combination of these feelings and emotional experiences for so long now that you think they are normal. They are not. Negative emotions and experiences are not a product of your job, your lack of wealth, your spouse, your boss, kids, bad luck, or the fact that the world as a whole just doesn't understand you. They are the result of inadequate planning and lack of control.

Think of a car without a steering wheel. No matter how big the engine, no matter how fast you choose to drive, you have no chance of getting where you want to go. Lots of power, lots of motion, but no control over your direction. That is how most people live their lives—constantly busy, constantly on the move, constantly expending mental, emotional, and physical energy. They are moving fast, but they are out of control. A written blueprint is like a steering wheel. It will give you control over your direction. You will be pleasantly amazed at the immediate positive effects your blueprint will have in your personal and business life. Should both you and your spouse create your own individual blueprints and then choose to support each other's dreams, goals, and values, even though they may be somewhat different, you will find a new level of synergy and energy in your relationship.

Your complete blueprint or life plan is made up of five separate sections.

1. *Dreams List:* an item-by-item list of what you would do with your life if you had unlimited time, talent, and money.
2. *Goals List:* a list of the specific results you want to accomplish during the next twelve months in both your business and personal lives.
3. *Values List:* a prioritized list of what you believe is most important to you in terms of relationships, concepts, and feelings.
4. *Action Plans:* a list of the objectives or steps that must be completed in the successful accomplishment of each of your goals. You will create one separate action plan for each goal on your goals list.
5. *Daily Activities List:* a prioritized list of all the individual activities, both business and personal, that you intend to accomplish during the current calendar month. The priorities determine those activities you intend to accomplish during the current day.

To create an effective blueprint, all five key elements must be defined clearly in writing. A full 50 percent of accomplishing what you desire in life—and most important, enjoying the experience—is dependent on how well you've drawn up your blueprint. If up to this point in your life you have not accomplished as much as you feel you could have, lack of ability is not the cause. It's your lack of a blueprint.

When you build a house according to a well-thought-out blueprint, all the pieces end up in place. They fit together and they work together. When you build your life around a well-thought-out blueprint, the pieces of your life fit and work together with far less stress and frustration. Your blueprint sets you up for continuous accomplishment instead of continual disappointment. It is the tool that will show you where you want to go, as well as the path you must take and the timetable you must follow to get there.

Success Strategy No. 9:

Organize your blueprint in a three-ring notebook.

It is important that you keep your entire blueprint together, since each of its five key elements is related to the others. The least expensive blueprint organizer is a three-ring, 8½ × 11-inch notebook. Put a label on the cover that identifies the notebook as your blueprint for the current year. Include your name, address, and phone number on a separate label on the inside cover in case your notebook is misplaced. This is a document you cannot afford to lose.

Lay out the sections of your blueprint in advance and identify each section with tabs. Here is my suggestion for how many pages to include in each of the sections.

Section	Number of Pages
Dreams List	4
Goals List	6
Values List	2
Action Plans	15–30 (1 for each goal)
Daily Activities List	20 (1–2 for each month)

Your original Dreams List will probably include twenty-five to fifty dreams and take up only one or two pages. But include a couple of extra pages in this section so you can add dreams as you think of them.

Your original Goals List will usually be longer than your Dreams List and it will be divided into two parts, business goals and personal goals. Begin the first page of this section with your business or career goals and the fourth page with your personal goals. There will then be plenty of space for listing additional goals of both kinds.

Your Values List will probably take about two pages. I'll show you how to determine those values and align them with your goals in Chapter 8.

The section in your blueprint for your Action Plans will require the greatest number of pages. You will use one page to make an Action Plan for each goal, listing on each page all of the objectives or steps required to accomplish that goal. If you run out of space, you can list additional objectives on the back of the page.

Your Daily Activities List will probably require two pages for each month. One page can be used for planning and prioritizing your daily business activities and the other for planning and prioritizing your daily personal activities.

Your Daily Activities List will, in general, take the place of any daily planner or planning system you are using now. If you wish to continue with your current planning system and it is contained in a three-ring notebook, you can add your Dreams List, Goals List, Values List, and Action Plans to the front of your planner. In that way you can convert your daily planner into the far more effective SuperSelf format.

To keep your blueprint up-to-date, your Daily Activities List should be removed from your notebook at the end of each month, after you have copied any uncompleted activities onto next month's list, and kept in a file folder. In that file, at the end of each year, you will have a complete record of all your business and personal activities for the entire year. I can't think of an easier way to keep a diary—and a record of the progress you are making toward the achievement of your goals and dreams.

Success Strategy No. 10:

Use the Givenizer for the ultimate in planning and control.

The Givenizer® is a complete system for planning and controlling your life. Specifically designed to incorporate all the strategies you can use to create your own blueprint, it includes sections for your Dreams List, Goals List, Values List, Action Plans, and Daily Activities List. The daily activities forms are printed on the reverse side of a foldout calendar for the month so that you can note on the calendar specific appointments for specific days. In the permanent records section of the Givenizer, you can also note important information like names and addresses, phone and fax numbers, birthdays and anniversaries, and data on insurance policies and credit cards in case you need immediate access to this information. Other forms are also included or available to help you organize specific areas of your life. For instance, if you manage people or projects, we have designed special forms that make staying organized and on top of your entire life a breeze. You can get more information about the Givenizer or order one by calling Charles J. Givens Organization at this toll-free number: 1-800-365-4101.

In the following chapters, I'll give you more details about how to create and complete your blueprint. But here, in general, is how your blueprint for maximum effectiveness will look:

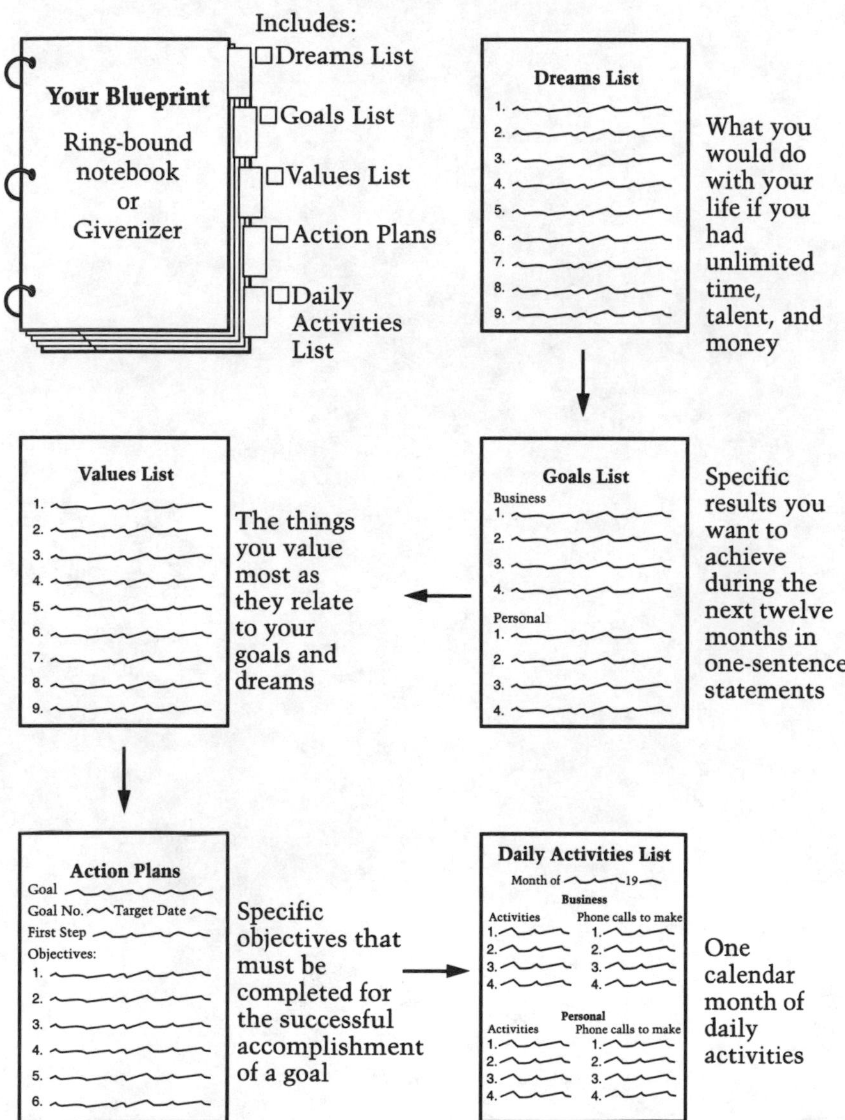

CHAPTER 5

Discovering Your Dreams

Our life is what our thoughts make it.
—Marcus Aurelius

When I was just eighteen, I quite inadvertently did something that changed the rest of my life. I created a Dreams List, which was to set my direction and give me the momentum to make something of myself. I had just graduated from high school and was working for eighty-five cents an hour at Tolly's Market in Decatur, Illinois, helping to support my mother, who could no longer work because of cataracts, and my brother, who was just starting high school.

I've already told you about the turmoil and disasters of my early life, and as a teenager I had long spurts of feeling sorry for myself and inwardly asking, Why me? What did I do to deserve this? I thought, felt, and acted like a victim. As a result, I was constantly unhappy and unmotivated. With that kind of attitude, it was about all I could do just to survive. I gave up my ability to dream. I lost my ability to see the future since I was totally caught up with my problems in the present.

Then when I was sixteen it all changed. I had gotten so low that I contemplated suicide. But when you hit bottom, you let go of all expectations. I realized that my expectations of how the world should be, how my parents should act, how my teachers and even my relatives should have greater concern for straightening out my disastrous life had little to do with reality. If I wanted my life to work any differently, it was up to me and no one else. I suddenly understood that my only alternative was to get back up on my feet and stop wallowing in self-pity. In other words, I took total responsibility for my life, day by day and hour by hour—no more blame, no more criticism, no more complaining.

My life immediately began to take a 180-degree turn. I was in action. I tackled new projects and new ideas with a zest for living I had missed since before I was ten. As success bred success, I began to feel I could do anything. I had no money, no specialized education, no contacts, and only a small amount of rapidly growing self-confidence, but my life was losing its shackles, its self-imposed limits. For the next two years, I found that the more I viewed myself as totally responsible for my life, the more in control I seemed to be of the goals I wanted to achieve. More and more, I could see possibilities instead of only problems. Then one day I said to myself, What if you could become everything you admire in others? If you could do, have, and be anything you could think of, what would that be? What would it include? That was when I created my first Dreams List.

I cannot fully describe the power over my life doing this simple exercise gave me. You will have to experience that for yourself. My objective here is to convince you of the importance of this exercise, because it is from your Dreams List that both the plan and control of your life will flow. Much of what you will be able to achieve from here on in will stem from this single element of your blueprint.

My first Dreams List was more than 50 dreams long, and over the next few years I added to it until the number exceeded 180. There is no limit to the number of dreams you can include on your own personal Dreams List. You are limited only by the power of your imagination.

Success Strategy No. 11: Begin your life's blueprint with a Dreams List.

Think of your Dreams List as the script for a movie about your life. You are the writer and you can take the movie in any direction you choose, filling the script with as many positive experiences and adventures as you can imagine or desire. But instead of writing the story of how you have lived your life so far, write the story of how you would like to live your life in the future. Create your Dreams List as if you were outlining the high points of your autobiography *before* you have lived it. Writing about your past limits you to the experiences you have already had. Writing about your imagined future has no such restraints.

A movie script begins with a written outline of what up to that point were only random events, scenes, and experiences. Your Dreams List is similar because it is an outline of the major events, scenes, and experiences in the most successful and satisfying life you can imagine for yourself, unaffected by any current realities, family circumstances, level or lack of wealth, past or present pressures, or your own current level of confidence or ability.

Success Strategy No. 12:

Prepare your Dreams List as if there were no limits to your life.

It is easy to view your life and where you are now as a product of its limits. These limits often become excuses for not reaching out for more of life's golden opportunities. The major limits in everyone's life seem to be these:

- Limited time
- Limited money
- Limited knowledge, talent, and ability
- Limited opportunity
- Limited self-confidence
- Limited support from spouse or family

These limits have power over your life and future only to the extent that you let them. All limits can be overcome, and the best way to begin is with a Dreams List without limitations. You don't have to overcome limits, disadvantages, or anything you feel you lack in order to imagine what you most want to experience from life. It takes no resources other than a small amount of time and mental energy. Yet outlining your dreams is the essential first step in creating your blueprint for more successful, satisfying living. It can help you spot possibilities and opportunities for your life and give you the confidence and motivation to overcome roadblocks and problems. Although some people may feel it's easier to attempt to avoid disappointment by not wanting much, remember, those who ask very little from life always get what they ask for—very little.

You can win the battle for success and accomplishment

only by clearly defining what you want. Your Dreams List is a critical part of that definition. As you think about and write down your dreams, you will find that, in general, they fit into just five categories:

- What you would like to have or own
- What you would like to do or create
- Where you would like to go or travel
- What you would like to be or become
- What you would like to contribute or put back

To get your mind working, think of the above categories as you create your Dreams List. Encourage family members to create their own Dreams List. Make it a fun, exciting family project, not a chore. There are no right or wrong dreams, only those which are identified and written down, and those which are not.

Success Strategy No. 13:

Crystallize your dreams by writing them down.

Hopes and wishes are generally random thoughts that possess little power or organization. A written Dreams List transforms hopes and wishes into a concrete framework for accomplishment. When you put your dreams down on paper, they become real, they become permanent, they crystallize.

You will discover that some dreams on your list are more important to you than others. The pursuit and accomplishment of those dreams will tend to generate a greater sense of personal satisfaction than those that are less important or even whimsical. List them all. It's easy to get so involved in just making it through the day, day after day, that your dreams are left in the dust, buried and untouched in your subconscious mind. It's time to get your dreams out in front of you where they will continually become the major focus of your life.

Now let's get started with your list. To make it easy, I have divided the process into six steps.

Step 1: Sometime today, find a quiet time and place where you will not be disturbed for at least twenty to thirty minutes.

Step 2: Open the notebook in which you are going to create your life's blueprint, and at the top of the first page write "My Dreams List" and the current date.

Step 3: On the next line write the following statement: "If I had unlimited time, talent, money, knowledge, self-confidence, and support from my family, here is a list of everything I would like to do with my life."

Step 4: Now begin to list each of your dreams as it comes to mind. Don't rush. Wait a few seconds or even minutes if necessary for the ideas to flow. Don't evaluate the possibilities or probabilities of achieving each dream based on your current circumstances. This is a Dreams List, not a shopping list. Let your imagination run free.

Step 5: Write down everything that comes to mind no matter how silly or outrageous. Later you can edit your Dreams List if you choose. For now, your objective is to get it all down on paper without mental reservations. There are no limits to a Dreams List, so put them all down.

Step 6: Keep going until you have listed a minimum of twenty-five dreams, no matter what they are. There is no correct length. Just put down everything that's been rolling around in your mind but that you've never written down before.

Your Dreams List, unlike the Goals List you will make later, is not a commitment, but a method of clarifying what excites you. It has nothing to do with what is practical. It is a description of your life in terms of what is possible.

As you list your dreams, you'll discover that dreams are not something you are "dreaming" up. They have been a part of you all along, stored away in your subconscious mind. But you may have thought, Possibly, someday, or when times are better or different, or when I have time or get the bills paid, or when the children are grown, or after my divorce is finalized. Your mind becomes filled with dream-busting excuses for inaction, but in truth, once your dreams are down on paper excuses lose their power and your mental, physical, and emotional energies are regrouped and refocused like a laser beam.

Once you have completed your Dreams List, you will begin to feel that the simple step of writing down your dreams is redirecting your life toward the accomplishment of what has always been important to you. You will experience a renewed sense of what I call "aliveness," an inner excitement at the new prospects for the positive experiences that await you. Even without periodically reviewing your Dreams List, you will see some of your dreams immediately take form as probabilities instead of only remote possibilities.

You will want to review and revise your Dreams List at least once a year. As you accomplish each dream, record the date on your list. But leave the dream and date on the list as a reminder of your ability to both create and live out your life plan—your personal movie script. Remember, your Dreams List is a lifelong project. You'll want to add to it continually as new dreams come to mind.

Occasionally you may delete a dream from your list. For instance, on my original list I wrote as one of my dreams, "Cross the Sahara Desert from east to west." That dream probably found its way onto my list because I knew that it had never been done before. When I later actually spent time under the scorching sun of the Sahara, I could easily see why. But more importantly, I began to realize that the risk/reward relationship just wasn't there. Even if I accomplished the trip, my reaction would have been more "so what" than a great feeling of accomplishment. I removed the dream from my list, not because I felt that it couldn't be achieved, but because the price in terms of time, money, and endurance would have been far in excess of the potential reward. Over the years, you may find yourself removing a dream here and there from your list just because the price exceeds the potential reward.

Once you have created your Dreams List, you will find that from time to time and in the most unexpected ways opportunities will arise to achieve even your most far-out dreams. Of course, it is your responsibility to take advantage of those opportunities. That's exactly what happened to me in May 1988, when Adena, my son Chuck, his wife Amy, and I were spending a few weeks in Egypt exploring that mystical, ancient culture. Two of the dreams that I had put on my list almost twenty years before were to climb the Great Pyramid of Giza, and to enter the Great Pyramid and make my way through the myriad of ascending tunnels into the great chamber in its very center.

Just seeing the Great Pyramid was an experience of a lifetime, and in the 110-degree burning daytime sun, we walked around the huge structure and admired the Sphinx. While the four of us stood there in amazement at those great monuments, my mind wandered back to the days when I had first written those two dreams on my list. Here I was—half the battle was over—but I was still 455 feet, or forty-five stories, from the top of the pyramid and the climb looked like a gargantuan physical effort. I asked the guide about climbing the pyramid and he laughed. "No," he said. "It is against the law. And the government has decreed very long jail sentences to deter any Egyptians from even the thought of going up the face of the pyramid. However, that doesn't seem to apply to foreigners."

So it *was* possible, I thought, realizing there would be no reason to issue a decree if nobody could make it anyway. That night, we came back to the site of the great pyramids, only a short way out of Cairo, to see the evening sound-and-light show. While we were sitting there, in the middle of a conversation about something totally unrelated to pyramids a waiter walked up to me, tapped me on the shoulder, and asked, "How would you like to climb the Great Pyramid?"

Amazing, I thought. Here was another one of the hundreds of opportunities I've experienced just by being clear about what I was after. "Of course," I said. "What does it take?"

He replied, "If you're willing to be here at 3 A.M. when most of the guards are gone, I will meet you and we can pay off one of the soldiers. I have a friend who knows the path up to the top of the Great Pyramid."

"How much?" I asked.

"Four hundred dollars" was the instant reply. "But," he added after a moment's hesitation, "maybe you can bargain the guard down a little bit."

The sky was a slight midnight blue when my alarm went off at 2:45 A.M. Chuck, Adena, and I made our way down to a taxi, and headed out through the streets of Cairo. There was not a soul in sight. The cool desert night air had a sense of mystery and intrigue as we arrived on the site. There were no lights—it was pitch black. The three of us started walking toward the Great Pyramid after exiting the cab, since the cab driver would go no farther. We were completely surrounded by darkness when suddenly a flashlight came on. "Hello, my friend," said the voice of the waiter. I said to myself, Well, he showed up, something the waiter was probably thinking as well. We walked through the night toward the Great Pyramid, turning the flashlight on and off intermittently to avoid arousing suspicion.

Soon we came upon two soldiers with automatic rifles and, in Arabic, our waiter began negotiating. The waiter told me, "Four hundred dollars." "One hundred dollars," I replied.

After five minutes of bargaining, I pulled out two hundred-dollar bills and the soldiers let us pass.

At the base of the pyramid, having snuck in as quietly as the night itself, and in bare feet, was the waiter's friend, who knew one of the few paths up the pyramid. Adena didn't think she could make it all the way to the top, so Chuck and I decided it would be best to leave her up about three stories where no one could bother her. Then we would continue the arduous climb, hoping to reach the top of the pyramid in time to watch the sunrise.

Some of the stones were four feet high, and we had to climb and not merely step to go from layer to layer. In other places the stones were cracked or chipped, so we could get enough of a foothold to make climbing easier. Just going up the first three stories was a great effort. In the dim starlight, we could barely see the ground. We had forty-two stories to go.

We left Adena between the crevice of two stones, and after we had been gone fifteen or twenty minutes, she became bothered by the massive number of mosquitoes in the area and thought maybe if she turned on her flashlight, it would attract them away from her body. Well, the flashlight also attracted some desert nomads passing by on the opposite side of the pyramid, away from the soldiers. When they saw the light, they turned their camels around and rode over to the pyramid and motioned for Adena to come down.

They yelled at her in Arabic, but she didn't move. Then one of them started climbing the pyramid, as if to get her, and suddenly Adena felt she had somehow been cast in the movie *Raiders of the Lost Ark.* She knew we were so far up now that if she screamed, not only would we not hear her, but we couldn't have gotten down by the time the desert nomad reached her. Just in the nick of time, the soldiers rounded the side of the pyramid, saw what was happening, and chased the men away. Not bad service for a bargain price of only two hundred dollars.

It took Chuck and me at least two hours of hard climbing to reach the top of the pyramid, and when we did we couldn't see a thing below us. We had made the climb in starlit darkness, following our barefooted guide and hanging on tightly enough to each steep-faced stone so as not to slip. Although we couldn't see the bottom, we knew it was a long way down, especially if we fell and began bouncing off the stones.

The stones at the top had been worn away, and instead of a point there was a flat area about fifteen by fifteen feet. Even that high, the mosquitoes were swarming, and we spent much of the next half hour before sunrise fighting them off. As the sun came up and we could hear the desert and the city below, I experienced one of the most incredible feelings I've ever had —that feeling I so often describe as the "peak of aliveness."

Through my telephoto lens, as it became lighter, I saw Adena on the ground now, standing by the next of the three pyramids. After I took pictures of the sunrise and surrounding area, we started to climb back down. It took a little less than two hours, and I knew that after that effort, if I could even walk for the next two days it would be a minor miracle. But when you accomplish one of those dreams that has seemed at times both impractical and impossible, both your physical and mental energies operate at their peak.

As if the climb were not enough, later that afternoon we actually had the opportunity to go through a small, formerly secret door in the pyramid and climb through the inside into the great chamber. Although the interior of the Great Pyramid had been closed for most of the previous twenty years, the government of Egypt had decided to open it and let a limited number of people actually experience the pyramid from inside.

Two impractical dreams became reality within a twenty-four-hour period. Those kinds of experiences have been commonplace for me in the past twenty-five years. I know it's because I long ago discovered the technique of crystallizing my dreams on paper and then watching them come to fruition through opportunities I might never have noticed otherwise.

You will have the same experience. Opportunity will present itself, but you have to be the one to go for it or to let it slip by. In life, it is possible to lose your money, your home, or your spouse, but the memories, the excitement, and the emotions associated with the accomplishment of any of your dreams can never be taken away from you.

Success Strategy No. 14:
Allow your Dreams List to expand to form the framework for your entire life.

When you first discover some of those long-buried dreams and enter them on your Dreams List, they may seem as unattainable as a trip to a distant galaxy. But if you keep your Dreams List in front of you and work to achieve your dreams step by step, even the most distant ones will over time become attainable destinations.

For instance, after writing my original list, I could see that dreams about traveling to distant and exotic places came up over and over again. Some were well defined, like climbing the Rock of Gibraltar and the Great Pyramid, while others related to quantity—"Travel to fifty different countries." For someone who was then earning less than a dollar an hour and had no real knowledge of the world, even the possibility of such travel would have been discounted by a "practical" person.

However, I had discovered that what excited me then, and would for the rest of my life, was exploring the entire world, and my Dreams List built the framework from which my specific travel goals would emerge. I was just over forty years old when my original goal of fifty countries was reached. The process was so exhilarating and exciting that my dream was expanded many years ago to exploring every country, territory, and island group on the planet. According to the United Nations' list there are 260, and according to the more expanded list of the Travelers Century Club (of which I am a member) there are 311.

So far I have created the opportunity from the framework of my original Dreams List to explore 212 of them, more than all but a handful of people on the entire planet have visited. I expect to have explored them all by 1997.

In the process, those around me have also benefited from my dreams. My son Chuck has been to eighty-five countries with me, my son Rob to sixty-five, and my wife Adena to ninety-six. In addition, my sons and I have financed and personally conducted private expeditions into the most remote, uncharted jungles of the world where tribes still live a Stone Age existence. We have rafted the white-water sections of the Alas River in West Sumatra through jungle too thick for human inhabitants, but where tigers and elephants still roam wild. We have traveled up the rivers of the Asmut region in Irian Jaya, one of the least explored areas of the world, and lived from village to village with tribes who are still cannibals and eat the brains of their slain enemies to acquire their mental powers. We have traveled by old riverboat down hundreds of miles of the Amazon and its tributaries in South America, catching and eating piranha for lunch and hunting (but not hurting) crocodiles at night for sport. We have tracked tigers in the black of night, running barefoot so as not to make a sound through the jungles of southern Nepal.

It all began with the simple process of creating a Dreams List. That list has produced for me more excitement, adventure, wealth, and experience than I have seen in any Hollywood movie. I know your Dreams List will do the same for you and those you love, whatever your specific dreams turn out to be. No one is destined to a life of mediocrity and disappointment unless he or she allows it to happen by the omission of planning and control.

I have seen hundreds of truly inspirational and heart-warming experiences happen to people, all beginning with the creation of their Dreams Lists:

- A sixty-six-year-old Ph.D. spent his birthday hang gliding with me off the huge sand dunes at Kitty Hawk, North Carolina.
- A fourteen-year-old boy started his own successful business.
- A forty-five-year-old recently separated housewife with no previous sense of adventure rappelled straight down a two-hundred-foot cliff, then rode a zip line sixty feet in the air three hundred yards across a valley at forty miles per hour hanging from only wrist straps, an experience that gave her renewed self-confidence.
- A thirty-five-year-old mother swam and played with dolphins at Kings Dominion Park in Virginia, a dream she had had since she was a child.
- A twenty-eight-year-old European immigrant, who barely spoke English, built a $5 million fortune in five years, starting with a $6-an-hour job. I will never forget the tears of joy in his eyes as he sat in my office in Orlando, telling me the story of his success and the part my strategies had played in his life.

Live your life around your dreams and you live your life like the movie it was meant to be. Live your life without dreams and you live a life full of frustration, problems, and discouragements. It's your choice. And you begin exercising that choice when you create your Dreams List.

CHAPTER **6**

Generating Goals

Who dares nothing, need hope for nothing.
—Johann von Schiller

A goal is a specific, measurable result that you want to produce at a determinable time in the future. Your goals are the stepping-stones toward the realization of your dreams, the second key element in the blueprint of your life.

Goals are experiences you have not yet had, places you have not yet been, people you have not met, a level of income you have not achieved, a type of relationship you are not now enjoying, or having something you don't currently own. Like your dreams, there is no limit to the number of goals you can set other than the limits of your imagination. And although goals represent what you intend to achieve in the future, they are always set and worked on in the present.

A study of university business school graduates who had been out of school for ten years was conducted to determine how they were progressing toward their goals. Amazingly, 83 percent of the graduates had set no goals at all. This 83 percent reported that they were working hard and staying busy but had no specific future plans. Another 14 percent had goals, but their goals were mental, not written. However, this 14 percent was earning on the average three times the income of those who had no goals at all. Only 3 percent of the entire graduate group had written goals. That 3 percent was earning a whopping ten times what those with no goals were earning.

The message is clear: goals, particularly written goals, make the difference in your overall level of accomplishment. Among the business school graduates in the study, the short time they spent establishing clear, written goals made a dramatic difference in their income levels. Over the past twenty-eight years since I first discovered the incredible power of dynamic goal setting, I have seen equally dramatic differences in the lives of thousands of individuals and families. In fact, I have yet to observe any individual or family with specific, measurable goals who did not experience an immediate and continuous pattern of increased effectiveness in producing results.

Don't confuse your goals with your expectations.

Establishing goals has a positive impact on your life. But if what you hope to achieve in life is based on your expectations, rather than on working to reach established goals, you are setting yourself up for the possibility of disappointment. Expectations have to do with how you believe other people should behave, and how the world should bend at your command. Your expectations may result in a large amount of grief, whereas established goals will result in a large amount of satisfaction and success. The winning choice is clear: develop your goals, drop your expectations. It is a mistake to expect that you will accomplish any goal because you deserve it or because there is something in your past that entitles you to it. Unfortunately, there is no such thing as "deserve." You end up achieving in life because of planning and control, not because you have "paid your dues."

Defining what you are after is 50 percent of the battle in getting there.

Given the importance to your life of establishing goals, you would think that libraries and schoolrooms would be full of goal-setting rule books. They are not, and unfortunately that is one of the biggest handicaps in our educational system. Unless your teachers and parents directed their lives with written goals, and encouraged you to do the same, it is unlikely that you understand their importance.

The concept of goals is also one that is often either overlooked or overworked in personal and business success programs. Yet even among those who write about or teach goal-setting techniques, few understand the necessary strategies and systematic approach required for maximum effectiveness.

There is little question that goal setting works, at least among successful or soon-to-be-successful people. And once you learn how to power up your goals with the necessary strategies, you can create a level of accomplishment and control over your life that at this point may be beyond your imagination. In fact, you can become so good at generating goals that it will be necessary for you to be careful what you plan or ask for because you will most assuredly experience it.

Goal setting is as important to the successful operation of your life as eating or sleeping. The only difference is that your life won't end if you don't set goals. However, without goals directing your life, you will miss out on much of your potential for experiencing the positive emotions of excitement, aliveness, enthusiasm, joy, and even happiness. Without goals, you can end up living from problem to problem instead of from opportunity to opportunity. Setting goals will steer you toward opportunities while enabling you to overcome the obstacles and break through the barriers necessary for their accomplishment. Running your life without goals is about as effective as attempting to drive your car from the passenger's seat. To be effective in the goal-setting process, you must go far beyond the usual ideas of how to set goals.

Make choices, not excuses.

There are many excuses for not setting goals, and I've heard them all:

I don't have time to set goals. I'm too busy.
I don't set goals so I won't be disappointed.
I'm really not sure what I'm after.
I set goals but they just don't seem to happen.

You have the right to make excuses, but excuses won't produce results. In reality you have one of two choices: you can design and direct your future by setting goals and working to achieve them, or by default you lose the opportunity to create and control your own life. In the latter case, you allow not only your future but also your present to be controlled by other people, events, and daily pressures, all of which produce plenty of stress and frustration but not a feeling of accomplishment. Harsh but true. There are no other alternatives. Wishing or pretending it should be different won't make it so.

But when you set goals, they become your navigational tools, guiding you toward a predictable future or destination despite the sometimes not-so-predictable events that may occur along the way. And as you begin to define your life in terms of goals, you automatically increase your level of excitement, aliveness, enthusiasm, self-confidence, and self-motivation.

Success Strategy No. 15:

Set goals to organize and structure your mind for maximum effectiveness.

When I was twenty-six, I read what I consider one of the greatest books ever written, *Psycho-Cybernetics* by Maxwell Maltz. "The mind is a goal-striving mechanism," Maltz said. I understood intuitively what he meant, and I never forgot it as I observed people year after year. Those who were not committed to striving for goals seemed to have several emotions in common. Unfortunately, they were negative emotions like frustration, boredom, anger, depression, fear, loneliness, and lack of aliveness. These people were busy but never seemed to be continuously happy, content, or at peace with themselves. It was as if they were waiting for something to happen, but weren't quite sure what it was.

Without goals, negative emotions are the predominant experience. But once you've learned the fine art of establishing goals, instead of negative emotions, positive emotions become your experience—emotions of motivation, excitement, a sense of achievement, a feeling of being in control, a dramatic increase in self-confidence and the ability to weather storms along the way. Another reward of taking the time to establish your goals is greater happiness. Happiness is the overall experience of positive emotions. As with other benefits of goal setting, greater happiness is an automatic result.

Accelerating your life by setting goals also accelerates but does not create the problems and setbacks you'll encounter.

Setting goals won't rid you of all the obstacles and setbacks you will face in your life. That's not the purpose or the value of setting goals. As a matter of fact, you may find that you encounter stumbling blocks at an even more rapid rate. But that's good news, not bad. Because you will be moving toward your goals at a greater velocity, you may encounter in a month what it would have taken you twelve months to encounter at the snail's pace at which you were moving before. You are not facing additional obstacles, you are just facing the same obstacles at a faster pace. If the pace gets too frantic, you can choose to slow down. When you're in control, it's your life.

But remember, once you've worked your way to the other side of a brick wall, there's seldom a reason to climb back over. You're ready for the next challenge. The mind is indeed a goal-striving mechanism. Without goals, without destinations, without something to shoot for, you might as well hang it up. There's no way around it.

The difference between dreams and goals is in commitment and the length of time required to achieve them.

Dreams generally require more than a year to achieve, while a goal is something that can be accomplished or reached in less than a year. Of course, if everything fell into place or you suddenly confronted an unexpected opportunity, even a dream that at first appeared to require many years might be realized within one year. On the other hand, sometimes your dreams may require most of a lifetime, because so many other things have to happen first.

Goals are commitments, dreams are not. Remember how you made your Dreams List? You wrote down everything you would like to do, have, and become, without evaluation, even without consideration for its effect on those around you. As part of your blueprint, you must also make a Goals List, and when you write down a goal on your list, you define it and make a plan to take the steps necessary to achieve it. You commit yourself to its achievement no matter what roadblocks you encounter.

Your Goals List will focus on practicalities, whereas your Dreams List contains remote possibilities and even fantasies, dreams so big that when you first write them down it appears likely they would require most of a lifetime to accomplish or experience. Dreams are ends in themselves; goals are normally means to an end. In other words, goals generally fit together like pieces of a puzzle so that when all the pieces are in place a dream is realized. For instance, let's say you own your own company and your dream is to be the biggest and most respected in your field. Before realizing that dream, it is likely that dozens of related goals must first be achieved.

Another example from my own Dreams List was to wing walk, the feat of standing on the top wing of a biplane in flight. It has the earmarks of a dream.

- To be accomplished within one year? No.
- A fantasy? Yes.
- Of importance to my overall plan? No.
- A commitment? No.
- A stepping-stone to something larger? No.

As you can see, dreams are different from goals, but both are descriptions of what you want to do with your life. Those dreams on your original Dreams List that are the prime candidates for inclusion on your Goals List should meet one or more of three criteria. Create goals out of those dreams that:

- you chose to accomplish within the next year.
- are related and necessary to any goals that you would like to accomplish within the next year.
- you are willing to commit to because they inspire you, excite you, or fulfill a strong desire.

As you identify a dream that qualifies as a current goal, copy it from your Dreams List to your Goals List. Don't remove it from your Dreams List, just duplicate it on your Goals List. When you have achieved that goal, cross the goal off both your Goals List and your Dreams List.

Success is the progressive, timely achievement of your stated goals.

Using this definition, you can easily see that success and all the positive feelings associated with it are directly related to establishing goals. So let's begin by looking at the rules and strategies that must be applied to establish your goals and maximize your ability to achieve them on a timely basis.

Success Strategy No. 16:
Make your goals specific and measurable.

Imagine setting out on a two-week vacation with your car fully loaded, but with no maps and no predetermined destination. You would be lost from the moment you left your driveway. No matter how fast you traveled, you would not be going anywhere. There would be nothing to measure your progress, and no matter where you ended up at the end of each day, you would have no way of knowing if you were where you wanted to be or how far you still had to go. That's the way life works —or rather doesn't work—without goals. As my old friend Jimmy Alford used to say, "We're lost but we're making good time."

Your goals are the signposts along the roadway to your dreams. But a signpost is only useful if it tells you in what direction you should travel to get where you want to go. The way to turn each of your goals into a signpost is to define it in terms that are both specific and measurable. *Specific* means that you define a goal in terms that create a clear, concise mental picture of what you are after. *Measurable* means that you quantify each goal, making it objective instead of subjective. With money that's easy. If your goal is to have money in an investment account, you make that goal measurable by determining the exact amount of money you want to have in the account, whether $1,000 or $1 million. Without being quantified, a goal is like clay that has not yet been shaped into a beautiful, usable vase.

The more specific and measurable your goal, the more quickly you will be able to identify, locate, create, and implement the use of the necessary resources for its achievement.

Resources and strategies are necessary for the accomplishment of any goal. Resources you will normally need include time, money, materials, knowledge, and assistance from others. All must be brought together in a coordinated plan. The length of time necessary to reach your goal is generally a function of how quickly you can gather these resources and put them to use.

If your goal is unclear or nonspecific, the processes and resources necessary for its accomplishment will also be unclear and the pathway will often be confusing. That's why you should define each goal in specific and measurable terms. The test is simple. If a goal does not seem clear and precise in your own mind, it will not be easily reached.

For example, let's say you want to buy a newer car to replace your old "clunker," which is beginning to give you lots of trouble and is costing too much money. If you define your goal as simply wanting to buy a newer car, dozens of unanswered questions remain: what kind of car, what price range, what color, what make, what year, what model, what options? Without specifics, your mind ends up with confusion and questions instead of answers and directions.

However, once you define the car you are after in terms that are specific and measurable, the process becomes simpler. Your goal becomes easy to visualize. Let's say you specify your goal by stating, "The car that I want to buy is a two-year-old Lincoln Continental Mark VIII. And I want to buy it at 50 percent or less of the retail price of a new one." Now your goal is specific. From hundreds of types of cars made in different years, you have defined your goal as to manufacturer, model, and year. You have also made your goal measurable by stating the amount you will pay for the car. Your goal would be defined on your Goals List as follows: Buy a two-year-old Lincoln Continental Mark VIII at less than 50 percent of retail.

Now that you have a specific and measurable goal, the resources you will need and the procedures you will have to follow become clearer. As you conduct your search for the car, whether through newspaper advertisements or other sources, the cars available for sale that fit your parameters become easier to spot. In fact, they become so apparent, opportunities will seem to pop out from everywhere.

The more specific and measurable your goal, the more quickly it can be accomplished.

When you make your goals specific and measurable, you effectively link them to the power and abilities of your mind. Your mind operates like a magnet, attracting to you the opportunities necessary for their accomplishment. Therein lies the real creative power of your mind, and the power that is most often overlooked.

You've heard scientists say that we use no more than 5 percent of the power of our minds. If you are like me, the question has always been, How do I tap into at least some of the balance of that 95 percent? One answer is to establish goals. Your mind is constantly creating your future either by plan or by default. Default occurs when the mind has no specific plan on which to ply its power. Your mind power is wasted and your life seems to wander from one problem to another. With goals, you have assigned the power of your mind to specific tasks and your life will have a purpose and a direction.

Part of your mind, the subconscious, never sleeps. It operates twenty-four hours a day, organizing, reorganizing, and testing different combinations of potential resources and strategies necessary to accomplish your goals. Those brilliant ideas you sometimes seem to come up with in an instant can be the result of many hours of effort and tens of thousands of calculations performed by your subconscious mind, a process of which you are seldom aware. The clearer the input—the more specific and measurable your goal—the more powerful your subconscious mind becomes in working toward achieving it.

It is all too easy to state any goal in nonspecific terms. Your thoughts concerning your retirement program could be stated thus: "I need to put more money in my retirement account this year." That statement is not a goal because it is not specific and measurable. The word "more" is nonspecific, nebulous, and indefinite. It could represent any amount from one cent to the legal maximum allowed in your retirement plan.

Suppose your goal is to have a better relationship with your spouse, son, or daughter. Nothing seems to be inherently specific and measurable about that goal. And yet you know that unless your goal is stated specifically, not only will it be far more difficult to reach, you may never be quite sure when it has been accomplished.

Even goals such as better relationships or desired changes in your emotional patterns must be stated in terms that are specific and measurable if they are to be effective. Begin by thinking of how you would define a better relationship and identify the parts of the relationship that you feel are not working as well as you would like. Included might be lack of communication, very little time spent together, continuous arguments, the inability of either of you to discuss with integrity your thoughts and feelings, and the level of irritation you experience from the behavior of the other person. This list of problems represents the aspects of the relationship that you would like to change. What you want to accomplish in each of these areas can then be stated in measurable terms.

For instance, if you've identified that normally in your relationship you end up in two or more arguments a day, your goal may be to reduce the number of arguments to no more than two per week. Of course, as with all goals, you then keep score. You monitor what happens when you begin to criticize your spouse or mate, which only adds to the chance of the full-blown argument you seek to avoid. You make the determination at that point that your goal is more important than proving your point, so you rein in your emotions and get on with the accomplishment of your plan for fewer arguments. An argument, by definition, requires two people. Although you cannot control the other person, you certainly have the ability to control yourself and your actions, and in the process make the progress you are after.

To enable you to make seemingly nonspecific goals more specific, ask yourself these questions:

- What will the result look like?
- What signposts will help me know when I've accomplished my goal?
- What am I willing to contribute or change to get the job done?
- What specific commitments am I willing to make?

If, for instance, your goal is to spend more time with your spouse and you realize that the word "more" is not specific, your goals can be stated as:

- Spend thirty minutes together each Tuesday evening communicating our thoughts and feelings about our relationship.
- Go out to dinner together twice each week.

Adena and I go out to dinner several evenings each week, but recently she said, "You know, you don't seem to take me out to dinner as much." Surprised, I said, "Adena, what are you talking about? We went out to dinner three nights this week." She replied, "No, you don't understand. You don't seem to take *me* out to dinner as much. Lately we've always been with a group of people."

My mind, trained for maximum effectiveness, had begun combining personal and business dinners to accomplish multiple objectives. But Adena, correctly, wasn't buying the notion that our dinners out together were the same as dinners together with other people. Time alone with Adena was not the same as entertaining others with Adena. She was aware of it; I wasn't.

Adena wasn't being accusatory. She was saying unemotionally that she preferred to spend more time with just me. That was not inconsistent with one of my primary goals, which is to spend as much time as possible with my family—Adena, my sons and daughter-in-law, and now my grandson. They are my best and closest friends. Now, once or twice a week Adena and I may take guests out or invite them to our house for dinner, but the rest of the week it is just us. We set a mutual goal to spend more time together and did it by limiting the time we spend at dinner in the company of other people. We were clear about what we were after and established a specific and measurable goal to accomplish that result.

When setting your goals, avoid subjective words and phrases like:

a lot	more	most
much	less	greater
fewer	better	highest

These subjective words make for nonspecific, ineffective goal statements. For instance:

Put *a lot* of money in investments.
Have *fewer* nights of lost sleep.
Argue with my spouse *less often.*
Become confident *most* of the time.

Although subjective words and phrases may help define quality, they do not relate to specific quantity. When you quantify your goals, you have an objective target to aim for, and a way to measure your success when you hit that target.

The above goals can be made specific and measurable, as in these examples:

Accumulate *$50,000* in investments.
Sleep comfortably and soundly *every night.*
Argue with my spouse no more than *once per month.*
Become confident *twenty-four hours a day, every day.*

Success Strategy No. 17:
Make your goals believable.

Doubt is the opposite of belief. Doubt is temporary disbelief in your ability to accomplish, and it neutralizes your power to achieve your goals. When you do not believe achieving a goal is possible, chances are you will not achieve it no matter how badly you wish you could and no matter how many strategies you apply. The greater the distance between where you are and where you want to be, the easier it is for doubt to become a factor.

If strong belief is like pressing down on the accelerator toward your goals, then strong doubt or disbelief is like letting up on the accelerator and even applying the brakes. Doubt often shows up in random or continuous thoughts regarding the improbability or impossibility of reaching your chosen destination within your time frame, or even reaching your destination at all. Doubt is negative thought energy.

The impact of doubt is directly proportional to both the level of difficulty in achieving a goal and the intensity of the doubt.

The greater the level of difficulty you anticipate in reaching your goal, the easier it becomes to trigger doubt. Doubt often arises when your goals are out of phase with your past experiences and expectations. If a goal you have set appears unrealistic to your conscious mind for any reason, doubt will be triggered, and your mind's vast storehouse of positive energy will be watered down. It's like entering a prizefight against a strong opponent with one hand tied behind your back. Doubt only adds to any other handicap you may have.

To eliminate destructive doubt, state your goals in terms that are believable to you. In this case, no one else matters. For instance, you may believe that sometime during your lifetime the possibility exists that you could travel to the moon. You may believe that it can and will happen, coupling possibility with probability. However, if you set a goal to travel to the moon by your next birthday, it is probable that your mind will be filled with doubts like:

- Impossible. There are no scheduled moon flights.
- The government has not approved civilian space flights.
- There is no place to purchase tickets.

Mentally check each of your goals to determine if you actually believe accomplishment is possible in the time frame you have allotted. I call this process the believability test. After you've established each of your goals, apply the believability test by reading your goal and monitoring what thoughts pop into your mind. If you experience only excitement at the thought of accomplishing your goals and experience no doubt, you're on the right track. If, however, your mind suddenly fills with all the reasons that are going to make the accomplishment of your goal improbable, you still have some work to do in correctly defining that goal.

Success Strategy No. 18:

Overcome doubt with positive, present-tense affirmations.

Your doubt about the accomplishment of any goal may be the result of your past experiences, a low level of self-confidence, or other attitudes about yourself programmed in your subconscious mind. In this case, the doubt has little to do with the probability of accomplishing your goal. You are doubting yourself.

You can begin to override those negative thoughts with constant positive affirmations. For instance, your goal may be to have your MasterCard bill paid off by the end of the year, which requires no longer charging on the card and then making extra payments on the balance each month. If your experience in the past does not support the probability that you will stick to the regimen, positive affirmations may do the trick.

Phrase your affirmations in the present tense as if your goal has already been achieved. For instance, "It is December 31 and my MasterCard bill is completely paid off." Repeat the affirmation to yourself ten, a hundred, even a thousand times, over and over again whenever doubt creeps in or when you have the short-term desire to skip the extra payment or to charge something new on the card. Take the card out of your wallet. Don't cut it in half, but instead clip a note to it that says, "I have my MasterCard bill completely paid off." Through repetition your positive, present-tense affirmations can override the potentially self-defeating doubt programs in your subconscious mind.

Success Strategy No. 19:
Commit your goals to a written list.

To qualify as a goal, whatever you want to achieve must be written down. Nonwritten goals, therefore, are not goals at all. Don't catch yourself saying, "I have goals and I know what they are, so I don't need to write them down." Nonwritten goals are unclear and nonspecific, with details that tend to change each time you think about them. Putting each goal in writing crystallizes it into a set of fixed details. The clearer the goal, the more easily it can be achieved.

In the notebook that you are using to create your blueprint, turn to the page you have labeled "Goals List" and write down each of your goals, one on each line. Refer back to the Dreams List you have already made to see if the achievement of each of your goals will help you realize your dreams. If so, you are heading in the right direction. Also review your Dreams List to see if any of your dreams qualify for immediate inclusion on your Goals List. Keep your blueprint someplace handy where you can update your Goals List and refer to it often. When you have accomplished each goal, cross it off the list. Remember, each goal you accomplish takes you one step closer to the life of your dreams.

Increased clarity equals increased opportunity.

The number of opportunities you will take advantage of during your lifetime is directly proportional to your clarity of vision and your willingness to take action or risk. That's where your Goals List comes in. An immediate result of determining specifically what you are after is increased clarity. Increased clarity is what it takes to recognize an opportunity and seize it. The goals on your Goals List are the action steps toward the realization of any dream, and where action and opportunity meet, events begin to move in your direction. When you know where you want to go and what you have to do to get there, you are in control. You have by choice established the goals that are most important to you. Why invest your time and energy in anything else?

Success Strategy No. 20:

State your goals as single, concise sentences beginning with action verbs.

Each of your goals should be stated and written in one complete, powerful sentence beginning with an action verb. Action verbs establish movement, and the essence of any goal lies in moving from where you are to where you want to be.

On the following chart you will see 109 action words that are appropriate goal-sentence starters. Notice that all words describe a specific action you will take.

Add (information)
Apply
Ask
Avoid
Become
Begin
Bid on
Borrow
Build
Buy
Call
Carry
Change
Check
Choose
Combine
Complete
Compute
Consider
Contact
Contribute
Convert
Copy
Correct
Create
Cut
Decline
Decrease
Deduct
Delay
Determine
Develop
Divide
Do
Drop
Eliminate
Enjoy
Enroll
Examine
File
Finance
Find out
Fix
Formulate
Get
Give
Go
Hire
Identify
Incorporate
Increase
Instruct
Insure
Invest
Join
Keep
Learn
List
Locate
Make
Maximize
Meet
Minimize
Move
Obtain
Open
Operate
Overcome
Own
Participate
Pay
Photograph
Prepare
Protect
Purchase
Put
Qualify
Raise
Read
Reduce
Refinance
Remove
Rent
Replace
Roll over
Select
Sell
Send
Set up
Shop for
Show
Sign
Spend time
Start
Stop
Store
Structure
Substitute
Subtract
Take
Teach
Time
Train
Turn
Upgrade
Use
Withdraw
Work
Write

Action words set direction and establish momentum. As you are stating your goals in writing, refer to this list until you get the hang of it. You may wish to add words of your own. The list is meant to get you moving and not to limit you in any way.

Success Strategy No. 21:

Set a realistic target date for the completion of each goal.

Setting a target date is essential to the effective completion of each of the goals on your list. A target date is the realistic date by which you think your goal can be completed or reached. A target date is based in part on desire and in part on what is both possible and practical.

As you write each of your goals, set an initial target date for its completion. Since, in general, a goal is something you intend to have accomplished within one year, your target date will normally fall within the next twelve months. There is, of course, a fine line between desire and possibility. Though you might desire to accomplish your goal by tomorrow at the latest, the reality is that the accomplishment of any goal takes time. The amount of time required is usually a function of the resources, money, and knowledge needed, as well as the number of other steps you must take to accomplish the goal. Your aim is to pick a target date that combines the best of desire with the best of what's possible.

There is also a fine line between realism and doubt. Once you have written a goal, negative thoughts can creep into and muddy the process. Thoughts like "I don't really have the money or the smarts" may make the goal seem unattainable, or the time it will take seem infinite. You have within you the absolute power to accomplish any realistic goal on your list, so mentally eliminate doubt from the process at the outset.

When you first write any goal on your list, you probably won't have at hand all the resources required for its eventual accomplishment. If you did, it is a safe bet that your goal would already be a reality. Your strategy in picking a target date is to calculate mentally the reasonable time it will take you to gather the resources and the additional knowledge necessary to achieve your goal. Don't spend a lot of time picking your target date, since later you will have the option of lengthening or even shortening it as you discover in more detail what will be required.

Setting target dates for all your goals establishes the velocity at which you will work to achieve them. If you double the time you expect it will take to achieve each goal, obviously you have to put in only half as much effort and time each day to meet your target date. However, the downside is you could have accomplished twice as much in the same amount of time and you will not experience the same level of satisfaction that you would from accomplishing more in less time.

Conversely, if your target dates are not realistic and far too short to be practical, you can create feelings of frustration because things are not happening according to schedule, or you may even begin to feel that you are just not a person capable of achievement. Feelings of frustration and self-doubt are unnecessary and can be eliminated by setting realistic target dates. There is no way to cook a three-minute egg in two minutes. Reaching goals does take time. Push yourself into action but allow yourself adequate time.

Let's take a look at how the whole process works by following the thoughts of one of my students, Bill, who decided to put my goal-setting strategies to work. "What are some of the things I'd like to do?" Bill thought as he began to prepare a list of his goals. "Let's see, I'd like to be in business for myself, in something that relates to boats." So Bill wrote down his first goal: *Start a successful boating business.* Was this goal specific and measurable? Yes. A single, concise sentence beginning with an action verb? Yes. Then Bill thought, "Well, if I'm going to start my own business, I've got to stop working so hard. These sixty-hour work weeks are eating into my personal and free time." Bill's second goal: *Cut work time to forty hours per week.* Does it follow the strategies? You bet. "The kids are getting older," Bill thought, "and I haven't done much planning for college. One of my goals is certainly to invest enough money to see that they get a college education." So Bill added this goal to his list: *Set up a college investment plan for Sandy and Tom.*

As the weeks went by, Bill added to his Goals List, while looking for opportunities to move in the direction of accomplishing the goals already on his list. He also set up realistic time frames for the goals on the list. When he was finished, Bill's handwritten list looked something like this.

Bill's Goals List

Goal	Target Completion Date
1. Start a successful boating business.	________
2. Cut work time to forty hours per week.	________
3. Set up a college investment plan for Sandy and Tom.	________
4. Teach children in the YMCA tutoring program.	________
5. Lose ten pounds.	________
6. Learn and apply relaxation techniques.	________
7. Stop criticizing Marjorie.	________
8. Create my financial plan, following Givens strategies.	________
9. Contribute $6,000 this year to my 401(k) plan.	________

Now, following Bill's example, draw up your own personal list of at least ten goals you would like to accomplish within the next year.

The more of a dreamer you are, the longer your Goals List will be from the start. However, if you've never set goals, you're going to have to "kick-start" yourself into the thinking process to get it done. Once your goals start flowing from your mind, they will continue. There is no limit to the number of goals on which the mind can work at one time. Although you may be initially limited in the time you have each week to pursue your goals, that will change. Once you're clear about what you're after, you will begin to find more and more time you didn't think existed for pursuing the very things that are the most important to you.

Someone once said, "If you can dream it, you can do it." The statement is true, but it can be more accurately phrased, "If you turn your dreams into specific, measurable, believable, written goals, you can anticipate their accomplishment."

Success Strategy No. 22:

Keep a copy of your top ten goals where you will see it every day.

It is easy to become distracted from spending your time and energy on what you have chosen as the most important parts of your life—your goals. Keep yourself on track and heading for your goals by continually reminding yourself of what those goals are. I have already shown you how to include your Goals List in your overall blueprint, which will serve as a permanent record of your progress. But it's also a good idea to keep a list of your top ten goals someplace where you will see it every day.

Here are some suggestions:

- the bathroom mirror
- the refrigerator
- your middle desk drawer at the office
- Scotch-taped to the top of your desk or computer stand at home
- on a card in your wallet or purse
- on the sun visor of your car, held in place by rubber bands

Twenty years ago, while I was experimenting with how to display my goals in places where I would bump into them every day, I used one strategy you will not want to repeat. I decided that an effortless way to remind myself of my goals every morning was to write them on my bathroom mirror with a piece of soap. I am so creative, I thought. Now the first thing every morning, I will face myself, my goals, and my day with renewed motivation and inspiration. Alas, it was not to be. When I took a hot steamy shower, my soap-written goals dissolved and ran down the mirror in an illegible blur.

Keep a list of your top-priority goals where you will see them the first thing every morning and the last thing every night. If you choose the bathroom mirror, just be certain you use a written or typed list on a piece of paper fastened with tape.

CHAPTER **7**

Seeing Success

A picture is an intermediate something between a thought and a thing.

—CALVIN COOLIDGE

Now that you have made a list of the important goals in your life and have decided on the first steps you must take toward achieving them, you are ready to use another strategy that will dramatically increase your momentum: the power of visualization.

Visualization is the process of creating a mental picture of what you want to happen as if it has already happened. For example, let's say that one of your goals is to own a weekend retreat in the mountains. Now make a mental picture of that goal. Visualize the landscape, the house, yourself *in* that house on a summer weekend, looking out over the scenery.

Success Strategy No. 23:

Visualize your goals clearly to achieve them more quickly.

How well you visualize depends primarily on how you have used or can train your mind. Some people can create intense mental pictures of the accomplishment of their goals in living color and vivid detail. That's great if you can do it, but without training most people can conjure up only a vague impression or a very hazy mental picture.

To determine how well you visualize, close your eyes and think of a bright red fire engine—a big hook-and-ladder truck. You've certainly seen one before, so you do have a vivid, detailed picture of one stored in your subconscious memory bank. How well you are able to recall or visualize that fire engine depends on how well you are able to search your memory bank and bring the already existing picture into your conscious mind. Do you see the fire engine as clearly as if you were looking at a sharp snapshot, or is it blurry and not too clear? Now think again of that vacation retreat or another one of your goals. How clearly can you see it in your mind's eye?

From my own experience, there is no question that the speed with which you are able to achieve your goals is directly related to how clearly and how often you are able to visualize your goals. The more clearly you can mentally picture how your life will be when your goal has been achieved, the easier it is for your mind to search out and spot the opportunities that are essential for accomplishment. The power of visualization will expand your horizons. If you can see your destination clearly, you know the direction you have to go to get there.

The power of visualization is also a strong motivator. It's

like adding an afterburner to a jet engine, or a four-barrel carburetor and fuel injection to an automobile engine. You are upgrading the engine from good performance to high performance. In this case, the engine is your mind. Its effectiveness in accomplishing your goals in minimum time and with minimum effort is greatly enhanced when you add the power of visualization. Your mind goes from good performance into high performance.

Whatever you visualize clearly and often will eventually become part of your reality—your experience. Sometimes even the most remote possibilities, even the seemingly impossible, becomes probable. Let me give you an example from my own experience.

For fifteen years in SuperSelf workshops I described again and again my progression from the cowardice I experienced as a child to the courage that is now part of my life after the total elimination of fear. (Something I'll help you with in Chapter 21.) Part of courage is the mental realization that when you find yourself in stressful, dangerous, or even life-threatening situations you are a totally capable person able to remain calm but alert and to make instantaneous, positive, self-preserving decisions without panic. That experience of courage is part of your SuperSelf.

As an analogy, I would ask the group, "How would you feel and react if you were suddenly placed in a small room with a several-hundred-pound wild tiger and no way out because it was between you and the door? My SuperSelf," I would continue, "is now so in control that I would not experience fear or panic, only the calm ability to make decisions based on the actions of the cat."

Somehow that example had an almost fairy-tale-like quality to me as I visualized it over and over through the years. Although I know all things are possible, facing off with a big cat in a small space was nowhere to be found on either my Dreams List or my Goals List. Then it happened.

In 1991, Adena and I were on an adventurous, nine-country

trip through South America. We had been gone for a few weeks and she wanted, if possible, to fly from Quito, Ecuador, back to Orlando to spend Thanksgiving with her parents, and then in a few days fly south to meet me in Trinidad. Of course, it was possible. I put Adena on the plane home and caught another flight to Cayenne, French Guiana, a small country on the north coast of South America.

French Guiana is a country of dense jungles; 97 percent of its 100,000 people live on the coast. It was originally colonized by European prospectors with dreams of finding gold, but the prospectors quickly died off, as did the accompanying soldiers, from malaria and other jungle diseases completely unfamiliar to the Europeans but manageable by the few native Carib Indian inhabitants. The country still operates as a French protectorate and most of the people speak French but not English.

In Cayenne, I hired Jack, a laid-off shrimp boat worker, to take me as far back into the jungles as we could get in a day. Jungles are my favorite places in the world, and I have conducted private expeditions into many of them.

There are only two roads in French Guiana, the coast road and the convict-built road that heads straight into the interior. As we traveled that road, Jack said he knew of a place where some animals and reptiles that had recently been taken out of the jungle were kept and we drove for some time to get there. The animals included a beautiful 200-pound jaguar, a massive, fast-moving, tree-climbing member of the cat family and king of the South American jungle. The cat was kept in a cage ten feet by fifteen feet, surrounded by chicken wire, with an eight-foot tin roof to keep out the hot sun.

"Want to see if we can get close enough to pet him?" Jack asked, challenging me. "I can get permission from the guard and help from the man who feeds him."

"You bet," I said, thinking only of the incredible story that could be told—if we survived.

The three of us—Jack, the animal feeder, and I—entered

the jaguar's domain watching two huge eyes watching us from a platform built to simulate a tree branch about six feet off the ground at the end of the cage. I couldn't help thinking of a clip I had seen just two days before of a 1950s Ed Sullivan show on which the great animal trainer Clyde Beatty had declined at the last minute to go through with his lion act. The cage was too small because of the size of the stage. But Sullivan persuaded Beatty into working in a fifteen-foot-by-fifteen-foot cage, and, true to form, one of the lions jumped him. It took five minutes and the repeated firing of Beatty's blank-loaded gun to get the lion to back down.

As anyone knows who has seen the pictures on my animal wall at the Givens Organization, I had already overcome all of my childhood fears of animals and have held or played with water buffalo, wild rhinoceroses, snakes, spiders, and crocodiles around the world. And now, here I was a few feet from one of the most ferocious animals of the South American jungle, often known to attack local Indians when cornered.

I was loving it. There was not an ounce of fear on my part, just the excitement of the opportunity to do something few people have ever done: face off with a big cat. In less than a second, the cat leaped almost silently to the ground, and I saw that he was as big as I was. Jack and the feeder backed up against the wire at the far side of the cage. I was left in the middle and the cat began circling, never taking his eyes off me. His paws made no sound, just like a house cat, and he began murmuring a low growl which I imagined to be friendly. As he continued to circle me, it was easy to see which of us was cornered and which was in charge.

Suddenly the cat broke the circle and jumped to my side. I let my hand dangle so he could smell it, just as you would with a dog. This magnificent animal came up to my waist. His huge, sandpaper-like tongue began to lick my hand as the guard and the feeder began talking quickly in French and then a few words of English I didn't understand.

"Face him, face him," Jack said nervously in broken English. It took me a few seconds to figure out that he was telling me to turn my whole body toward the jaguar to show that I had no fear.

In an instant the cat opened his huge jaws and in another second had my entire right thigh in his mouth. I could feel the teeth clamp down through my black cotton knee-length shorts, just hard enough so I could almost count the teeth. Then the cat released his grip and backed off for a moment, watching to see what I would do. He got around behind me, brushing past my leg, still uttering that guttural purr.

"Face him, face him!" came the screams. I turned to face him as the cat took one leap, propelled by his giant hind legs and feet. I braced myself for the inevitable, and he hit me squarely, as if he were leaping into my arms.

With his hind feet on the ground, the cat stood six feet high. He opened his jaws and put the entire side of my face in his mouth. I was looking at tonsils. Still I didn't get the sense that he wanted to harm me. He was just playing with me like a toy. His upper teeth were across my nose, and his back teeth were at the back of my head. I felt one tooth pierce the skin on the back of my neck and another scrape along the side of my nose. At that tense moment, I couldn't help think about how often I had stressed in the SuperSelf program the importance of facing your fears in breaking through your limits.

After what seemed like a minute, the cat let go of my head and walked to the other side of the cage, growling low, almost as if he was laughing. Then he leaped at me again, and this time I caught him as I would a child leaping into my arms. He was all I could hold, and he grabbed my waist with his powerful tree-climbing hind legs as if I were a tree trunk. Now his head was higher than the back of mine, and he again opened his huge mouth and wrapped his jaws around my head.

When I released my grip from around the jaguar's body, his hind feet hit the ground, but his paws were still on my shoulders and he was staring me straight in the face. That was our goodbye. We had had all the fun I could handle for one day. I backed away from him, and as I ducked through the small door of the cage, I put my hand on the back of my neck where it felt as if blood was running down. It was, from two perfect punctures made by the cat's massive pointed teeth.

"Any problem?" I asked Jack who was startled at the sight. "Any problem with rabies, I mean."

"No problem at all," he said. "From monkey bites and dog bites, yes, but not from jaguar bites."

Later I again thought of how often I had asked the participants in my SuperSelf workshops to visualize how they would react if they found themselves facing down a big cat. "If you can visualize it," I had often said, "it will become part of your experience." Admittedly, it was an extreme example, but this too had become part of *my* experience. In fact, visualization is such a powerful tool for achieving your dreams and goals that as you become a pro at this life-experience-creating strategy, you must be careful to watch what you ask for, because surely you will get it.

Success Strategy No. 24:

Make visualizing your goals a regular habit.

Visualizing a goal is like giving a direct order to your mind to apply its full power to the goal's accomplishment. But unfortunately, the picture you have created of your goal is not the only data being received by your mind. In fact, it is only a minuscule percentage of the incoming data, part of which may even be negative information—reasons why you think you *can't* achieve your goal. Block out those negative thoughts with positive visualizations. As yet there are no scientific instruments to measure the power of visualization. Science has not yet advanced to the level of being able to measure consciousness or thought other than as changes in brain-wave patterns. But don't wait for science to catch up. There is no doubt that the more often you visualize what you are after, the more quickly you will see and experience tangible results.

For instance, if your goal is to be the vice president or executive manager of your department or company, visualize yourself in your new office, smiling, satisfied with your new nameplate as VP or executive manager on your desk. No, you don't have to envision the current VP jumping out a tenth-story window to clear a space for you. No, you don't have to envision some male chauvinist, whom you perceive as standing in your way of becoming the first woman executive, getting hit by a train. All you need to do is see yourself where you want to be—and then, one by one, take the steps that will get you there in ways that do not harm other people. No guilt about accomplishment required. You worked for it.

Remember, the greater the detail and clarity of your thought pictures and the more often you picture what you want, the more quickly you are likely to see results and to overcome the apparent obstacles between where you are and where you want to be.

Success Strategy No. 25:

Add momentum to your visualizations with some high-powered emotions.

As the saying goes, "Get into it." Get into visualization of your goal by generating some positive emotions and feelings about it. In your mind, see it, touch it, taste it, feel it, believe it, experience it, live it. It's your goal, and your goals are something to get excited about.

Visualizing your goals with positive emotions and enthusiasm is one of the best ways to put down doubt. Don't let negative thoughts and emotions enter the picture. With positive feelings of accomplishment and excitement, you can leave feelings of doubt and inadequacy in the dust. No, you're not just faking it.

Success Strategy No. 26:

Visualize your goals just before you go to sleep.

Your mind never sleeps—at least not your subconscious mind. And it is your subconscious mind that sparks your ability to transform an imagined goal into reality. That's why a great time to visualize goals is while you are on the way to the Land of Nod. Keep a copy of your Goals List next to your bed and glance at it before you turn out the lights. Then visualize the accomplishment of as many of your goals as possible.

During the six to eight hours you are asleep, your subconscious mind will continue the process. It will organize, categorize, explore options and alternatives, and even come up with some of the elusive answers you've been looking for about how you are going to get from here to there.

This process is no stranger to you. You have already had the experience of going to bed with something weighing on your mind only to awaken with ideas, alternatives, and even answers as if they came out of nowhere. All you are doing with this strategy is consciously controlling the input and data your subconscious mind will be working on overnight. The results are astounding. Give it a shot a few times. Even if the answers and alternatives don't come immediately upon awakening, you'll find that they'll pop into your head while you are sipping your breakfast coffee or when you're on your way to work.

There is also a side benefit to closing your eyes with your goals in mind. You may find that the process enables you to go to sleep more easily and quickly. If you have trouble falling asleep, positive nighttime goal visualization will edge out the negative thoughts or worries that seem to be running at lightning speed through your mind, keeping you wide awake and staring at the ceiling.

Success Strategy No. 27:

Visualize your goals as if you have already achieved them.

If you visualize your goals as something you will reach in the future, your accomplishment of those goals will be constantly pushed into the future rather than experienced in the present. You may not prevent your goal from becoming reality, but you will lengthen the amount of time required to achieve it. Remember the old saying, "Tomorrow never comes." Always picture your goals in the present tense. Instead of mentally asserting, for instance, that you *will* become a vice president of your company, picture yourself as already the vice president—now! Visualizing your goals in the present tense instructs your mind to compress time and bring the accomplishment of those goals as quickly as possible into the present. No, you are not lying to yourself. Remember, everything created by man or woman was once an idea, a thought, a vision before it became a physical reality, including the chair you are sitting on.

Once you get into the habit of constantly visualizing the results you are after, you will notice that your self-confidence and, therefore, your level of enthusiasm increase. You will even get to the point, as I eventually did, where your pictures of the future will seem like your experience of the present. Once you can visualize your dreams and goals, you are well on your way to their accomplishment.

CHAPTER 8

Aligning Your Goals with Your Values

Success is getting what you want. Happiness is wanting what you get.

—CARL TRUMBELL HAYDEN

In the late 1970s, when I lived in Washington, D.C., I was introduced to an attorney at a Capitol Hill cocktail reception. This man had spent his entire life working to build one of the biggest law firms in the country—384 lawyers in Boston, Washington, and New York. To strike up a conversation I innocently commented, "You must really be proud and excited about what you've accomplished. Lots of lawyers have the dream you had, but couldn't pull it off. You did."

I expected a simple response like "Thank you." Instead, his face softened and after a long sip of his scotch he replied, "Son, let me tell you how I feel about what I've accomplished. From the time I was in law school—even before—my dream was to become the best and the biggest. I had a burning desire to build the largest law firm in the country. I married my college sweetheart while we were still in school, and soon after receiving my law degree I started working day and night to realize that dream. When my wife began telling me that she wanted to spend more time with me, I'd say, 'But honey, I'm doing it for you.' She said that if I really wanted to do something for her, I could spend more time with her instead of with my job.

"Our first child came, and then our second. I was not there when they were born. I was off opening offices in other cities. Again, my wife begged, 'You've got to spend more time with us.' And my standard reply was 'I'm too busy right now but it will change.' It never did.

"I'm seventy-four years old now. My wife left me twenty-five years ago and I never remarried. At the time, I was shocked because I thought I had made it possible for her to have every material thing a woman could want. I know now I was wrong. I gave her everything *I* wanted her to have.

"My kids and I don't know each other and never did. I'm retired from the law firm now. I just don't have the energy for it, and I've got nothing left to prove. I've got grandchildren I have never seen. Since I never related to my kids, they've never had any reason to bring their own kids to see me."

By this time, the man had a trace of tears in his eyes. "If I had it to do over again," he said, "I would first determine what was really important to me and build my life around that instead of what I thought was supposed to be important to me. But it's too late now."

His words hit me like a hammer. Then and there I began to realize the importance of knowing your values in the pursuit of your dreams and goals. His story made apparent to me the dangers of conflicts between goals and values.

Conflict inevitably occurs when your goals and values are out of alignment.

When what you think you want, your goal, is in conflict with what you think is important to you, your values, the result is a feeling of emptiness when that goal is achieved. You look around wondering, Is this all there is? Why am I not as excited and as enthusiastic as I thought I would be? The reason is that when your goals are not in alignment with your values, their accomplishment does not trigger the positive emotions of excitement, aliveness, and enthusiasm.

To put it simply, values are the things, people, concepts, and feelings that you rate the most highly in your life. They constitute your personal philosophy of life and will give you the greatest sense of satisfaction and feelings of self-worth and accomplishment. But when setting personal goals, very few people are wise enough to ask, Do these goals *really* reflect what I value most in life?

The truth is that most people don't spend a lot of time thinking about their values or even what their values are. Or they often accept without question the values of others, only to realize at some later date that they do not share those values. As a result, they spend a large part of every day, and thus a large part of their lives, working toward goals that have little to do with what really matters to them.

An understanding of what you value the most is essential in determining your priorities and setting your goals in life. Without an awareness of your values and a cross-check against your goals, that great sense of accomplishment results only by chance, when you have been lucky enough to inadvertently align a goal and a top value. A lack of satisfaction upon achieving your goals can then deter you from setting new goals that are more in line with your values.

Your values can, and will, change as you go through life. What is important to you in your twenties may be less important in your forties or fifties. Or you may have simply overestimated the importance of a value. That's why it is essential to continually ask yourself:

Am I designing my life around what I value the most?
Is what I am trying to achieve something I truly value?
Am I experiencing any conflict between my goals and my values?
Has the accomplishment of goals in the past produced an empty or an excited feeling?

Success Strategy No. 28:

For maximum enjoyment of success, first determine your top ten values.

If this is the first time you have thought about "values," you may think that there are dozens or even hundreds of them. If so, you will be surprised to learn that if you compiled a list of the different values expressed by ten thousand or even a hundred thousand people anywhere in the world, they would all tend to fall into just twenty-five categories. I have talked to people in a hundred countries from hundreds of different cultures, but the things they value the most are always the same. These values cross all cultural, ethnic, racial, and sexual lines. Once you strip away externals, the sameness of all of us underneath becomes so apparent that the differences disappear. That sameness lies in our values.

Chuck, Rob, and I and another member of the Givens Organization spent five weeks in Papua New Guinea in 1991. We got so far back into the interior that many of the people there

—the elders and the children—had never before seen white people. They have no newspapers, no radio, no television. They don't even have the wheel, which is why scientists classify them as still living in the Stone Age. Because I'd seen the sameness when it comes to hopes, dreams, and values of people all over the world, no matter what their culture or background, I wanted to know if that was still true in a village of Stone Age people.

We were climbing a mountain called Mt. Gillaway and were a couple of thousand feet up when we arrived at a little village where several families lived. The people were so friendly they gave us one of their huts for the night and two complete families crowded into another. The hut was made of straw, with a dirt floor and a hole carved in the middle of the dirt for a fire. There was no place for the smoke to escape, so if you built a fire (and it was very cold at night that high up on the mountain) the hut filled with smoke. To the villagers, we were unique, and that evening they all came to the hut to see us.

In Papua there are seven hundred different languages. Each tribe has its own language. But in every village at least one person spoke a common language made up of German, English, and a couple of dialects, which is called pidgin. Our guide had lived in Papua for eighteen months and could speak pidgin. He translated what we said in English into pidgin, relaying our words to the one person in the tribe who also spoke pidgin, who then translated our words into the local village language for the people. You can imagine how long it took to communicate back and forth that way.

These were the questions I had for the villagers:

Where do you think you came from?
Where do you think you're going?
What do you want for your children?
What are your dreams and goals in life?

What I found out about these Stone Age people was that they had the same hopes, dreams, and values that all of us have. They wanted better things for their children. They wanted to do better financially, which meant raising better crops of Ca Ca (sweet potato) and owning more pigs, since pigs are the real wealth. They wanted to believe that there was something to look forward to after death and they wanted peace of mind, a long life, and good health. They wanted to travel, but felt they couldn't because they were surrounded on all sides by tribes they considered enemies. Most had never been more than five miles from the village. And while they did not use words like "fame" or "career," they implied that status and meaningful work or craftsmanship was also important to them. This group of people who had almost no contact with the twentieth century had hopes, dreams, and values not so much different from those in our own super high-tech world. Strip away the façade, I thought to myself, and people everywhere are virtually the same. The experience brought a whole new meaning to me of the concept of the "Brotherhood of Man."

Now take a few moments to review the Values List I have created for you on page 127. They are the twenty-five values I have found to be the most important to people all over the world. What you personally value most will tend to jump out at you as you read the list. Note on a piece of paper all the values that seem important to you. From that list choose what you consider your top ten values and arrange them in the order of their importance to you, from one through ten. This is your Values List. Keep it in your overall blueprint for ready reference and for frequent comparison with your Goals List to make sure they are in alignment.

Don't confuse your values and your goals. A value is something you believe in, feel, or think about yourself. A goal is something you intend to change or accomplish. Although, as you will see, it is extremely important that your goals and values are in alignment and work in harmony, they are not at all the same.

Values List

1. Peace of mind
2. Security
3. Wealth
4. Good health
5. A close relationship with spouse/mate
6. A close relationship with children
7. A close relationship with parents or other family members
8. Meeting the "right" person
9. A meaningful job or career
10. Fame
11. Power
12. Free time
13. Happiness
14. A close relationship with God
15. Friendships
16. Retirement
17. Contributing time, knowledge, or money to others
18. Knowing accomplished and successful people
19. Controlling my own business
20. Overcoming all my problems
21. Living to an old age
22. Personal possessions—cars, houses, jewelry, etc.
23. Travel to exciting places
24. A sense of accomplishment
25. Respect from others—being thought of as a good person

Success Strategy No. 29:

For maximum satisfaction and effectiveness, align your goals with your top values.

When your goals are in line with your top values, your time and your mental and emotional energy will be invested in working toward and achieving the goals that you feel are most important to you. To live your life successfully, it is imperative that your goals and top values be in alignment. The most satisfying and fulfilling goals that you will ever accomplish in life will match your top five values. You will experience pleasure and reward from those goals you reach that match values six through ten, but not to the extent that accomplishing the goals in alignment with values one to five will produce. Achieving the goals on your list that don't match any of your top ten values will leave you with the Is-that-all-there-is? feeling. Even when you achieve those goals on time and with great struggle, you will have the feeling that you have been wasting time.

Let me share with you a real-life example of values conflict. When a woman from North Carolina named Patrice participated in one of my SuperSelf seminars, she had already set as her top one-year goal to remodel her home, and was allocating much of her time and money to this plan. But when she ranked her top ten values, nowhere to be found was any value that was served by remodeling her home. As a matter of fact, she began to see, and told the group, that this goal was already becoming a source of major conflict in her life.

The top values on Patrice's list were spending time with her family and experiencing peace of mind, and these two values were in direct conflict with the process of tearing up her house and having it remodeled. When the realization struck her, Patrice crossed her remodeling project off her Goals List. She had never questioned the project from the time she had conceived it, but once she saw that goal was out of alignment with her top values, the conflict was obvious. When she really thought about it, Patrice admitted she actually enjoyed her home just the way it was, and couldn't think of a single truly significant benefit in making all the changes. With some of the funds she had saved for remodeling her house but no longer needed for that purpose, Patrice was then able to take her whole family on a long vacation and spend some real quality time with them in a relaxing environment, which also contributed to one of her top values—peace of mind.

The only thing more destructive to your life than setting goals that are out of alignment with your values is setting no goals at all.

You can leave conflict and inefficiency behind and instead experience satisfaction and effectiveness through the habitual use of my simple values alignment exercise. Aligning the goals you set with your values is the first step in fine-tuning your blueprint for successful and effective living. As Ted, who attended one of my SuperSelf experiences, said, "It seems to me that if we have mixed values, mixed objectives in our lives, we end up not really caring about ourselves and, as a result, we don't contribute too much to the betterment of our own lives, nor to the betterment of other people's lives."

To complete the values alignment exercise, simply compare the lists you made of your top ten goals and your top ten values. For example, Mary, a divorced personnel manager in her mid-fifties, developed the following one-year Goals List.

1. Obtain a 10 percent raise in salary.
2. Be promoted to personnel director.
3. See each of my five grandchildren once a month.
4. Visit Europe for two weeks.
5. Lose fifteen pounds.
6. Design an exercise program and do it three times a week.
7. Start a home business in needlework.
8. Meet a wonderful man.
9. Eliminate interruptions from my life.
10. Buy a new car.

Mary's top five values were:

1. A close relationship with family
2. Travel to exciting places
3. Retirement
4. Peace of mind
5. Security

When she compared her goals to her values, Mary discovered that a couple of the goals she had thought were most important were not in alignment with any of her top values. The potential result? Values conflict. One of her top values was retirement. Therefore, her objective of working harder and longer with the hope of being promoted to personnel director in one year was in conflict with the value she placed on retirement and spending more time with her children and grandchildren.

Mary's goal of starting a needlework business had come about as the result of the passion for needlework she shared with her daughter, and the thought that in a business they could spend more time together. In talking to her daughter, Ann, Mary discovered that now that Ann's children were older, she was interested in participating more actively in the business idea, and might even be able to run it full-time. Mary revised her Goals List to align her goals with her values.

1. Retire from my current job by age fifty-eight (retirement).
2. Write a business plan for the needlework business with Ann (security, retirement, and close relationships with family).
3. Save and invest an additional $2,000 per year (security and early retirement).
4. See each of my five grandchildren once a month (close relationship with family).
5. Visit Europe for two weeks (travel to exciting places).
6. Eliminate unnecessary interruptions from my life (peace of mind).

If your goals are not in alignment with your values, either revise your Values List and set new goals that reflect your values, or reexamine your goals and eliminate those that no longer seem important. (Mary did both.) When you have verified that each of your goals meets one of your top ten values, write the number of the value as shown on your Values List next to your goal.

On the following page, in graphic form, is what happens when you create a blueprint for your life in which your dreams, goals, and values are in alignment.

The Interaction of Dreams, Goals, and Values

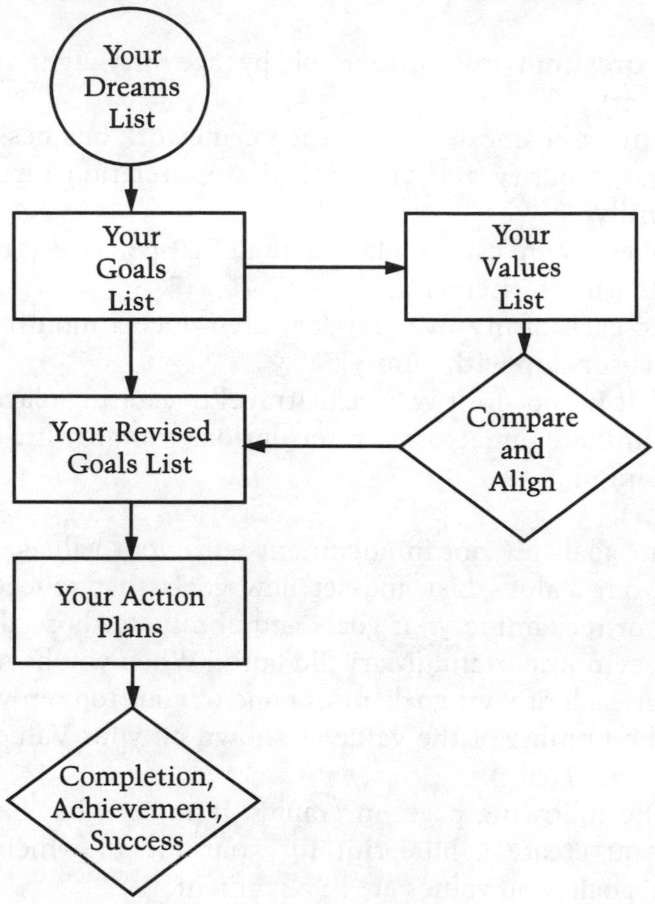

You have limited time and energy—we all do. That's a fact of life. Don't waste your precious energy achieving goals that will not create the sense of accomplishment and satisfaction that will give real meaning to your life. Remember, as you grow older and wiser your values may change. Be certain your goals change along with them.

CHAPTER **9**

Operating with Objectives: Your Action Plans

If you don't know where you are going, you will probably end up somewhere else.

—Laurence J. Peter

Now that you're certain your goals and values are in alignment, it's time to swing into action and start working to achieve your goals. But first, to save time and energy, and to achieve maximum effectiveness, you should create an Action Plan for each goal. An Action Plan is a list of the successive steps or actions you must take to achieve each goal, and it includes target dates for their completion. An Action Plan will enable you to conceptualize and pursue a goal as if it was a single project, which is exactly what it is. All the necessary steps and strategies for completion are in one place, on one page, which makes monitoring your progress an easy task.

Keep all your Action Plans in your blueprint. Action Plans will become a major part of your planning and control system for both your business and personal life.

Success Strategy No. 30:

Complete one Action Plan for each goal on your list.

A goal is a destination, but along the way many individual steps will be required to achieve it. The steps necessary to reach your goal are your objectives, all of which must be accomplished before that goal becomes a reality. Whereas your goals are the stepping-stones toward your dreams, your objectives are the lampposts that illuminate the path to each goal. The accomplishment of each objective brings you one step closer to your target. To complete one Action Plan for each goal:

1. Copy or duplicate the Action Plan format on page 135. Make one copy for each goal on your Goals List.
2. Copy a single goal on each form, using the one-sentence description from your Goals List.
3. Include the number of your goal from your Goals List and whether the goal is business or personal. Note the date you are beginning the action form, and the target date for completion.

Action Plan

Check one: Goal Number: (from Goals List)

□ Business □ Personal

Goal: ______________________________

Today's Date: ______________ Target Date: (from Goals List)

Start Date	Objectives	Completion Date
	1. (your first step)	
	2.	
	3.	
	4.	
	5.	
	6.	
	7.	
	8.	
	9.	
	10.	
	11.	
	12.	
	13.	
	14.	
	15.	
	16.	
	17.	
	18.	
	19.	
	20.	

Success Strategy No. 31:

Specify a first step as the first objective on your Action Plan.

It has been said that the longest journey begins with but a single step. The same is true of the journey along the path toward your goals. One big difference between doers and talkers is the initiation of that first step.

After you have written a goal on an Action Plan, write a short sentence describing the initial action you will take toward its accomplishment. The first step is your first objective. The toughest part for most people is just getting started, overcoming inertia. A clear description of the first step you must take will give you both momentum and direction.

You activate opportunity by getting into action.

To succeed in reaching any goal requires:

- the presence of opportunity, and
- taking advantage of the opportunities that are present.

Opportunity is an option that, if exercised, will move you one or more steps toward your predetermined goal. Life is full of opportunities, the vast majority of which go unexercised.

Imagine yourself standing in an eight-by-twelve-foot room with bare walls and not a stick of furniture or other adornments. Every sixty seconds someone drops a $100 bill through one of a dozen holes scattered throughout the ceiling. Those $100 bills represent your opportunities. That means there are opportunities all around you every minute of the day. All you have to do is keep your eyes open and grab them as they float by.

The problem is that you are blindfolded. Opportunities are falling all around you and you cannot see a single one. You can grope in the dark and occasionally grab one of them out of thin air, but most will just float right by, untouched, untested, and unconcerned about whether you take advantage of them or not. Opportunities are neutral. They don't become more prevalent or more accessible because you "deserve" them, or because you have "paid your dues." The only way you can take advantage of the opportunities all around you is to take the blinders off, to know exactly what you are looking for and then to reach out and grab it.

Listing a first step as the first objective at the same time you first pull out each Action Plan will get you into action, and action will allow you to seize the moment—to seize the opportunities that are constantly passing you by. Sometimes the first step toward your goal is clear and apparent. More often than not, however, you will need additional data just to get the process started. Then the first step will be the gathering of additional information or knowledge. You will want to write the first step in the same format as the goal—beginning with an action verb. You might use action verbs from the list like:

learn determine find out talk to locate

Even if you don't know exactly how to proceed, you will know what you need to know or find out to get going, so research becomes the first step in achieving your goal.

Success Strategy No. 32:

Break each goal down into a set of manageable objectives.

1. List additional objectives in the order you think of them.
2. To the left of each objective on your Action Plan, note the date you began to take action to achieve it.
3. To the right of each objective, note the date it has been completed, and then cross it off the list.
4. Add objectives to your list as they become apparent and necessary.
5. When you have achieved your goal, also cross it off your Goals List and file the corresponding Action Plan in your blueprint file.

All goals can be accomplished by being broken down into manageable, step-by-step objectives. Say your goal is to start a part-time carpet-cleaning business, which you hope will eventually produce enough income to allow you to quit your job. This goal stems from one of your dreams, which is to establish a successful full-time business of your own, netting you $50,000 per year. Ever since you wrote that dream down on your Dreams List, you've been looking for a business you could start for less than $5,000. You found your opportunity when a friend in another city who is in the carpet-cleaning business offered to give you his help and advice.

You can now list your goal as: "Open a carpet-cleaning business." You will notice that this goal is specific, can be visualized, and you believe you can accomplish it. However, before you can actually open the business, there are a dozen or more steps that you must take. These steps are your objectives, which you will put in writing on your Action Plan. Here are some examples:

1. Write a detailed, one-year business plan or pro forma with expected monthly income and expenses (with the help and advice of your friend in the business).
2. Find an investor who will put up half of the $5,000 required, and list those who might invest.
3. Determine what equipment is needed and how much inventory will be required.
4. Locate the manufacturers of carpet-cleaning equipment.
5. Determine if anyone sells reconditioned or used equipment.
6. Establish a trade account with wholesale suppliers.
7. Talk to other carpet-cleaning companies about what equipment they recommend.
8. Obtain equipment prices from manufacturers and retailers.

As you list each objective, you are creating a simplified, step-by-step path toward your goal. List all the objectives you can think of in the order you think of them. You can reorganize or remember them later if necessary. Some objectives will necessarily precede others. For instance, before you can get prices, it is first necessary to locate the manufacturers or retailers that sell carpet-cleaning equipment. And you'll realize that your carpet-cleaning business, like any business, will require as much marketing as actual carpet cleaning. You first must have carpets to clean, so next you list the objectives related to advertising and marketing.

1. Find out how other carpet-cleaning companies advertise.
2. Check with the local newspaper about its Sunday television supplement and rates.
3. Determine how early an ad must be placed.
4. Determine if the newspaper will extend credit or if each ad will have to be prepaid in cash.
5. Design preliminary ads based on what seems to be successful for others.

Once you've gotten your mind working on establishing your list of objectives for any goal, you will find that you are constantly adding to your list. And as you accomplish an objective, you will cross it off the list. Thus, your list of objectives will give you a sense of purpose and direction, as well as a sense of satisfaction and success as you complete each objective and cross it off your list.

Each question you must answer becomes an objective. Each action you must take becomes an objective. Each resource you must gather becomes an objective. When taken together, all these objectives become a dynamic, step-by-step Action Plan.

By the yard, it's hard, but by the inch, it's a cinch.

Breaking down goals into written objectives is one of the greatest secrets of superachievers. Working on the accomplishment of individual objectives is all that's necessary to reach any goal you wish in your life. In the process, you double both your power to accomplish and your personal effectiveness. When you think of a major goal as a giant step from where you are to where you want to be, uncertainties, unknowns, and doubts can permeate your mind. But when you think of a goal as the end result of a series of small steps, there will be no more doubt in your mind that you are going to make it happen.

CHAPTER **10**

Prioritizing Your Activities

We first make our habits, and then our habits make us.
—John Dryden

There is one final set of strategies necessary to speed you on your way to the accomplishment of your objectives and goals, and hence the realization of your dreams: your Daily Activities Lists. An activities list is your prioritized daily agenda. Line by line it shows what you intend to accomplish during the current day and, in fact, up to the end of the calendar month.

There seems to be no limit to the long list of activities on which you can choose to spend your time. Therefore, there will seldom be a day during your life when you feel "caught up." Think back. Can you ever remember a day when you felt that you had accomplished all the things you needed to do and would like to have done? I certainly cannot remember one. However, what's important is not that everything gets done during a specific day, but that the activities that are most important to the accomplishment of your dreams and goals have been completed on a schedule set by you. To feel good about how you use time does not require being busy every moment, or constantly playing "catch-up." Positive feelings and the mental rewards associated with real accomplishments are produced through effectiveness, since only effectiveness produces results.

Think of it. If you can double your effectiveness, by definition you can accomplish twice as much in the same amount of time. You will double the speed at which you accomplish your objectives, and you will cut in half the time it takes you to achieve your dreams and goals.

Success Strategy No. 33:

To double your effectiveness, apply the 20/80 rule.

Just 20 percent of the activities on which you could choose to spend your time will produce 80 percent of the results you're after. Conversely, spending time and energy on the other 80 percent of your possible activities will produce only 20 percent of the results you're after—including only 20 percent of the total sense of satisfaction from accomplishment.

When it comes to achieving your dreams and goals, just 20 percent of your activities will take you along your pathway faster and farther than others. Identify that 20 percent and then spend the majority of your time and mental and physical energy each day on their accomplishment. Focusing first on the commencement and completion of that 20 percent is what transforms energy-wasting efficiency into results-producing effectiveness.

In the purest sense, it would be a waste of your time, talent, and energy to spend time on anything not in the top 20 percent of the activities on your list, at least until that 20 percent has been totally completed. That's the point.

The mind tends to take the path of least resistance.

If the 20/80 rule is not applied in prioritizing your activities, your mind will automatically involve you in activities that are easier to do and require less thinking instead of the more important activities. Dropping off your clothes at the cleaners may be an easy activity requiring very little planning, stress, or mental energy, but it certainly won't bring you closer to your dreams and goals. If you instead arrange to have your dry cleaning picked up and delivered, and spend the hour you've saved working on the résumé you've been meaning to update to get the new job listed on your Goals List, you're prioritizing your activities according to the 20/80 rule.

Practiced consistently, carefully, and continuously, this rule will eventually develop into a habit of maximum personal effectiveness. You will find that you are getting up to twice as much done in only half the time. Remember, the priority activities are not ones that are being forced on you; you are doing them by choice.

Applying the 20/80 rule also reduces the stress that often occurs when you feel you're getting behind or just aren't producing enough results for the time and effort you are expending. With the application of the 20/80 rule, you will have learned to compress time—to accomplish in one day what previously would have required you two, four, or even ten days to accomplish. With practice, your skill level will develop, as it did for me, to the point where you are able to accomplish in one year what it will take those around you ten years to accomplish. Real effectiveness gives you the experience of new success and power and enables you to find balance and control for your life. Your SuperSelf operates best using the 20/80 rule.

Success Strategy No. 34:

Transform efficiency into effectiveness with a prioritized activities list.

As you put your personal blueprint into action, you will come to be aware of the great difference between efficiency and effectiveness.

- Efficiency is the process of staying busy all the time, with no idle moments.
- Effectiveness is the process of producing the maximum results in the minimum time, with the minimum effort.

Most people spend their lives attempting to become more efficient. Yet efficiency is not the key to getting more done. How many times have you thought to yourself at the end of a day: I was so busy today I just couldn't seem to catch my breath, but I still didn't get much done. That feeling is the trademark of efficiency—lots of action, but lack of results.

Your dreams, goals, and Action Plans are all about results. They have little to do with the process of staying busy. In fact, there is some conflict. Look again at the definition of effectiveness and you will notice that the objective is to produce results with minimum time and effort, not maximum "busyness" and hard work.

You become effective by working smart instead of working hard.

Efficiency is often a mental trap. You think that, because you're so busy and moving so quickly, you must be getting somewhere. In fact, the reverse is often true. The "I-have-never-worked-so-hard-and-got-so-little-done" feeling is an indication that results are not being produced commensurate with the effort expended.

You will achieve your goals on schedule only by learning to transform efficiency into effectiveness. You will then discover that:

- Every action has a purpose.
- Interruptions are consciously eliminated.
- Rushed motion gives way to rational movement.
- Unbalancing surprises become a thing of the past.
- You are seldom caught off guard.
- Your life is planned, stress-free, and seldom behind schedule.
- Excuses for being late are left behind.
- Deadlines are met.
- Your life and your time line are under your control.

Any day of your life can be divided into a series of activities, from brushing your teeth to stopping at the cleaners on the way home from work to writing an important letter or even calling your mother. Not all of your daily activities are of equal importance, and your mission is to organize and prioritize all activities into a working plan. You then work your plan in order, from the high-priority activities to the low-priority activities, until all are complete or you run out of time at the end of the day. If you're as busy as most people, you will find yourself running out of time far more often than you complete your list. No problem. There is always tomorrow. However, it is the number of priority activities you can complete each day that will determine how many of your goals and dreams you achieve each year.

Use the 20/80 rule to prioritize your daily activities. Once you have identified the 20 percent of activities on your list that are the most important, divide these activities into "must-do" and "should-do" categories. Must-do activities are those that if not accomplished by a specific time or deadline will create additional undesirable, time-consuming problems. Give these must-do activities your top priority. They will include activities such as:

1. Paying a parking ticket today to prevent the fine from doubling.
2. Attending your daughter's play at 8 P.M. Yes, all personal activities should be included and prioritized, as they are no less important to your success and sense of values.
3. Showing up for the departmental meeting at 3:15 P.M., as requested by your boss.
4. Putting gas in the car on the way home so you won't run out on your way to work tomorrow.

Often, must-do activities will contribute to the accomplishment of your goals and dreams, but many of them, although necessary, are not the most productive. However, you are still being effective when you spend time on the necessary but not-so-productive must-do activities, because the noncompletion of these activities would cost you additional time and energy later on. In other words, you either do these activities now or pay an even greater price later on.

If your life is already under some control, these must-do but nonproductive activities will take up only a small fraction of the hours in your day, and you will complete them each day before you begin the should-do activities. Your should-do activities are directly related to the accomplishment of your dreams and goals and will also be given top priority on your list. These activities include the objectives that you have taken directly from your Action Plans, but they can be the easiest to put off or postpone if you instead stay busy handling low-priority activities. Your should-do activities for the day might include:

1. Writing that new brochure for your small part-time business to increase sales.
2. Applying for an equity loan on your home to give you money to pay off and reduce the interest rate on your consumer debt.
3. Balancing your checkbook and credit card statements to prevent costly errors.
4. Calling five potential prospects, even though you don't like making phone calls.
5. Spending quality time with the kids, even though all your business projects aren't complete.

Don't keep your Daily Activities List on random scraps of paper that can easily get lost, or on the pages of a daily or weekly desk calendar that are usually torn off and thrown away. The correct place to write down and prioritize your activities is on the activities pages in your blueprint. Since you don't know in advance how many activities you will be able to accomplish in a single day, your "Daily" Activities List should include all activities you anticipate accomplishing, or desire to accomplish, during the rest of the calendar month. You then choose and prioritize these activities on your plan for the current day. Mark the approximate 20 percent of your activities that are in the top-priority category with a "p" or an asterisk (*), or, if you choose, you can number them 1, 2, 3, . . . in the order in which you intend to accomplish them.

Many people, indeed many planning systems, encourage you to create a new "To Do" list each day by transferring all noncompleted activities from today's list to tomorrow's list. From the time I first began controlling my time with Daily Activities Lists, that has never made sense to me. First of all, there is nothing magical about accomplishing every item on your daily list on the day you first write it down. Second, you will find yourself spending an unnecessary ten to twenty minutes every day transferring uncompleted items to another list, which will chew up as much as three thousand to six thousand minutes a year, or an incredible fifty to one hundred hours, all an avoidable waste of time. Third, if you are ambitious and positive you will generally put far more on your list each day than can reasonably be accomplished, so you could, with so much left over, end up every day feeling like a failure instead of the success you may actually be.

The winning strategy is simple: Avoid wasting time and energy by expanding your Daily Activities List to include one calendar month. That way, you transfer uncompleted items to another list only at the end of each month. In addition, you don't have to wait for an upcoming day before you can enter the activities associated with that specific day. Instead, you can list all of the daily activities you intend to work on during the entire month, which will enable you to better identify that month's most important priorities.

Success Strategy No. 35:

Divide your activities list into four sections.

The best and easiest format to use for your activities list is to divide it into four sections: business activities, business phone calls, personal activities, and personal phone calls (see opposite).

The Four-Section, One-Page Activities List

Daily Activities List

Month of ______ 19__

Business

Activities	Phone calls to make
1.	1.
2.	2.
3.	3.
4.	4.

Personal

Activities	Phone calls to make
1.	1.
2.	2.
3.	3.
4.	4.

The Two-Section, Two-Page Activities List

Daily Activities List

Month of ______ 19__

Business

Activities	Phone calls to make
1.	1.
2.	2.
3.	3.
4.	4.
5.	5.
6.	6.
7.	7.
8.	8.
9.	9.

Daily Activities List

Month of ______ 19__

Personal

Activities	Phone calls to make
1.	1.
2.	2.
3.	3.
4.	4.
5.	5.
6.	6.
7.	7.
8.	8.
9.	9.

Although business and personal activities are equally important if you want to maintain the balance in your life, it is easiest to work from your activities list when you separate the two. Depending on the number of activities you schedule in one month, you can either list all activities on one page or list your personal and business activities on separate pages.

You have already chosen the goals that are most important in your life, and in your Action Plan for each goal you have listed the specific steps you have to take or the objectives you have to reach in order to achieve that goal. At least once a week, go through your Action Plans forms and pick one, two, or three objectives from each plan that you would like to accomplish during the calendar month. Write each of these objectives under the appropriate section, business or personal, of your Daily Activities Lists. Your objectives are scheduled for action and accomplishment as soon as they are transferred to your activities lists.

To keep track of your progress, note on the Action Plan the date that you copied the objective to your activities list. When you have completed the activity, cross it off both your activities list and your objectives list, also noting the completion date on your Action Plan. When you have reached all of the objectives you listed on your Action Plan, your goal should be complete.

Success Strategy No. 36:

Record and prioritize on your activities lists all important phone calls and appointments.

Phone calls that have top priority on both your business and personal activities lists should be identified and prioritized with a "p" or an asterisk (*), just as prioritized activities are marked. Cross off the phone calls when you have completed them. Use the code "N/A" for "no answer" to remind you that you have already called, or "C/B" for "call back" if you need to receive or give more information. If you note on your list both the name of each person or company you are calling and the complete phone number, you will lose no time looking up phone numbers. When you include appointments or meetings on your activities list, note the specific time of each.

Remember once a week to compare your activities lists with your Action Plans for each goal. Those objectives that have been accomplished you can cross off your Action Plans. At the same time, you can transfer additional objectives from your Action Plans to your current activities lists. The process doesn't take long, and it will keep your plan organized, focused, and under control.

Your Dreams List, Goals List, and Action Plans are the decision and planning tools incorporated into your blueprint. But it is from your Daily Activities Lists that the real action and control of your life emanate. Focus your mind like a laser beam, paying total attention to your top-priority activities. From day one you will produce greater positive results, as well as the positive emotions that accompany real accomplishment. These feelings alone are worth making a change in the way you schedule your time.

Success Strategy No. 37:

Review and revise your blueprint at the end of each calendar year to assess your past progress and chart your future direction.

At the end of each calendar year, in the week between Christmas and New Year's Day, allow yourself about an hour to review and update your blueprint. Label a file folder "Blueprint 19______" and use this folder to file all of the completed items from the year's blueprint. Noncompleted dreams, goals, Action Plans, and activities should remain in your blueprint.

This is the time to add new dreams and goals, along with the Action Plans and activities you will have to pursue and accomplish in order to achieve them the following year. The end of the year is also a good time to recheck your Values List and make sure that what you have accomplished is in alignment with your most important values.

As you review and revise your blueprint at the end of each year, you will have a feeling of great satisfaction at how much you have accomplished. You'll have a sense that every day of the year has had a direction and a purpose. "Where you is" now is not "where you was" a year ago. You will have made significant steps toward the realization of your dreams and goals. Your blueprint is giving you the power to plan and control your future, and you will look forward to the upcoming year with anticipation, and with the self-confidence and momentum necessary to surmount whatever obstacles may lie ahead. You are your SuperSelf—and nothing can stop you now.

PART III

Doubling Your Personal Effectiveness

CHAPTER 11

Doing Discipline

Let him that would move the world, first move himself.
—SOCRATES

Your life's blueprint is your master plan for success. Once you have created it, your aim will be to put that plan into action in order to achieve the results you want within the time frame you have set for yourself. But what if I told you that there are strategies you can use that will dramatically decrease the time it takes you to reach your dreams and goals? If you can increase your personal effectiveness, then it follows logically that you will accomplish more in less time. That's exactly what the use of these strategies will do. In fact, they will *double* your personal effectiveness.

I can state the first of these strategies in just one word: discipline. No matter how conscientiously you have created your life's blueprint, you cannot hope to reach your dreams and goals unless you follow it. That takes discipline, which is a key ingredient to achieving success and essential to doubling your personal effectiveness.

You've probably said to yourself time and time again, If

only I had more discipline, then I could get more done. The truth is, there is no such thing as a nondisciplined person.

Discipline is a choice, not a legacy.

Discipline is not an innate human characteristic—something you were born with or without. To be disciplined or nondisciplined is a choice you make every minute and every hour of your life. Discipline is nothing more than the process of focusing on any chosen activity without interruption until that activity is complete. Discipline is something you do and not something you have. You therefore have the freedom to choose to act with discipline and decisiveness. To become what others refer to as a disciplined person requires only that you "do discipline" over and over as a conscious act until repetition makes discipline a subconscious habit. Doing discipline means that you choose not to allow fatigue or interruptions to become an excuse for inaction or a change of plan.

From the time we were small children, we were lectured about the virtues and importance of discipline, but no one ever seemed to define discipline, and our role models all too often did not act with discipline or focus. In reality, personal success requires both. Here are some facts that will help you zero in on the power of discipline.

- Discipline is the process of total time control.
- Discipline is the ability to stay focused on your chosen action path without detour, distraction, or interruption.
- Discipline is the ability to keep all agreements with yourself and with others, without blame, excuses, or caving in to obstacles.
- Discipline is the ability to show up on time, every time.
- Discipline is the ability to complete important personal or business projects on schedule, even on budget.

- Discipline is the ability to keep your mind, body, and emotions in balance, no matter what's going on around you—even when what's going on around you produces fear, anxiety, embarrassment, or guilt.
- Discipline is the power to keep going forward when everything around you seems to be pulling you back.

The result? Discipline generates trust and confidence in yourself, and attracts trust and confidence from others. The constant act of discipline magnifies your power to accomplish at least 1,000 percent. Plus, discipline frees up hours of personal time each day, which can be invested in what you value most, such as family, health, peace of mind, and financial security.

Success Strategy No. 38:

Increase your level of effectiveness by learning to maintain focus.

One important reason for controlling your time through planning strategies like goals, objectives, and activities is that without them your mind will wander, seldom staying focused on what you think needs to be done.

Focus is the process of keeping your thoughts, attention, and energy totally on the task at hand.

By learning to maintain focus, at your own personal speed you will accomplish the most in the least amount of time—the essence of effectiveness. Discipline is all that is required to maintain your focus, and focus is the key to getting the important things done.

Allowing interruptions or delaying the start of a project until you "feel like it" results from failure to make the choice. Your mind is an obedient servant. It will do exactly what you tell it to do—provided you tell it, and then by your actions prove that you mean business. But like an unruly, unsupervised child, when not controlled and monitored your mind and thoughts will often take you in a multitude of random directions. For instance, your mind is great at making excuses or finding reasons for not starting or sticking to a project.

The process of monitoring your mind to ascertain that you are maintaining focus is what discipline is all about. Discipline means that you choose to operate in the "no excuse, only action" mode. At any moment you can make the choice to "do discipline," no matter what you did or didn't do the moment before. Doing discipline has nothing to do with what kind of person you are or aren't. It is true you must continuously make the choice to do discipline, over and over many times a day. But eventually discipline will become a habit, and when it does your ability to accomplish will run on automatic pilot without your needing to resort to excuses for inaction.

Doing discipline will help you stay focused beyond distractions, disruptions, fatigue, and low interest levels. You succeed by consciously and continuously choosing to act like a disciplined person.

Success Strategy No. 39:

Increase your effectiveness and earn the confidence and trust of others by keeping your agreements.

No aspect of discipline is more important than keeping your agreements—doing exactly what you say you will do, exactly when you say you will do it. An agreement can be made with yourself, with someone else, or with a group, and failing to keep an agreement, even with yourself, can have lasting repercussions in both your business and personal life.

In today's world, inability to keep agreements and commitments seems to be epidemic. I first realized this fact when I was about twenty-five years old and working at Genesco. Zeke Zimmerman, who ran one of Genesco's computer departments, had just gotten married. He and his wife Betty decided they wanted to show off the home they had just moved into, so they invited twenty-five couples over for a party on Friday night. Zeke passed out written invitations that contained an RSVP request. All twenty five couples said they would be there, including my wife at that time, Bonnie, and me.

The party was to begin at 8 P.M. and last until 10:30. At 8:15, when Bonnie and I arrived, we were the only ones there besides the hosts. We all talked for fifteen minutes, and at 8:30 another couple arrived. Now there were four guests. When 9:00 came, no one else had yet arrived. Ten o'clock came and went, and still no other guests. A very embarrassed Zeke and Betty ended the party at 10:30, and Bonnie and I and the other couple went home.

On the way home I wondered how it could possibly be that twenty-three couples had not shown up. After all, each had made a commitment to attend the party. All they had to do was keep it. Curious to find out what had happened, the next Monday morning I went around to all of the people who hadn't kept their commitment and asked, "Why didn't you show up last Friday?" The answers I got were unbelievable.

"We couldn't get a baby-sitter."

"My family dropped in from out of town."

"I just plain forgot."

"The car broke down."

"I was too tired."

I heard one excuse after another, some repetitive, some original, but all acceptable in the minds of those who had failed to keep their commitment. They were not acceptable reasons for failing to show up at Zeke and Betty's party. All could have been overcome with the decision to do so. Take a cab! Bring your family! Find another baby-sitter! All the obstacles were minor, but it had dawned on no one that a commitment is more important than a minor inconvenience. From that moment on, I made a commitment to keep my agreements every time and all the time—no wavering, no excuses. If I make an agreement, I know and everybody else knows that I will be there when I say I will, and I will be there every time. I will do what I say, and I will do it every time. That is my unwavering commitment to myself and it has served me so well that I hope I can convince you to make it yours.

Agreements to those who desire success are as nonconditional as heartbeats are to those who want to live. Your ability and willingness to keep your agreements are a direct measure of the level of control you have over your life. If you want to win, you must be willing to keep your agreements in the face of all excuse-producing obstacles. Determination is all that is required to remove most obstacles, and a powerful level of determination can be achieved just by placing a priority on keeping your agreements.

My life changed when I made a decision to keep all my agreements, and yours will too. Keeping your agreements reduces stress because it does not require any further thought or last-minute decisions. Keeping your agreements eliminates the potential of guilt and gives you a well-defined, predetermined track on which to run. In short, keeping your agreements keeps your life simple and manageable. In addition, keeping your agreements builds trust and confidence in yourself and from others—the trust of family, friends, and coworkers. When you keep your agreements, people know they can depend on you to do whatever you have said you will do. As a result, your career moves faster, your business becomes more successful, and your personal life is under your control. Your confidence increases as you discover that you can eliminate the obstacle, rather than break your commitment.

People spend a great deal of time changing plans and breaking agreements, both sure signs that their lives are racing out of control. Keeping your agreements is one of the most powerful SuperSelf tools you can apply in your quest to double your personal effectiveness.

The loyalty and trust of other people generate the cooperation necessary for achieving your dreams and goals.

I once negotiated a deal in which an associate would receive a 10 percent interest in a new business we would start. I would provide the investment capital and the use of my name and the infrastructure of my companies. He had asked for a 50 percent interest, but my standard percentage for division heads is 10 percent of net profits. However, when I wrote out the agreement memo, I mistakenly entered 50 percent instead of 10 percent as his share. Over the next several months, he went into action on this business endeavor under the assumption that he was entitled to 50 percent of the profits, not 10 percent. We never in the meantime discussed our terms. Eventually I discovered my error. I wasn't thrilled about it, but the path to follow was clear. I had made an agreement and my agreements are not changeable. He received 50 percent of his division's profits. Instead of our having an argument about his percentage, with him questioning my integrity and maybe even quitting, he went on to build the second biggest division in terms of both revenue and profit. The decision has made me millions of dollars and, of course, my associate is now an extremely wealthy man.

Recently, in a meeting with him he expressed his loyalty and trust in me and my organization. As a result of my honoring my agreement, he said it was his intention to be involved with me and my organization for the rest of his life. He even wanted his kids to be involved eventually. That kind of loyalty is more rewarding to me than any amount of money.

Excuses are only made for failure, never success.

Growing up, most people come to believe that breaking agreements is okay as long as they can come up with a good excuse. As a result, much of their lives and relationships are conducted in the context of broken agreements. But there are no "good" excuses. Excuses by nature are detrimental to your success, wealth, and well-being. You can automatically avoid the necessity of making excuses for failure by keeping your agreements.

I'm sure you can recall many times in your own life when people didn't do what they had agreed to do. Unkept agreements, for example, occur when people:

- Say they'll call and then don't
- Agree to get together with you and then cancel
- Say they'll respond to your proposal by a certain date but do not
- Quote a price in an advertisement and then add extra costs when you buy

Success Strategy No. 40:
Promise only what you can deliver, and deliver what you promise.

An important measure of your control over your own life is the percentage of agreements you keep. Your objective, of course, is 100 percent. When you keep your agreements, you are doing it not only for the sake of the other people involved, but also for your own personal benefit and success.

Why, then, do people make agreements they are relatively certain they can't keep? One reason is the desire to please others and to avoid potential conflict. For example, let's say your boss asks for a report on Friday and you know it can't be ready by then, but you don't want to upset him, so you agree. Short-term gain in this case will result in long-term pain. When the report isn't ready by Friday, your boss will be *really* upset. You could have told him you couldn't possibly have the report ready by Friday so he wouldn't make his plans based on a date that was unrealistic. But you didn't. You might have suggested ways in which you could finish the report by the hoped-for deadline, such as some additional assistance. But if that was not practical, you should have both agreed on a deadline you could make.

Fear is another reason for making commitments you cannot

keep. Let's say you've made plans to meet for dinner and the theater with your wife at 5:30, but at 5:00 your boss asks you to work late to finish a critical project. You know your wife has already left for the restaurant, but you're afraid you may be passed over for a promotion or even yelled at if you turn your boss down. So you leave a message for your wife at the restaurant, telling her you can't make dinner and she might as well go on to the theater without you. You then grit your teeth and do the work, distracted, feeling guilty, rushing to finish, operating under stress and interrupted by several phone calls from your wife. When you have finished the job, you get to the theater just in time to see the third act. And your wife, needless to say, is annoyed and angry. In this situation, you have two commitments, one to your wife and the other to excellence on the job. Both are important, but you made the commitment to your wife first, and keeping it is your first priority. Explain the situation to your boss, without making excuses or apologies. "Bill, I'm meeting my wife at 5:30 for dinner and the theater, and I need to keep that commitment. I'll come in tomorrow morning at 6 A.M. to finish the project." You are not breaking one commitment at the expense of the other. You have figured out a way to honor both.

A third cause of broken agreements is the desire to please. Say, for example, your parents invite you for dinner at 7 P.M. on Sunday night. You want to come to please them, but you're playing in an amateur golf tournament. If you're lucky, you might be able to get to your parents' on time, but in all probability, you know it will be unlikely. Still, you don't want to disappoint your parents, so you agree to be there at 7:00.

Sunday night comes, you're on the eighteenth hole, it's already 7:15, and your parents' house is half an hour away. Now you're miffed at your parents, yourself, and the slow foursome ahead of you. You feel like a victim because rain has slowed down the play, and you know that when you finally get to your parents' house, they will hardly appreciate the inconvenience their invitation has caused you. You will probably hear sarcastic remarks about how everything is more important than time with them. You've set yourself up to lose again.

Don't make agreements you can't keep just because you want to please the people involved. Tell your parents you would love to have dinner with them, but you probably won't be able to make it by the time they have chosen. The alternative? Agree to have dinner later in the evening, or suggest another night. Conflict eliminated.

It is easy to make commitments based on short-term pleasure or the short-term avoidance of conflict, hurt, or emotional pain, simply hoping that in the long run "maybe it will work out." You know better. A commitment is a choice, and you may have to make many additional choices in order to keep it. But it always pays off—short-term *and* long-term.

I remember when I was first teaching SuperSelf-type programs in the seventies. I lived in Washington, D.C., and traveled throughout the Shenandoah Valley conducting my workshops. One day I was scheduled to teach a program at 10 A.M. in Charlottesville, Virginia, almost a hundred miles from where I lived. I started out with plenty of time, and as always got a thrill out of driving through the tight mountain curves in my 240Z. But that day, the fan belt broke and the car immediately began overheating. I had a choice. I could either stop and let the car cool down, or I could push it to the limit by continuing to drive and look for a gas station where I could replace the belt and add water to the radiator. I was in the middle of nowhere. There wasn't a farmhouse, a filling station, or anything else in sight—nothing for miles but trees and mountains. So I made choice number two—to drive on with the thought that my engine might hold out until I found a place where I could add some water and get a replacement belt.

The car decided not to follow my plan and in a few minutes the engine froze up. At that point I had another choice. I could have said to myself, Oh, well, I'm still closer to Washington than I am to Charlottesville, so I guess I'll just call someone and get a ride back home. Surely people will understand. After all, it's going to cost me a lot of time and money to get this car running. Or I could have become the victim by thinking, Poor me, what am I going to do next? I'm in the middle of nowhere. Why did this have to happen to me when I have people waiting and a workshop to conduct?

However, there was only one logical choice as far as I was concerned: get to Charlottesville the best way I could without my car so I could keep my commitment and conduct the workshop.

I calmly and unemotionally took my briefcase out of my car, stood on the edge of that deserted mountain highway in my suit and tie, and stuck out my thumb. There wasn't much traffic, but in only ten minutes I was given a ride by a man who was going to Charlottesville. Just my luck, I thought, smiling. As we drove into Charlottesville, I told him why I was going there, and not only did he deliver me right to the doorstep but by the time we arrived I had convinced him to enroll in the program!

I was actually on time, and I conducted the workshop as if nothing at all unusual had happened. Then at the end of the program, I simply said, "Look, I don't have a ride home. Is anybody here heading for Washington?" About ten hands went up. I doubted that all of them were really going to Washington, but they may have been thinking, Man, if we could just get Chuck Givens in a confined space where we could bend his ear for an hour or two . . . So I got a ride and the person who drove me home got to pick my brain. We both won. At the end of that day, I felt calm and successful instead of angry and frustrated. I had made a challenge out of getting to Charlottesville instead of becoming buried in the process. And I had yet another success to reinforce the fact that events did not control my life, unless, of course, I chose to give them that power.

Treat every agreement or promise as a nonchangeable commitment. Follow through on your agreements even in the face of:

- Potential additional costs
- Potential lost opportunities
- Unforeseen interruptions

As a result, your ability to keep your agreements will:

1. Result in a clearer, more direct path toward your objectives and goals
2. Eliminate guilt, indecision, and stress
3. Heighten your sense of self-confidence and control
4. Produce more predictable outcomes to the events in your life

The winning strategy is clear. Physical discomfort, inconvenience, or extra costs are not valid reasons for breaking an agreement. From this moment on, make a promise to yourself that you will keep your agreements in the face of all of life's little tests.

CHAPTER **12**

Controlling Your Time Line

You will never "find" time for anything. If you want time you must make it.

—CHARLES BUXTON (ENGLISH AUTHOR)

Time is the element that makes your blueprint work. It is part of the environment in which you are required to operate. You get 24 hours a day just like everyone else, and you are powerless to change that fact. Where your potential power does lie is in how you organize and use that time. Your objective is to get 36 hours of accomplishment out of every 24 hours of time.

When you add it all up, there are precious few hours each week to work on your dreams and goals. That is why maximum effectiveness is the most important key to accomplishment. Let me show you what I mean. There are just 168 hours in each week—24 hours a day for 7 days, the same for everyone. Let's construct a time graph of a typical week to show

how quickly those hours are eaten up by repetitive, sometimes necessary but often mundane, nonproductive activities.

First, let's eliminate from your available time the amount of time you are asleep. If you sleep 8 hours per night, you have already used up 56 of your 168 hours.

Now, let's say that it takes you an hour in the morning to get ready for work from the time the alarm clock rings through showering, brushing your teeth, eating breakfast, and heading for the office. Of course, if you have kids to get off to school, you can probably add another half hour, but for now we'll use 7 hours a week as get-ready-in-the-morning time. We'll add another 3½ hours at 30 minutes every day for the time it takes to wind-down, get ready for bed, and go to sleep. Now the total time left is down to about 101.5 hours.

Sleep 56 Hours
Prep & wind-down 10.5
Time Left 101.5 Hours

Now, let's say that your commuting time to work is 45 minutes one way or 1½ hours a day for 5 days a week. Each week you spend 7½ hours commuting.

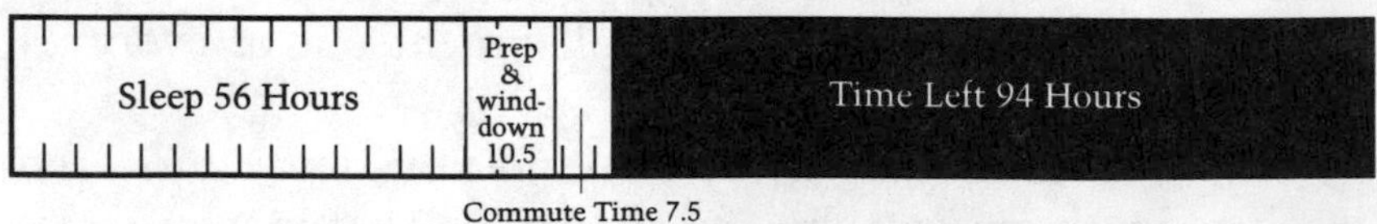

Now, let's assume that including your lunch hour, you spend 9 hours a day for 45 hours a week at your job. Your time line now looks like this:

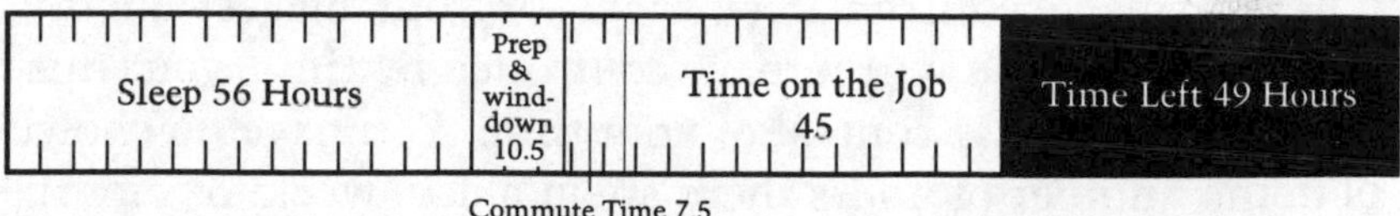

Finally, let's allow for an hour for dinner each night 7 days a week and all you're left with is 42 hours a week, or an average of 6 hours a day, weekends included, to get done everything else that is really important to you.

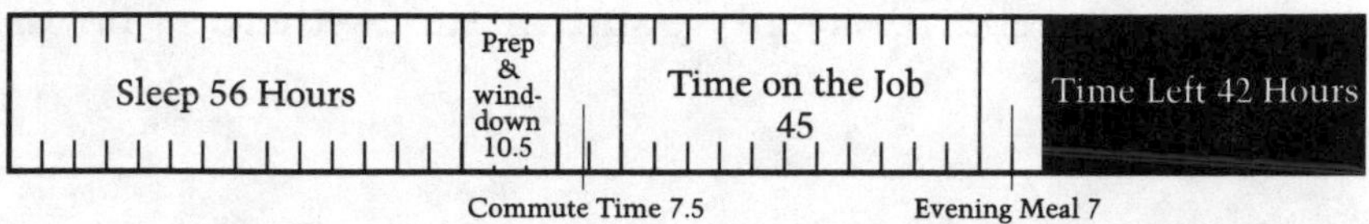

Out of each week you have already used up 75 percent of your total time and have only 25 percent left to live out the rest of your life. The time left for both your personal life and the accomplishment of your dreams and goals is far less than the number of hours you sleep or work. And during that small percentage of remaining time, you must also allot time for:

- Your spouse or mate
- Your children
- Television
- Hobbies or interests
- Sports and/or exercise
- Housecleaning, yard work, home and car maintenance
- Friends
- Errands

I'm sure you could add another dozen items that eat up your spare time. All that time gone, all those time-consuming activities remaining and you haven't even allocated one hour to working on the accomplishment of your long list of goals and dreams.

Time can be your greatest friend or your biggest enemy. While most people will remain controlled by time, your mission is to take total control of your time. You have no choice as to the number of hours there are in a day, week, or month, but you do have unlimited choices as to how you will spend that time. You also have a choice about whether any moment of your time remains under your control or whether you pass control of your time, your mind, and your life to an event, worry, fear, fatigue, or another person. You are either in control or out of control at any point in time—there is no in between.

Success Strategy No. 41:

Take control of your time or time will control you.

Think of your day from the moment you get up until you go back to bed again at night as your daily time line. A daily time line for most people is fifteen to eighteen hours long. Within that time frame lies all of your potential for accomplishment. You control how quickly your planned future develops by how well you control your daily time line.

Your day can easily become filled with stress, worry, frustration, anger, boredom, interruptions, temporary mental and emotional imbalances, busywork, and rushing without results. Or it can be planned, calculated, smooth, stress-free, and full of accomplishment. It's up to you.

You maintain control of your time line when you:

- Plan your objectives and activities each day in advance
- Prioritize your daily activities

- Start on time
- Show up on time
- Refuse to get sucked into confrontations
- Eliminate interruptions
- Separate your emotions from the events that occur around you
- Maintain a positive, can-do attitude
- Plan your work, then work your plan
- Complete your day by prioritizing your activities for the following day

You lose control of your time line when you:

- Start late for work or an appointment
- Arrive late, making excuses
- Allow interruptions to detour your planned activities
- Become rushed and pressured and, therefore, under stress
- See unforeseen events as "big deals"
- Become the victim with thoughts like "Why me?"
- Feel exhausted and depleted at the end of the day
- Finish your day by complaining about what went wrong
- Measure your day in terms of what didn't get done instead of what did

Dozens of unexpected situations can occur during your day that may make you feel your life is running out of control. They all begin to have a cumulative effect, like the snowball rolling downhill that eventually creates an avalanche. The good news is that 95 percent of these unplanned, unexpected events are avoidable—*if* you plan ahead to stay in control of your time line.

Here are just a few of the signposts along the way of losing control of your day:

- Running out of clean clothes
- Losing your car keys

- Skipping breakfast because you are late
- Answering the telephone while rushed for time
- Not allowing extra time for unforeseen delays
- Blaming others and external events for your lateness
- Keeping other people waiting
- Always leaving late, then rushing in traffic to make up time
- Making "To Do" lists on scraps of paper, only to misplace them

Let me share with you some of the strategies I have developed and used for the past twenty-five years to keep control of my time line. These strategies are so simple and yet so powerful that when used together as a system, they will instantly allow you to restructure your day for maximum effectiveness with minimum delays and detours. Your objective is to consciously incorporate these strategies into your daily life until they become subconscious habits.

As with all good strategies, once discovered and applied they become common sense. But what we call common sense is often not common knowledge. Common sense doesn't run your life. Old subconscious habits do, and these habits may be causing you to lose control of your time. These strategies will help you develop the habits and patterns necessary to regain and keep control of your time.

Success Strategy No. 42:

Avoid triggering the no-slack principle by making and sticking to your plan.

While striving for success, there is one principle you can count on—one that you cannot avoid. I call it the "no-slack" principle. The no-slack principle states, as in Murphy's Law, that whatever can go wrong will go wrong, and it will go wrong at the worst possible time. And once things begin to go wrong, they will continue to go wrong until you consciously take back control. No slack means there is no extra margin for error. It is as if the universe is constantly saying to you, "Either you plan to get it right, or you will soon learn the fallacy of your plan."

The no-slack principle can also be stated, "If you allow one thing to go wrong, it seems as if everything will go wrong." If there is a pinhole in the bottom of a bucket, *all* the water will run out—regardless of the size of the hole. Therefore, your daily plan and activities must be continuously monitored. You must stay on time and on target.

Let me give you an example of a no-slack scenario to demonstrate how if you let one activity get out of control, your entire day begins to run out of control.

1. You plan to fill the car with gas on your way home, but since you're so tired you decide to wait until tomorrow.
2. The next morning you leave late for an important appointment and run out of gas on the way attempting to get there on time.
3. You swear at yourself because you know you should have stopped to get gas last night.
4. As the engine starts to sputter you discover you are in the center lane, and you cannot get your car through traffic to the side of the road before it quits.
5. You realize it is rush hour. Just your luck! You now fear someone won't see you and may hit your car.
6. You see everyone staring at you and embarrassment sets in.
7. You rush to the trunk to get the gas can. As the lid comes up, you remember you left the can next to the lawn mower in the garage after filling the mower to cut the grass.

8. Traffic is now backing up, everyone is looking, and you feel pressured and stressed.
9. As you slam the trunk muttering, "Why me?" the sharp metal corner of the trunk lid rips the sleeve of your new $200 jacket.
10. You are now so distraught and angry there are tears in your eyes and a lump in your throat.
11. Finally someone stops, helps you get the car off the road, and gives you a lift to the gas station. After fifteen minutes and $20, a truck takes you and the gas back to the car.
12. As you approach, you see a patrol car and a policeman writing you a $25 ticket for illegally leaving your car on the side of the road.
13. As you jump out of the truck, you hit your shin on the side of the high step. It hurts like heck and is sure to result in a nasty bruise.
14. The policeman assures you he is sorry for your plight, but he has already written the ticket. He bawls you out for not having sense enough to put gas in your car. More anger and embarrassment.
15. When you finally get to your destination, the person with whom you had the important appointment has already left.

Fifteen trauma-producing events caused by one simple decision to tempt fate and *not* stop for gas! In the process you triggered the no-slack principle. The initial event, running out of gas, was preventable, but once you allowed that to happen, you lost control of the rest of your day.

The no-slack principle is around every bend in your day, waiting to catch you napping. You've been dealing with it your entire life. Sometimes you may even think the universe has something against you personally. But once you understand how consistently this principle operates, instead of cursing your bad luck, you may instead find yourself smiling and saying to yourself, Givens was right. There is no slack in life. Once you're on the no-slack merry-go-round, it's no use asking, Why me? The only solution is to take a deep breath, give up the anger and frustration, and get back to your plan. The angrier you get, the more frustrated you become and the longer you are going to perpetuate the no-slack principle.

How can you thwart the no-slack principle?

1. Make adequate preparations and plans, and then stick to them.
2. Respond quickly and decisively to whatever goes astray before it gets out of control.
3. Stay emotionally and mentally balanced, never allowing yourself to see yourself as the victim.

You will know you have become the victim when you hear yourself saying, "It's just one of those days." Take the position of the victim and you give the no-slack principle power to dominate the rest of your day and to control the direction of your life. The best way to deal with the no-slack principle is to keep it from happening in the first place. I'm now going to share with you a series of simple but effective strategies that will give you immediate power over the small things that can go wrong during the day. Make these strategies an integral part of your daily life. Together they form a control system to keep your daily time line under your control.

Success Strategy No. 43:

Arrive on time, every time.

You establish your credibility primarily through demonstrating your ability to keep your agreements with yourself and others, and only secondarily by how you look when you get to your destination. A good gauge of your ability to keep your agreements is how many times you are late—for work, for appointments, for meetings, or leaving the house for the airport or even a movie. Being consistently late is feedback that your time is not "your" time at all, but belongs instead to a constant stream of interruptions and unnecessary delays. Poorly planned time lines are the real cause of leaving late and arriving later.

Arriving on time begins with leaving on time. Make leaving on time a priority, a personal challenge. If you make a commitment to yourself that being on time is your number-one priority, even if you must walk out of the house with your hair a mess, without your makeup, jewelry, or tie on just one time, you will dislike the feeling so much that you won't allow it to happen again. You may find yourself putting your shoes on in the car, but the next morning you will be ready on time.

Success and accomplishment often require breaking old failure habits. No matter how small they seem, if they are automatically repeated day after day they are cripplers to effectiveness. If you have a habit of being late, break it.

Success Strategy No. 44:

Arrive early, but never late.

It's okay to arrive fifteen minutes early, but it is not okay to arrive fifteen seconds late. Making excuses for why it wasn't "your fault" won't get you there any earlier the next time. In fact, excuses are an attempt to put a stamp of approval on failure, much like "I tried."

Chronic lateness is not caused by any one event. It is a symptom of how your entire life is working in terms of your ability to plan your time and work your plan. Lateness should be viewed as an indication that your life is suffering from a lack of total time control. Time will work for you or against you. It is your choice. Time marches on with or without you and regardless of your attitude about it. But if you want to master time, master the following strategies—no excuses—and I guarantee you'll arrive on time, every time.

Success Strategy No. 45:

Don't make getting ready the last thing you do before leaving the house.

Proper preparation begins with proper planning. Before going out, do you wait to bathe, dress, and get ready until the last possible moment? That's an invitation to disaster. If getting ready is the last thing you do before leaving the house, rest assured you will leave late as often as not. If it normally takes you about forty minutes to get ready from start to finish, the logical tendency is to leave a time slot of—you guessed it—about forty minutes. During that forty minutes one or more interruptions or surprises are bound to occur that will add a minimum of five to ten minutes to the total time required. Count on it. Remember the no-slack principle? Don't fight it, plan on it.

Your strategy is to plan a nonpriority event or activity in between getting ready and the time you intend to leave the house. Plan time to do some paperwork or make a phone call. Then, if you get into a time squeeze, the time lost can be made up by skipping that nonpriority activity, and you still leave on time. Those who are habitually late are generally still getting ready when it's time to leave.

Ever lose your car keys? What a question! Couldn't remember what pants or pocketbook you left them in? Common sense would ask how many times car keys have to be lost before it becomes obvious that a systems approach is needed for keeping track of those elusive little rascals. Although systems approaches may be a part of your everyday business or career life, few people have employed the power of systems, even simple ones, to their personal lives.

Let's begin with a systems approach to getting ready, and getting where you're going on time. Let's say that you're leaving home for an important appointment. You've misplaced your car keys again and it takes twenty minutes to find them. What happens to your attitude? You get angry at yourself or whoever misplaced the keys, and suddenly you're operating under stress. After you finally find your keys and race to the car, you continue experiencing the no-slack principle as you find yourself slowed down by heavier than usual traffic that causes you to hit every red light. Now your whole day is rolling downhill out of control. By noon you're saying to everybody, "It's just one of those days." And it all began with one minor, easily preventable event—misplaced car keys. Without a systems approach to that problem, the same scenario is destined to repeat itself over and over no matter how vehemently you swear that it will never happen again.

Success Strategy No. 46:

Leave your car keys in the same place every time you arrive home.

The lost key syndrome is easily overcome if your keys are readily locatable every time you need them. Here's how to ensure it. Put a bowl, tray, or other decorative object on a table as close as possible to the door you normally enter, and where you will automatically see it when you arrive home. Each time you or anyone else using a car walks through the door, make it a rule and a habit to drop the keys into the bowl. Normally your keys are in hand as you step into your home after unlocking the door. Should you occasionally leave them somewhere else, like the kitchen, bathroom, bedroom, a pants pocket, or a purse, as soon as you spot them shift them immediately to the bowl.

Anytime you or anyone else leaves the house, the location of the keys is predictable and they are accessible. It's so simple, yet so effective—no more lost car keys. If you set up systems like this one for all of life's repetitive small challenges, and there are dozens of them, it will amaze you how much more simple and stress-free your life becomes.

In our Orlando home, Adena and I use a beautiful Lalique crystal bowl as our key depository near the door to the great room where we normally enter the house. We use the same system in our other homes, and keys just don't get lost.

Success Strategy No. 47:

Combine all frequently used keys into complete duplicate sets.

Most people have a separate set of keys for each set of locks, and often end up at the right lock with the wrong keys. Let's say you are a multiple-car family, plus you have keys that open your home and office. Normally, there are one or more keys for each car and another set for home and/or office. Stop the fumbling and the wasted motions. Incorporate the keys for all important locks into one complete set, and then make as many duplicate sets as necessary.

Here is an example of a complete set:

- Key to house
- Two keys to the Chevy—door and ignition
- Two keys to the Toyota—trunk and ignition
- Your office key
- Spouse's office key

Once all keys are in complete sets, no matter which set you pick up you will never be locked out of your home, office, or the car you choose to drive. Keep two extra sets for the rare occasion when keys do get misplaced. No more concern about who has which keys. Several sets will be in your key receptacle where and when you need them, and any set will do since they are interchangeable. Simple but effective.

Success Strategy No. 48:

Change your door locks so that one key fits all.

Houses normally come with a "set" of keys—one for the front door, one for the side door, another for the back door, and maybe even another for the lock to the shed or garage door. Any multiple-lock setup requires multiple keys and an excessive amount of labeling and duplication. What a potential waste of time and effort! Call a locksmith and have all the locks in your home changed to use the same key. Tell the locksmith exactly what you want done over the phone so that two trips won't be necessary. The complete process can be done for well under a hundred dollars. The doorknobs and locks don't have to be replaced, only the internal lock mechanisms. Then, one key fits all—no matter which door you choose to use. Two, three, or more keys per set are replaced by just one master key for your entire home. Your complete key sets now require only one key for the entire house.

At our Orlando home, in addition to the front and side doors, there are sixteen sets of double French doors, two west-wing doors, an upstairs balcony door, a boat house door, a garage door, and an atrium door, all with locks. Can you imagine how much time could be spent just looking for and duplicating keys if all those locks used different keys? In our home, one key fits all. No matter how few doors you have now, a good system like this one will save you time and trouble.

Success Strategy No. 49:

Ignore the telephone and doorbell when getting ready.

Have you ever noticed that when you're getting ready to go somewhere, people seem to gang up on you? They phone or stop by unexpectedly, and as a result you end up late. The solution is easy. To pick up the phone in the middle of getting ready is to invite disaster. Let it ring, or dead-end the phone into an answering machine. Handle the call on your schedule—when *you* have time.

Don't answer the door while you're getting ready. You won't miss a thing, but you will be ready to leave on time. Sure it's tough to resist when your mind tells you that maybe someone is at the door with a check for $10,000, though it's really a kid selling magazines. If someone is at your door with a package and you don't answer, either the package will be left by the door or with a neighbor, or you'll find a note indicating where you can pick it up. Your mission and priority is leaving on time so you will arrive on time. To accomplish that objective requires ignoring telephones and doorbells.

Success Strategy No. 50:

Plan ahead for dual use of the shower or bathroom.

One of the silliest, most frequent causes of lateness is conflict over using the same bathroom at the same time. There are twenty-four hours in a day and yet two people want to take a shower at exactly the same moment. There are two success strategies: You could build an additional bathroom and get a note from your doctor for the IRS that says the new bathroom should be tax deductible because it is necessary for your mental health (but I would not advise it). Or to be more practical, just plan your time lines so the two of you don't conflict. Nothing will ruin your beautiful evening out or your morning at the office as quickly as an argument over who should get first last-minute use of the plumbing.

Conflicts over the bathroom, like other relationship conflicts, often begin with the absolutes "always" and "never." One says, "You *always* want to get in the bathroom at exactly the same time I do!" And the other retorts, "Well, you *never* give me the consideration of allowing me to use the bathroom when I want to. There are two people who live here." Now, there are two problems to deal with: the shortage of available bathrooms, and an angry spouse or mate. The solution is simple. Just sit down calmly and agree on who will use the bathroom at what time and then write it down as if it were a business plan. Life doesn't have to be complicated. Proper planning reduces perpetual conflicts.

Success Strategy No. 51:

Practice effective time management on yourself, not those around you.

One person in a relationship is often better at time management than the other. Don't allow that difference to create a conflict. If you're standing by the door ready to leave and your mate is not ready, you have alternatives other than anger and frustration. It is better to deal unemotionally with the lateness of the person who is not ready on time. Remember, you always have choice. You can leave on time and arrive on time without the other person. Or you can wait calmly until the other person is ready and go together. Effective time management can only be practiced on yourself. Demanding that others do the same just won't work.

Success Strategy No. 52:

Fill up your tank on your time – not at stress time.

You would think that a majority of experienced drivers would have a system to prevent unnecessary, time-consuming, lateness-creating stops at the gas station. It's just not so. Most drivers push an empty tank to the limit, breathing fumes through the carburetor before they are willing to pull over to the pump. If you're one of them, you know that the results are always the same. Stress and frustration are produced by:

- Leaving too late to stop for gas and still arrive on time
- Feeling there is a fifty-fifty chance you can make it without running out of gas, so you pray and curse under stress the entire way
- Kicking yourself for not having filled the tank yesterday
- Slowing at each gas station you pass but making a last-minute decision to drive on
- Finally deciding to play it safe and pull over only to find a line at the pump or the slowest customers and clerks you could imagine

- Getting angry because someone else in the family drove the car without having the courtesy to refill the tank
- Discovering you have only a couple of dollars in cash because you didn't plan to stop for gas
- Worrying that your credit card is over the limit or that where you stop won't take credit cards

Sounds like anything but fun. Again, it's the no-slack principle in operation. Your mind becomes consumed with negative thoughts and emotions, all for lack of a predetermined system for something as simple as keeping gas in the tank.

Here's how to put an end to the problem. Every time you stop for gas, fill up the tank completely no matter how rushed you are. When you get low and fuel stops are unplanned, you may find yourself asking for only $5 or $10 worth of gas to "save time." That guarantees you will have to spend *more* time getting gas again in a day or two, usually at the most inopportune time, wasting at least an extra ten minutes. Filling up completely requires no more than 120 extra seconds, but will save you at least one additional stop per week at the fuel pump. That's fifty extra stops a year, and you will have freed up more than five hundred minutes, or eight hours, for objectives far more important than pumping gas.

Use this same approach to all your repetitive activities and you can actually free up hundreds of extra productive hours each year. When the gas gauge gets down to one-quarter, STOP! Fill up the tank now. Don't push it until you trigger the almost-out-of-gas stress-and-frustration cycle. You've got to get gas anyway. Do it on your time, not at alarm time.

Success Strategy No. 53:

Add a ten-minute fudge factor to your travel time.

Why is it that our mathematical minds work backward? If it's seventeen minutes from your house to your destination and you must be there at 9:15, when do you leave? Two minutes to nine, right? That is, if you're not already late because somebody called and you chose to pick up the phone instead of staying committed to leaving on time.

Every time you allow only fifteen minutes for a fifteen-minute drive, the no-slack principle will take over your life. Traffic, construction delays, an accident, or something else will impede your path to prove to you that you didn't plan properly. Your strategy? Automatically add ten minutes to the travel time to any destination and set your mental clock to leave accordingly. Remember, there is no slack. Either you add the extra time or you will almost always be delayed for some unexpected reason.

When you get angry in traffic, it's generally because you are late or about to be late and you feel pushed. As much as you want it to be, it's not the fault of the thousand drivers who are there blocking the road in front of you, acting as if they were in a parking lot. And getting angry is not going to get you there on time. I know from my own experience.

The year was 1967. I was with a friend driving from stoplight to stoplight, late as usual. In those days I was a pro at getting angry with both traffic and the drivers who were the "cause" of it. I vented my anger by pounding on the steering wheel until the process became habit. "Those silly sons-of-guns," I'd say. "What do they think they're doing? What is this, a parade? A conspiracy? Is everybody out there 212 years old without a driver's license?"

I would go on and on until I worked myself up from fervor to frenzy. My face would get bright red as I yelled at other drivers from the protection of my own car and, of course, felt justified at my insane behavior. The more frustrated I became, the harder I would pound on the plastic wheel. It didn't matter to me who else was in the car. I knew I was "in the right."

That day in 1967 there I was again, up to my hubcaps in traffic, angry because I was late and blaming everyone else for the fact that time had slipped from my grip. As usual, I started pounding on the wheel. "Get out of my way! Don't you know I've got important things to do? If I had my way, nobody would drive on the highway when I'm using it!" Suddenly, with one solid hit—*crack!*—the steering wheel literally broke off. My anger instantly turned to embarrassment. Now what could I do? Hand the wheel to my passenger? "Here. You drive."

All those drivers who had seen me red-faced, waving and shouting, were laughing now. I felt one step beyond foolish. That's when the light bulb finally clicked on. If I was late and stuck in traffic, becoming frustrated, angry, and hostile didn't help me get to my destination a minute sooner. It was as if I were throwing gasoline on a house fire in a vain attempt to put it out. Now not only was I going to be late, I had rendered the car undrivable and had allowed the situation to drain me emotionally, ensuring that I would not be operating even close to my best when I finally did arrive at my destination.

At that moment, I mentally made the decision to change my losing habit of getting angry in traffic. Where I is, is where I is, I would tell myself, and getting angry will only make the situation worse. I began to add the ten-minute "fudge factor" and started leaving on time. Soon the process became habit and today, twenty-five years later, those around me know that they can bet on my being on time—every time.

Staying in control of your life requires emotional balance. Any time you "lose it" and get angry, you have passed control to someone or something else. When you say to a person, "You made me angry," you're actually saying, "You're now in control of my life." To prevent other people from controlling your life and your time, you must refuse to get angry.

I learned that lesson the hard way back in 1967, and partly as a result of that experience, I no longer get angry—not in traffic, not anywhere. It's simply a choice. Keeping your emotional balance allows you to save your potentially productive emotional energy for positive purposes, such as shooting for your dreams and creating positive, loving, conflict-free relationships.

Success Strategy No. 54:

Carry a local map in the glove compartment of your car.

Have you ever been on your way somewhere, even with verbal directions provided by someone else, and the street you were looking for couldn't be found? What a frustrating time waster! Always carry a map in your car of the area in which you are driving, no matter how well you think you know it.

Studies have actually now shown something I've been aware of for years. Many men are too proud to stop and ask for directions when they get lost. "Honey, just stop and ask directions," she says. "Not on your life," he says. "If I stop and ask directions, it's guaranteed we're going to be late. At least we have a chance of being on time if we just keep looking. This place has got to be here somewhere." At that point the no-slack principle is going to get you. If you don't already know where you're going, you have almost no chance of finding the place by trial and error in less time than if you stopped and asked for directions.

If you've got a map in your glove compartment, your problem is solved. Ask your passenger to read it, or pull over and read it yourself. Better yet, from now on consult the map *before* you start out, familiarizing yourself with the directions and estimating the time it will take to get there—even if someone has given you verbal directions.

Our road teams at the Givens Organization have been trained to follow a map procedure as a matter of policy. The first hour they arrive in a new city, they are required to stop and get a map of the area for each of the rental cars. Why? Because they're going to be lost for three days in that city without it. This is likely to happen even if they got verbal directions. One simple, extra procedure taking less than ten minutes saves hours and potential lost dollars. It's just as true in your own hometown.

Success Strategy No. 55:

Allow an extra five minutes to find the correct address or office.

Potential time-wasting events sometimes occur even after you reach your destination. Ever walk into a high-rise building and then attempt to figure out where you are going—when you are already late? Just reading the directory on the wall, if there is one, can take a couple of minutes, and if you have to find someone to ask directions from it may take even longer. If you have never been to a particular destination, add an extra five minutes to your travel time to give yourself time to find the office or address you are looking for.

After adding an extra ten minutes for the travel-time fudge factor and another five minutes to find the correct location or address, you will leave fifteen minutes earlier than the estimated time it will take you to reach your destination. That fifteen-minute margin will allow you to arrive on time every time. No more excuses, and no more stress and frustration.

Leave your life to chance and chances are you won't like the way you live your life.

There's nothing complicated about controlling your time line as long as you plan to give yourself enough time to get ready, and enough time to get where you're going. Plan your time line so the no-slack principle doesn't play "gotcha" with your life and your emotions. From now on, make it a priority to be on time, every time.

CHAPTER **13**

Prioritizing Your Personal Time

The business of life is not business, but living.
—B. C. Forbes

There are few truly successful people who haven't learned in some way to schedule their business time—whether with lists of activities on pieces of scrap paper or with an elaborate, $250 leather-bound time-planning kit. But even those who are good at scheduling business time often have little or no awareness of the importance of properly scheduling personal time. If you're one of them, you and I are going to have a heart-to-heart talk about how to balance your life and create more zing, excitement, and quality time in your nonbusiness, nonwork hours.

Success Strategy No. 56:

Schedule your personal time with the same priority and attention to detail as you schedule your business time.

There are 24 hours in every day, 168 hours a week—the same for everyone, no exceptions. No matter how your time is used, the maximum time available remains constant. Your waking hours are customarily divided between your business and your personal life. There is no one right time to stop thinking about your business life, any more than there is one right time to attempt to forget your personal life.

When you are living a satisfactory, successful life, your business and personal hours are closely intertwined, but you have learned to focus on business and personal activities at the appropriate times. On the job your primary focus is on business activities and goals. That does not mean that on company time you won't plan a golf game, have an interesting conversation with a friend or coworker about your personal thoughts and feelings, or think about how achieving your business and career goals will also help you achieve some of your personal objectives. The same is true when you leave your work environment. There is no mental switch that causes you to shut off thoughts about business activities and plans. In fact, it is when you're away from work that you may come up with your latest and greatest business-related ideas, even though your primary focus will normally be on personal activities and goals.

There is, however, one important separation that must be made between your business life and your personal life. Don't drag worry and stress from your work into your personal life, and vice versa. Through the use of the Success Strategies that follow, you'll find that job-related worry and stress levels can be reduced as much as 90 percent, leaving you more time and energy for personal activities like spending quality time with your friends and family.

No man on his deathbed ever said, "I wish I'd spent more time at the office." Yet business-time priorities often seem to take precedence over personal-time priorities. Don't let it happen. One reason you work hard is to have the money to do the personal things you've always wanted to do, such as travel, play more golf, buy a boat, and spend enjoyable, uninterrupted time with your family. Your personal time is just as important as, if not more important than, your business time. Don't allow business activities to cancel, interrupt, or control personal activities. If in your job or business you treat everything that goes wrong as an emergency, you will end up spending your life handling emergencies rather than spending quality time with those you really care about—your spouse, kids, parents, and friends. Jobs and businesses come and go, but these folks are with you for a lifetime. Start treating your personal time with them as the priority it should be.

Success Strategy No. 57:

Schedule your personal activities as if they were appointments that cannot be canceled.

If you and your spouse or mate have made a date to go out to dinner and a movie once a week, write the time on your Daily Activities List and mark it as a priority just as you would a business appointment. If you've scheduled a time to take your son or daughter fishing or to a football game, or if plan to attend one of their activities, write down the es and dates on your list as a priority. If you have important business appointments the same week, schedule them around your personal activities. The world won't come to an end. You'll just end up with greater control over your time with none of the guilt or self-criticism that occurs when you break personal commitments. Time lost with business activities that have interrupted personal activities seldom gets replaced.

Last year, as I was scheduling one of my many trips abroad, I received a call from Rick Frischman, the head of Planned Television Arts, who handles all my personal appearances on television shows. "Chuck, I understand you're going out of the country with your boys," he said, "but I think Oprah may want you in a week or so. Can't you reschedule your trip?"

My answer was the same as always: "Not on your life! Oprah will have to reschedule her time, or I won't be able to do the show." I made that statement knowing that the last time I was on "The Oprah Winfrey Show" her great audience responded by buying seventy-five thousand copies of my then new book, *More Wealth Without Risk,* which skyrocketed it to number-one on *The New York Times* best-seller list for the next eight weeks.

Tempting? Sure, but my personal priorities are just as important to me as business priorities or selling books. So, consistent with my goals and values, I turned down the opportunity, as I have in the past for many big shows. When I plan to travel or schedule other personal activities, nothing is going to change my plans. I've lived my life that way for thirty years and have still managed to find time to attain every business goal I've ever set. In reality, there is little in business that won't wait. That includes both events and people.

If you're a person with a demanding, high-stress job, it's even more important to schedule time for yourself and those you love. It is very likely that your performance in your job will be measured, at least in part, by how well you handle the conflicting demands on your time. You may feel you have to work long hours to get the job done, but your boss may feel that you're working overtime because you *can't* get the job done. A person who sacrifices his personal life for a job or cause often ends up lacking real happiness and a real sense of accomplishment. A balance between your job and your personal life is the key to success.

If your job is being a parent, you'll want to follow this same strategy. Mothers especially often fall into the trap of waiting hand and foot on the rest of the family and leaving no time for themselves. If this is your situation, again, balance is the key. Schedule your personal time with the same priority you schedule your household time. Give yourself time every day to do what you want to do and not just what apparently needs to be done. Make what you do for your family a willing choice, not a chore. Personal time and family time should be treated as a top priority in both single-parent households and households in which both parents work.

Success Strategy No. 58:

Don't allow job-related problems to interrupt scheduled personal time.

Your personal time is your mental-health time. The big mistake that many people make with their personal time is to say to themselves, "Well, when I get all the business done, then I'll spend some time with my family." Business is *never* done. Therefore, there is seldom any real time to spend with the family. It's the same thing as saying, "Well, when I get all my bills paid, then I'll start to invest the extra money." Have you ever noticed that there is never any extra money? Well, there's never any extra time, either, so it must be created.

Scheduling your personal time with the same priority as your business time is an absolute must for balanced, successful living. When there is a conflict, business can often wait, but not your family and friends. Your attitude should be: "No matter what comes up in business, I will not change the time I've scheduled for myself or my family." If you plan time with your family but are often interrupted by someone calling about job-related matters, turn off the telephone ringer and let the calls dead-end into your answering machine. The calls will wait; your family shouldn't have to.

Here's a short checklist to determine if you are in control of your personal time. If there are "yes" answers, you have work to do.

_____ Do you ever call home from work to tell your spouse, mate, or kids that you are going to be unavoidably detained even though you have made plans for the evening?

_____ Do you ever plan an evening with your family or friends and end up bringing work home from the office, which just *has* to be done?

_____ Have you ever scheduled vacation time and then canceled it for some business reason?

_____ Have you ever scheduled something to do with your kids on a weekend and then canceled because some business matter came up?

_____ Have you ever told your family you would spend a quiet evening with them, only to end up on the phone solving business problems?

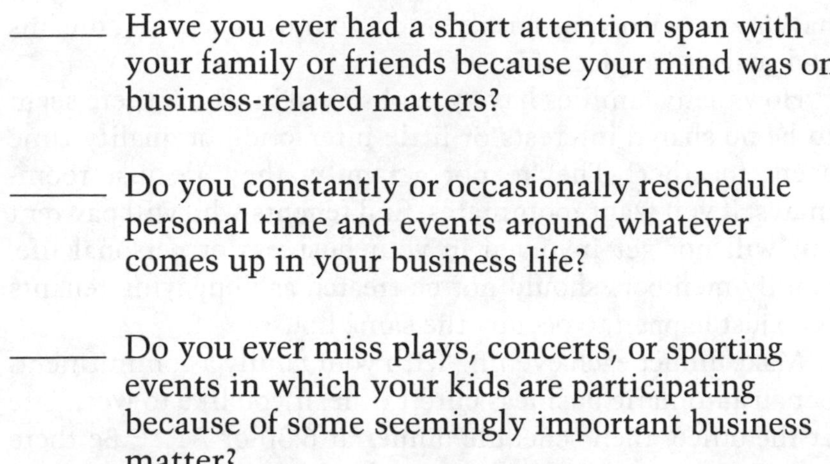

_____ Have you ever had a short attention span with your family or friends because your mind was on business-related matters?

_____ Do you constantly or occasionally reschedule personal time and events around whatever comes up in your business life?

_____ Do you ever miss plays, concerts, or sporting events in which your kids are participating because of some seemingly important business matter?

None of these interruptions will take over your personal life once it belongs to you. And the only way to take control of your personal life is to schedule your personal time with the same priority as you schedule your business time, then stick to that schedule. At first it might seem that you are missing out on some business opportunities, but you'll find that possibility usually exists only in your imagination. Your life will go on, and in the process you will build better relationships with those people who are truly important to you.

Success Strategy No. 59:
Stop treating your family as second-class citizens.

Your relationships may grow together or apart because of the priority you do or don't place on your personal time. Your kids are growing up. You are getting older. Time you could have spent with your family or on your own personal dreams and goals is irreplaceable.

How many families have you observed in which there seem to be no shared interests or little interaction or quality time spent together? They're not a family; they are just roommates. If you want roommates, find tenants who will pay rent but will not get involved in your business or personal life. Family members should not be treated as nonpaying tenants who just happen to occupy the same house.

Make dinner each evening with your family a commitment. Set an automatic business cutoff time. If you like to work late at the office, then schedule dinner at 6:30 or 7 P.M. Be there every time, no matter what you leave undone at the office. Don't worry, it will still be there tomorrow. Ensure that your family spends at least thirty minutes together at the table each evening with meaningful discussions, a lot of humor, a lot of fun. Make it a family tradition.

Adena and I have a tradition and a personal commitment to each other that every evening at 6:30 we will be together having dinner. No, not in our beautiful formal dining room. If we are alone and eating at home, we often sit on the floor and eat at the coffee table in our great room. We have our own chef, so neither Adena nor I has to think about preparing dinner, setting the table, or washing the dishes, but no last-minute business projects, problems, or appointments are allowed to interrupt that time together.

If you want to spend quality time with your family at dinner without one of you being stuck in the kitchen cooking, serving, and cleaning up, then bring home take-out or have someone cook and deliver. Or share kitchen chores as a family, making that part of the quality time you spend together. Get creative—it's your life.

If you become a slave to either office worries or to household chores, they will have power over your life. If, on the other hand, you treat your personal time as the most important time of your life, you will end up refreshed, less frustrated, and less stressed out, and you will have more positive energy each time you tackle new business situations and problems.

Schedule all of your personal activities on your Daily Activities List. Your daily business activities are scheduled on that same list. Compare the two schedules. Is there a conflict or the potential for conflict? If so, reschedule to avoid it. And remember, a scheduled personal activity, like a scheduled business activity, is an appointment that you are committed to keep. Don't lose sight of why you work so hard—to be able to enjoy your personal life and to finance your personal dreams and goals.

I schedule my personal time in detail—time with my wife and my sons, even how much time I intend to spend each day playing music at home, watching movies, playing golf, tennis, or video games, or jet-skiing on the lake behind our home. Nothing interrupts that time.

It's what you accomplish, not how long it takes, that determines your level of success.

Your mind has been telling you that to succeed you must work harder and longer hours. That's nonsense. When your personal and business times are balanced, there is less conflict and stress, and you become more effective and get more done in less time. Working hard has little to do with success; working with maximum effectiveness does. Work is hard only if you don't like what you're doing or don't properly plan and control your time. There's nothing hard about what you do in your business or career if you've chosen something you love. If you have not, then high on your Goals List should be to find a new job or career. Why spend eight or twelve hours a day doing something that is not personally rewarding and fulfilling? It doesn't make sense.

Stop taking your career so seriously. Make it fun. A hundred years from now, do you think that anybody will really care how many hours you spent at the office or what you did or didn't accomplish? Probably not. But right now everybody in your personal life cares about how much time and the quality of time you spend with them.

Longer work is not better work. If you work fewer hours and have a fulfilling personal life, doing the things you dream of doing and making living fun, you'll end up accomplishing more in your business life with far less stress.

Yes, you *can* have it all.

CHAPTER **14**

Managing the Mundane

Housework can kill you if done right.

—Erma Bombeck

Think of the number of hours in your day that you spend on activities that you find not particularly pleasurable or of little value. Some of these activities may be necessary, such as cooking to satisfy your family's desire to eat or buying a new battery for your car. The fact remains, however, that you spend considerable time on activities that don't contribute directly to the accomplishment of your dreams and goals. Since your dreams, goals, and values represent and are related to what you have determined to be important in your life, time spent on anything else is time that could be available for what you feel is important.

Success Strategy No. 60:

Increase your effectiveness by eliminating mundane maintenance activities.

All of the activities that do not contribute directly to your dreams or personal and business goals I classify as mundane maintenance. Sure, this stuff must get done, but not necessarily by you. Many of these routine or repetitive chores fit into four general categories: cooking, cleaning, home maintenance, and car maintenance. Here is a list of a few of the most common mundane maintenance activities that affect almost everyone in one way or another. I'm sure you can add plenty of your own.

- Taking clothes to the dry cleaners
- Shopping at the grocery store
- Painting the house, inside or outside
- Raking leaves
- Washing clothes
- Cleaning house
- Cutting the grass
- Putting gas in the car
- Shoveling snow
- Washing the car
- Ironing clothes
- Cooking meals
- Washing dishes
- Paying bills
- Fixing leaky faucets or a stopped-up toilet
- Washing windows
- Polishing furniture
- Planting shrubbery
- Changing oil or sparkplugs in your car

Probably up to half of your waking hours outside of your regular job are spent on activities like these that keep you busy but don't produce the satisfaction of real accomplishment. What a waste of your valuable time. Unless your chosen career is maid, butler, home maintenance expert, or auto mechanic, you may be sacrificing hundreds of hours per year on activities that are neither in alignment with your values nor contribute directly to the accomplishment of a single objective, goal, or dream.

Now, if one of the great loves of your life is the thrill of choosing and investing in lawn and garden equipment and then mowing, trimming, bagging, and raking your way to emotional bliss, don't let me convince you to drop those activities. But if for you lawn maintenance is the kind of necessary work that you least look forward to and that you would prefer to avoid with a passion, then using the following strategies will give you that opportunity.

Success Strategy No. 61:

Think of the cost of hiring out mundane maintenance as an investment, not an expense.

How do you get rid of mundane maintenance? The best and easiest way I know of is to pay someone else to do it. "Well," I hear you saying, "it will cost moncy to pay someone to do what I've been doing." Of course it will, but ridding yourself of time-consuming, repetitive chores is one of the most effective ways to increase your available time and emotional and mental energies to pursue what you have already decided is more important to you—your dreams and goals. The more time you can free up, the more effective you can become. Your objective is not to save money by doing low-priority jobs yourself; it is to free up time in order to pursue your high-priority activities. The cost is insignificant when compared to the incredible number of high-priority objectives you will be able to accomplish in that time. Using this strategy alone can double your effectiveness. It did for me.

When I first met Adena, almost ten years ago, I invited her to my ranch for dinner for our second date. I had an impressive home, complete with my own personal French master chef, Jacques—obviously a nice way to wine and dine a lady. We had a great meal and were having fun getting to know each other when suddenly Adena stood, picked up the dishes, and began carrying them into the kitchen.

"Whoa! What are you doing?" I asked her with some surprise.

She replied, somewhat startled, "Well, I just thought I would help clean up." Apparently she wanted to impress me with her willingness to pitch in and do the dirty work.

"Adena," I said as sweetly as I could, "let me explain it to you this way. If I need someone to wash the dishes, the windows, or the clothes, I can hire someone. What I would prefer in a relationship is someone who can share my time and the fun and excitement of life, not the housekeeping duties."

At that moment Adena thought to herself, as she told me years later, "Where do I sign up?" Obviously she did.

In all our years together, neither Adena nor I has ever washed a load of clothes, loaded the dishwasher, cut the grass, made beds, or vacuumed carpets. It is not because we are snobbish or feel we are above such activities. We are committed to spending our time on far more important things, such as building our relationship, building our businesses, and spending quality time with our families. If an activity doesn't relate to one of our top values, dreams, or goals, we pay someone else to do it. It is an investment, not an expense.

Actually, my awareness of the importance of freeing up more time began twenty-five years ago, in the sixties, when I was married to Bonnie and we were raising our two boys. I realized then that hundreds of freed-up hours during the year would be necessary if I was ever going to reach my goals during my lifetime or while I was still young enough to enjoy the rewards.

One day Bonnie called me at the office and asked quite innocently, "Chuck, please stop on the way home and pick up a loaf of bread for dinner. I'm completely out." "Bonnie," I replied too loudly and somewhat indignantly, "do I remind you of a grocery-store delivery boy? I'll never make us any money in a grocery store unless I own it, and I never will if I spend my time running errands. Just hire a neighborhood kid to go to the store for you. He will work cheaper than I am willing to work." Bonnie was shocked and didn't know what to say, so she just hung up. At that time she had no idea what I was talking about, but she soon realized that I was establishing a pattern of choosing carefully the activities on which I would spend my time.

I urge you or your spouse or mate to make a plan to do the same. Rid yourselves of those activities that won't take you closer to where you want to be. Hire someone else to do them. Sure, it costs money to get others to do what you've been doing unless you have a household full of kids who love to clean their rooms and mow the lawn. (Some chance.)

Success Strategy No. 62:

If the cost is less than your per-hour value, hire someone else to do the job.

Getting rid of all unproductive household chores might seem like a distant goal depending on what you're earning now, but when you have set a monetary value on each hour of your time, you can begin right now to shift mundane maintenance, chores, and other unproductive activities one at a time to those whose time is worth a lot less than yours. You will then free up one to five hours a day to devote to a combination of productive objectives such as:

- Spending quality time with those you love
- Working on your business and career goals and dreams
- Resting and relaxing
- Involving yourself in other personally rewarding projects and activities that are in agreement with your values

Getting rid of the mundane was how I began to free up the time to take total control of my life. I evaluated every moment of my time and how I used it, computing how much my time was worth per hour based on my current income. Then anytime routine and necessary chores could be done by someone whose time was worth less per hour than mine, I hired them out. There were no other considerations or decisions. Anytime a job required someone whose time was worth more per hour than mine and I had the skills, I did the job myself. Back then my time was worth a paltry five dollars an hour, and my yearly income amounted to only about ten thousand dollars. Twenty-five years later, and because of applying strategies like this one, my time, based on the same forty hours a week, is worth $12,500 an hour, which amounts to a personal net income of over $25 million every year. The drastic change was no accident. It was the result of a carefully calculated and conducted plan.

You have to start somewhere if you want to accomplish more and have the time to enjoy more of what you accomplish. Delegating mundane maintenance activities is a great starting place. How do you decide whether you are going to fix a leaky pipe yourself or call a plumber? Let's say that after checking you find that a plumber will cost $35 per hour. If the per-hour value of your time is less than $35, reach for your wrench. If the per-hour value of your time is more than $35, reach for the phone.

Success Strategy No. 63: When in doubt, let someone else do it.

Obviously when the dollar values of your time and someone else's, such as the plumber's, are about the same, there are other considerations as well. For instance, you would ask whether the plumber intends to charge for travel time to and from your house. If he is a half-hour away, the round-trip might tally up to $35 before he even laid a hand on the pipe. You're ahead of the game if you do it yourself because you're already at the source of the problem. Another consideration that affects whom you finally choose is your skill level. Pipes may not be your thing, and although you may be totally capable of learning, the required knowledge and even the parts and tools you need could take you several hours to acquire, while the plumber already has both. And, of course, if you are a total novice, you may make the problem worse and therefore more expensive to fix. For most mundane activities such as simple errands, mowing, cooking, and cleaning, you can bet it's more effective to get someone else to do them.

Obviously, the less you, or you and your spouse, make per hour, the more mundane maintenance you will have to do yourselves for a while. But as you make more, the less time you should spend on routine chores. It all depends on the value of your time. Look at "The Value of Your Time" table on page 210 to determine what each hour of your time is worth based on how much you are currently earning. You can

The Value of Your Time

Total Yearly Income	Total Number of Hours Worked Each Week			
	30	40	50	60
	Approximate Worth of an Hour of Your Time			
20,000	$ 13.34	$ 10.00	$ 8.00	$ 5.67
25,000	16.67	12.50	10.00	8.34
30,000	20.00	15.00	12.00	10.00
35,000	23.34	17.50	14.00	11.67
40,000	26.67	20.00	16.00	13.34
50,000	33.34	25.00	20.00	16.67
60,000	40.00	30.00	24.00	20.00
75,000	50.00	37.50	30.00	25.00
100,000	56.67	50.00	40.00	33.34
150,000	100.00	75.00	60.00	50.00
200,000	133.34	100.00	80.00	56.67
300,000	200.00	150.00	120.00	100.00
400,000	266.67	200.00	160.00	133.34
500,000	333.34	250.00	200.00	166.67
Total Number of Hours Worked Each Year (50 weeks)	1,500	2,000	2,500	3,000

also use the table to determine your hourly value at some increased level of income in the future.

To use the table, locate your total yearly income in the left vertical column. The four columns to the right represent the average number of hours you work per week: thirty, forty, fifty, or sixty. Read across the row to the right of the figure that represents your yearly income until you reach the column that most closely represents the total number of hours you work each week. The number at that point is the approximate current worth of an hour of your time. The total number of hours worked per year by someone who averages thirty, forty, fifty, or sixty hours per week is shown below each column at the bottom of the table. The yearly hours figure is calculated by multiplying the weekly hours worked by 50, allowing for a two-week paid vacation. The value of onc hour as shown in the table has been calculated by dividing the yearly income figures by the total number of hours worked each year.

Now that you know the value of your at-work time, you can figure out the cost of the time you now spend on mundane maintenance. Below you will find a list of activities that, in general, people find mundane in their lives. Jot down the mundane activities particular to your life, adding any that are not on the list. Next to each activity you listed, note the approximate number of hours you spend on that activity each month. If you perform the activity every day, you would multiply the number of hours daily by thirty to arrive at the number of hours you spend each month. If you perform the activity once or more per week, you would multiply the weekly hours by four to arrive at the approximate monthly figure. You get the idea.

Mundane Maintenance Activities

- Boat maintenance
- Car maintenance
- Cleaning garage
- Cleaning house
- Cleaning oven
- Completing tax return
- Cooking meals
- Dropping off and picking up dry cleaning
- Feeding pets
- Filling the gas tank
- Filling prescriptions
- Home repairs and maintenance
- Maintaining personal and business financial records
- Lawn and garden maintenance
- Making beds, changing linens
- Packing lunch boxes
- Paying bills
- Pool maintenance
- Running errands
- Sewing and clothing repairs
- Shining shoes
- Shopping
- Sweeping driveway/sidewalk/porch
- Shoveling snow
- Taking out garbage
- Washing/drying/folding clothes
- Washing/drying dishes
- Watering plants

Finally, total up the number of hours you spend on mundane maintenance each month and multiply that figure by the value you calculated as the worth of that hour of your time. That figure is the dollar amount you are currently spending on mundane maintenance. For example, let's say you spend two hours a weekend mowing the lawn, for a total of eight hours a month, and your time is worth $40 an hour. That's a total of $320 a month of your time. And if you live in a climate where you mow your lawn six months out of the year, you're spending almost $2,000 worth of your time on that activity alone. You could probably hire the most expensive lawn-care service in your community for half that amount and you would then have a total of forty-eight hours

—or the equivalent of more than one full working week—to devote to activities that will improve the quality of your life, not just the look of your lawn.

Here's another example. June, a mother who also works outside the home, was attending one of my SuperSelf workshops and was asked to list the mundane activities that came to her mind and the number of hours per week spent on each. She came up with the following list:

Activity	Number of Hours Per Week
Vacuum house	1
Wash clothes	4
Wash dishes	5
Wash car	1
Cook meals	5
Pay bills	2
Shine shoes	1
Drop off and pick up dry cleaning	1
Clean bathrooms and kitchen	3
Total	23

June was surprised when she realized the number of hours she spent each week on activities totally unrelated to her goals and dreams. When she multiplied that number by the value of an hour of her time, which she calculated at $30, and came up with $690 *per week*, she almost went into shock. That wasn't all. She knew there were only 168 hours in each week, and after deducting 50 hours for sleep, only 118 were left. June found out she was spending 20 percent of her total available waking hours on the mundane. If she subtracted 45 hours per week for work, 5 hours for lunch, and 6 hours of travel time to and from work, she had only 62 waking hours left, of which 23, or more than one-third, were spent on the mundane. June saw the light. She reorganized her life and doubled her effectiveness by hiring a part-time housekeeper for far less per week than the value of the time she had been spending on housekeeping chores and errands.

Success Strategy No. 64:
Begin giving up mundane maintenance now.

Go down your list of mundane maintenance activities and decide which ones you can give up immediately. Don't think about it for weeks. Positive, effective habits are built from action, not indecision. Your decision is neither permanent nor irreversible. You can always change your mind later. Your goal is to move forward now to free up as much of your valuable time as possible, and to give up later more and more of what is less and less important to the quality of your life.

Don't expect your husband to fix something every time it breaks. Call a repairman or, better yet, hire a handyman on a regular basis who will charge $8 an hour, a lot less than your husband makes. And don't expect your wife to be relegated to washing dishes, baby-sitting, vacuuming, and doing laundry for the rest of her days. That's not what life is all about. Remember that the purpose of this strategy is to free up time for both of you, not to free up time for one at the expense of the other. Work together, and you'll be amazed and surprised at the results.

Many of the mundane activities on your list could be combined and then performed by a lawn-care service, a home-maintenance service, or a housekeeper. Your kids can also pitch in, and you should make it a policy to pay them what you would pay an outside service to do the same job. Or you could work together as a family to do the chores you decide not to hire out, saving both time and money.

Go to it. Make a plan to get rid of the mundane and routine in your life. You and your family will then have more time to devote to really living your lives.

CHAPTER **15**

Eliminating Interruptions

All phone calls are obscene.
—Karen Elizabeth Gordon,
in *The Well-Tempered Sentence*

Odds are that interruptions are one of the main success and accomplishment killers in your life. Like most people, you are probably interrupted so often that you actually live life around interruptions instead of around your chosen activities. If so, you have fallen prey to the interruption gremlin—as have all others who have not incorporated interruption-busting strategies into their lives.

Success Strategy No. 65:

Take back control of your time by eliminating interruptions.

What is an interruption? An interruption is anything that diverts your attention from an activity you have chosen to do to an activity that someone else has purposely or inadvertently chosen for you. Interruptions are normally random and without any consideration for the importance of, or impact on, your time and your personal priorities. Interruptions chew up time and energy.

There are two major categories of interruptions you face daily at home or at the office: telephones and people in person. The telephone rings, and you automatically stop what you are doing to answer it. The doorbell rings, and the same thing happens regardless of the importance of the task at hand. Someone is forcing you to switch gears instantly even though it is not your choice. "I'm not interrupting, am I?" is the typical remark. "Of course not," you answer politely without an ounce of integrity. Whether people interrupt you in person or on the telephone, they always seem to have something on their minds that just can't wait.

The time wasted because of an interruption is longer than the time span of the actual interruption. For instance, you are concentrating on writing a report, business plan, or important letter when your concentration is broken by the ringing of your phone. Not only do you lose the time you actually talk on the phone, but it will normally take you several additional minutes to regain your focus and get back up to speed with what you were doing. Switching gears takes time.

The telephone has become the greatest source of interruptions. In fact, it is an electronic instrument designed to interrupt. For some reason you and I were taught to believe that when the telephone rings, all else must be dropped in a race to answer it before it stops ringing. That habit is like having someone follow you around yelling "Freeze" twenty times a day and expecting you to stop in your tracks for three to ten minutes each time. The danger is that old phone habits unnecessarily eat up hours of your valuable time—time that cannot be replaced. Your level of effectiveness in life is determined both by the number of hours you have available to work on specific objectives and by how effectively you use those hours. The more hours that are wasted, the less effective you become.

Answering the phone just because it rings means turning over your time and attention to someone else at a moment's notice. Obviously, achieving your goals and dreams becomes far more difficult when you are constantly working someone else's agenda and at someone else's pace.

The "answer the phone above all else" addiction cuts into your time not only at home and at the office but also at hotels and stores. Perhaps you can recall standing at a counter or waiting in line, only to hear the phone ring and watch the clerk stop instantly what he or she was doing to answer it. You and the other people in line were already there, having established a reasonable order of priority, and yet anyone who used the telephone was allowed to break into the line. Instead of answering the phone, the clerk should have picked it up, walked to the end of the line, set the phone down in its proper place, and just let it ring until the phone had worked its way to the head of the line.

The fact that a ringing telephone is given priority shows how illogical people have become about the use of the phone. Fortunately, there are ways to reestablish your priorities, break your telephone addiction, and regain control of your time.

Success Strategy No. 66:

Break the telephone interruption habit by ignoring the phone for an entire day.

To check the current level of control the telephone has over your mind and your life, do the following exercise. On a Saturday or other day off, note what happens whenever the phone rings. There is no written or unwritten rule that says you are required to answer it. But if you are addicted to the telephone, you will find your muscles automatically tensing the moment you hear the first ring. You will even notice that your body weight automatically shifts toward the sound. If the phone is in control of your life, you will find yourself having thoughts such as, What if this is an emergency? Is this call important? Does this phone call mean money to me? I wonder who it is. If these are your reactions and you then race to answer the phone, you're caught in the trap.

When I have people over to my Orlando home for either business or pleasure, it is interesting to watch their reactions if they hear a telephone ringing softly in another room. Now, mind you, this is my home and telephone, not theirs, yet people are so addicted to the phone that their minds have lost track of the difference.

One day I was meeting with four people in the great room when the phone rang a ways off in the kitchen. No phones are allowed to ring in the living area of the house, and the phone in the kitchen is for the staff. At the first ring the person talking to me stopped in the middle of a sentence, as if he expected me to interrupt by excusing myself to answer the phone. I didn't blink an eye since I broke my addiction to answering the telephone fifteen years ago.

The longer the phone rang, the more my guests began to

squirm. I could tell their minds were on the telephone and not on the business at hand. Their focus had been broken by someone who could not possibly be calling them. I could see a sigh of relief come over the entire group when the ringing finally stopped. I hadn't moved or even acknowledged that the phone was ringing, but it had completely taken over the thought processes of four people who were not in any way connected with it.

To break your telephone addiction, on a Saturday or the next day you plan to be home, make yourself a promise that from the moment you get up until the time you go to bed you will not pick up or answer the phone, no matter what. Let someone else do it, or let an answering device record the calls. Rest assured that nothing will happen other than that you'll probably have a more peaceful day than you have had in a long time.

An unanswered phone, at least until you break the addiction, may cause some stress, but the greater stress is caused by allowing your life to be controlled by a ringing telephone day after day. From now on, view every telephone call as a forced interruption and create a system that puts all calls and responses on your agenda, not someone else's.

Success Strategy No. 67:

Become the caller instead of the callee.

When there are people you must talk to, make it a practice to call them rather than risk being interrupted when they call you. It is your personal mission not to allow anyone to take control of your time. Most telephone calls waste time by stretching what could have been communicated in two minutes by a fax or a written memo into a ten-to-fifteen-minute conversation. Taking control of your telephone time does not mean that you stop talking to people; it simply means that you make as many phone calls as possible fit your schedule, eliminating the time-consuming, random interruptions that occur when you are forced to operate on other people's schedules.

Success Strategy No. 68:

Let an answering device screen and record your incoming calls.

One effectiveness-doubling tool is to get out of the real-time telephone loop altogether. The advent of telephone-answering devices has made that possible. No home or office should be without one. Think of the answering device as an interruption buster.

If you use an answering machine to handle your calls at home, you will want to pay close attention to your outgoing message. "No one is here now to take your call," the most commonly used home answering-machine message, may not be truthful and should not be used. Or if it is true, it could alert would-be burglars of the appropriate time to pay a visit.

If you begin your recorded outgoing message with the words "No one is *available* right now to take your call," your message becomes appropriate whether or not you are at home. Then follow up with these instructions: "At the sound of the tone, you may leave your name, telephone number, and the purpose of your call, and if necessary, someone will call you back." The use of the word "may" tells the caller that it is not necessary to identify himself or herself or leave a message, which will result in fewer unnecessary calls to deal with. Don't include the phrase "Someone will call you back." That implies commitment or agreement on your part to return every call. The words "if necessary" do not imply such an agreement. Who decides if returning a specific call is necessary? You do—not the caller.

You'll begin to notice that once callers learn you do not pick up the telephone at home every time it rings, your incoming calls will become less frequent, and the demands for your immediate response less urgent. Incoming calls to your office are, of course, a different matter. There, your availability to take calls and respond immediately may be an important part of your job. Even so, most offices now have some system to intercept and record incoming calls—receptionists or secretaries, an answering machine or voice mail. Here are additional phone-answering strategies you can use to minimize interruptions and maximize your effectiveness.

Success Strategy No. 69:

Check your incoming messages no more than twice a day.

You can waste valuable time by checking your home or office incoming phone messages continuously. Let them accumulate until you are ready to handle them. Twice a day is certainly sufficient at home and, when practical, at the office as well. Pick specific times each day to handle your messages. Instead of spending hours every day answering all calls just to determine the important ones, simply make a complete, chronological list of all your messages and circle those to which you will personally respond. Get over the feeling that if someone, anyone, took the time to call you, you are somehow obligated to return the call. Stop letting others control your time without your preapproval.

Success Strategy No. 70:
Make all callbacks at the same time.

One of the secrets to the effective use of your time and your telephone is to return all necessary calls at the same time. Set aside a period of ten to thirty minutes after you check your incoming messages and place *all* your outgoing calls at that time. Keep phone usage to just a couple of specific periods during the day instead of scattered throughout the day, and you will immediately become aware of the extra time and mental energy that you free up.

Success Strategy No. 71:
Use the built-in speaker on your answering machine to monitor for "must take" calls.

Once you break the telephone addiction, you will find that it may be necessary to answer the phone directly in only a few instances. For example, if the plumber is going to call you back to schedule a time to fix the leak in the pipe that is currently flooding your bathroom, you will more than likely want to take that call directly.

Almost all answering devices now have built-in speakers that allow you to monitor calls as they come in, coupled with a volume control that allows you to hear calls even from another room. You can listen and screen the calls as they come in and pick up on the one "absolutely necessary" call you are waiting for. If, however, you are still a telephone addict, you may find yourself rushing to monitor every call even when you are not expecting a "must answer" call. Don't let it happen. Turn on the speaker monitor only when you are expecting a "must answer" call. Keep the monitor off at all other times. Decide beforehand which call or calls you intend to answer directly and respond to no others.

I have not answered a telephone directly in fifteen years unless I was monitoring for an important call. Important calls in my life are limited to those from my sons and my wife. Yet there is no opportunity I have missed in that time—no so-called emergencies to handle. In fact, the hundreds of hours of time I saved have enabled me to create opportunities for myself in a stress-free and interruption-free environment.

I stopped setting such a high priority on answering calls when I finally figured out that checks don't come through the phone. At that point, answering the phone directly became far less important, and I learned to use the telephone as a tool of accomplishment instead of an instrument of forced interruptions. Remember, if you choose to continue to do things the way you have always done them, you will continue to settle for the life you already have.

Success Strategy No. 72:

Keep unwanted guests out of your bedroom.

Not only do most people allow the telephone to interrupt them both at the office and at home, even during dinner or their favorite television program, but probably 80 percent of American homes actually have telephones that ring in the bedroom. Talk about the ultimate interruption. Are you really willing to let people into your private sanctuary uninvited just because they know your seven-digit phone number? Sounds ridiculous, doesn't it? Allowing someone, anyone, to interrupt you day or night, even when you are in your bedroom?

Save at least a couple of rooms in your home where you can enjoy peace of mind without the interruption of a ringing telephone. I would imagine that your bedroom certainly should be one of them. Remember your logic when you first put a phone in the bedroom? Well, you thought, now that I have extra money, I'll buy some convenience. I'll put a phone in the bedroom so I won't have to get out of bed and walk into the next room or down the stairs to answer it. If you use my phone strategies, you're not going to answer the phone directly regardless of what room it's in. So it's not necessary that the phone ring in your bedroom. If you choose to keep a phone in your bedroom for the convenience of making outgoing calls, simply turn the ringer off. Other phones will ring but not the one in your bedroom. Better still, turn all the ringers in your house off and let your answering device do the work.

Adena and I do have telephones in our bedrooms—two lines and two phones, one for each of us. We can call out, but no one can call into the bedroom. With the exception of my sons and, of course, my wife when she is out, no one is allowed to call me at home at all on any phone at any time. That may seem strange to you at this point, but that is how important it is to me to protect my time from interruptions.

At first, people who call you may not be excited about your new phone procedures, but they'll soon get used to them. Remember, your objective in life is not just to please other people but to maximize your personal effectiveness.

Success Strategy No. 73:
Unlist your phone numbers.

Another strategy for eliminating unnecessary telephone interruptions is to have your personal phone number removed from the phone book and any other public records. Your name printed in the phone book is not a status symbol; it is only a method to ensure that random salespeople and crank callers have easy access to you. Think about it. If people you want to talk to are going to call, they already know your number. You've given it to them.

All of our personal home phone numbers are unlisted, and anyone who wants to reach me must first contact my personal assistant at the Givens Organization. She puts the calls on a list on my itinerary for the following day, and then I determine which, if any, I will return.

Success Strategy No. 74:

Install separate personal and business lines at home.

If you operate a small business from your home or use your home phone for matters related to your job, install both a personal line and a business line at home. Don't subject yourself to being available for business calls at all hours. You won't increase your effectiveness or your wealth, only your stress level. Dead-end the business phone at an answering machine after working hours. Both can be tax deductible. To think you're going to come up with some big business deal or revelation after 6 P.M. is usually nonsense. If somebody has an important deal for you, he or she will call tomorrow or can leave a message on your business answering machine. In the meantime, you have the opportunity to spend more quality time with those you choose. Now only personal calls will come through your personal phone line. The cost of an extra phone line is cheap compared to the value of the peace of mind it can bring.

Success Strategy No. 75:

Don't give your business number to personal acquaintances, and don't give your personal number to business contacts.

Once you've separated your phone lines, keep them that way by paying particular attention to which phone number you give out for which purpose. Put only your business number on your business card. Don't print your personal number on your card, as many small-business owners or salespeople do. A separate business number makes it possible for you to talk about work only when you choose to. You still won't miss any important calls. If you don't pick up, your answering machine will.

By the way, when implementing this strategy, you may flub a few times and give your personal number to business callers. If you do, in a year or so it may become necessary to change to another unlisted personal number just to wipe the slate clean. I've done it more than once over the past fifteen years.

Back in the seventies I accumulated about forty rental properties and did much of the management myself. That meant I had forty families who wanted to call me night and day, including weekends, to tell me what was wrong and what I had to fix instantly. Here is how I eliminated those interruptions: I installed a separate line into my home just for my real estate renters in addition to my personal phone line. When they signed a lease, I never gave my tenants my home address or telephone numbers. They received only the number of my special real estate phone line, which dead-ended into an answering machine in my office at home.

I told each of my tenants, "Look, if you ever have a problem, call me right away. In fact, call any time. You'll get my answering machine, but I check that answering machine faithfully once a week." Almost without exception my new tenants would say, "What do you mean? How can you do that? What if a diaper gets stuck in the toilet?" My answer was always the same: "Pull it out. I'm not coming over to put my hands in your toilet. My kids are grown, and I no longer do diapers." "Well," would often come the reply, "what if the place catches fire?" "Don't call me! Call the fire department," I said. "I'd rather not know what happened until I get the insurance check."

My tenants didn't call me directly because they couldn't.

I never once lost a prospective or even a current tenant because of my phone policy. They learned quickly to handle minor problems, and my peace of mind was preserved while my potential stress level was significantly reduced. That policy continued until I was able to afford to hire managers to handle all of my growing numbers of properties, and then they had to deal with the tenants. My time was by then worth more than a real estate manager's time.

Whether you own rental property or not, you get the idea. In order to keep your activities and time under your control, devise a simple telephone procedure that automatically produces the results you desire for the activities in which you are involved.

Success Strategy No. 76:

Stop playing switchboard for other family members.

With only one personal phone line into your home used by everyone, how do you predetermine who a phone call is for? You can't. And more often than not, the person who picks up the phone is not the person being called. The answerer has to ask who the caller is and who the call is for. If the callee is there, he or she must then be found and summoned to the phone. If the callee is not there, a message usually must be taken. When this happens to you in your home, you're wasting time playing switchboard for others.

The best way to eliminate this situation is to install a separate line for you, your spouse, and each of your children who are old enough to receive calls. Extra phone lines are cheap compared to the convenience and the time you will save.

Success Strategy No. 77:

Don't allow the thought of emergencies to compel you to answer the phone at all times.

One of the excuses I sometimes hear about hanging on to telephone addiction is "Well, what if it's an emergency and I miss it?" It seems that at some point in our lives we have all come to believe that answering the telephone is absolutely necessary because the call might be some sort of emergency that cannot wait and one we would be able to do something about. That may be true if you are 911, the police department, fire department, a doctor, or a hospital—the organizations and people in communities that do handle actual emergencies—but it doesn't ordinarily happen in the telephone lives of individuals or families.

Take a pen now and write down all the emergencies during your lifetime that originated as a phone call to your home and about which you were personally able to do something meaningful. No, I don't mean your son or daughter calling from college to inform you that he or she was short of money. I mean real life-threatening or health-threatening emergencies. How many can you list? The answer is normally none or at least less than two.

Even when such emergencies do arise, there are always alternatives for the caller. Answering the phone every time it rings on the off-chance of some real emergency that you will be able to positively affect is a year-after-year waste of time. A well-intentioned attempt to handle remote possibilities won't make you more effective, but implementing good solid time- and sanity-preserving telephone strategies will.

Success Strategy No. 78:

Install phones in your cars and use them for "callbacks."

There are telephones in all Givens family cars. My sons also have car phones. They are extremely cheap compared to the benefits you can derive. I paid $4,500 for the first car phone I bought eighteen years ago. The last cellular phone I installed had ten times the options of that first one and yet cost only $400.

Your time is a valuable part of your life. Not one lost minute can be replaced, and every minute has a measurable value. But if your mission is to get away from the interruptions of telephones, why, you might ask, would I suggest that you have telephones in your cars? Driving time is downtime, a time when little is accomplished except dodging traffic. It's not a great time to watch a television show, read, have a meeting, or relax. Driving time is the ideal time to make callbacks, whether personal or business. You can free up a half-hour or more per day, or 150 hours per year, by using the time in your car to make many or all of the calls you would normally make from your home or at work.

If you don't have a car phone, get one. No excuses. Even if right now you think it is a luxury and an extravagance, you will quickly find that it is an investment, not an expense. And, of course, your car phone is tax deductible when used for business.

Success Strategy No. 79:

Install a personal fax machine in your home.

A personal fax machine is another great effectiveness producer and interruption buster. You will find, as Adena and I did, that a personal fax machine is one of the best electronic time-savers.

A fax machine:

- Allows you to communicate instantly with other people who have fax machines without the necessity of tracking them down by phone
- Produces a written record of what you want to communicate
- Requires one and only one call, whether or not recipients are there since their fax machines are always there, ready and waiting
- Will call back until it gets an answer even if the line is busy, without the necessity of your remembering to do so
- Speeds up getting a response since both individuals and companies place a high priority on incoming faxes

Your personal fax machine can be used to:

- Send outgoing personal and business messages twenty-four hours a day
- Order items from catalogues without the necessity of wasting time on the phone
- Receive messages from those who want to contact you quickly without the necessity of your being interrupted

- Request and immediately get copies of bills, quotes, or other paperwork from banks, utility companies, department stores, or others with whom you do business

You can buy a thermal-paper fax machine for your home for as little as $400 and a plain-paper machine for about $1,000. Watch for the discount sales. You will want to get a fax with a telephone/fax switcher or buy one separately for about $80. The switcher determines from signals on the phone line which calls should go to your fax and which to your answering machine.

Once you install and use a fax machine in your home, you will wonder how you ever got along without it. In my experience, your home fax will become as important as your home telephone. Adena has purchased fax machines for all of her family members as Christmas presents, and they now communicate by fax with no interruptions and no delays. A fax works on your schedule, twenty-four hours a day.

Although years ago I began establishing a method of separating phone lines to create greater effectiveness, the process has grown into a phone system. You more than likely won't need a system as elaborate as we have, but I thought I would describe it to show how you can make the telephone work *for* you instead of *against* you.

The Givens' Orlando Home Phone System

Phone Lines	User or Location	Use
1.	Charles J. Givens	Personal, outgoing only
2.	Adena Givens	Personal, incoming and outgoing
3.	Security system	Auto-direct dialing if security is breached
4.	Estate manager	Incoming and outgoing

5.	Guest house	Incoming and outgoing for our guests
6.	Pager	800 number for paging estate manager
7.	Staff telephone	Personal for staff members who live on premises
8.	Fax machine	For CJG's home office
9.	Fax machine	For Adena's home office
10.	Fax machine	For office of Adena's assistant
11.	Computer modem	For direct computer link from home to computer services
12.	CJG's portable cellular phone	Outgoing only
13.	Staff portable cellular phone	Incoming and outgoing
14–17.	Car phones	Outgoing only

Yes, we have seventeen phone lines in our Orlando home. Communications worldwide are essential to us, but interruptions are not. Even with all these specialized phone lines, we follow the strategies that I have just outlined to you. If we didn't, our lives would be a turmoil of interruptions.

Nowhere on my Goals List or yours does it say, "Spend more time on the telephone." You have options when deciding how to run both your business and your personal life. Choosing carefully how you use your electronic communications time determines how much time you have left to live the rest of your life.

How important is it to take back control of your time and life from the telephone? Ask yourself how important it is to live out your goals and dreams. In your life there is nothing else with greater priority, and if your use of the telephone is impeding or interrupting your progress, rather than contributing to it, then it is time for a change.

CHAPTER 16

Intercepting Office Interruptions

If you don't run your own life, somebody else will.
—JOHN ATKINSON

You can apply the same interruption-elimination strategies to your business life, particularly if you work in an office environment.

At the Givens Organization, as in any business large or small, interruptions could easily become a way of life instead of the exception—but only if we let them. Here are some interruption-intercepting strategies that we have created and implemented in our offices that you can also apply in your work environment.

Success Strategy No. 80:

Install voice mail on your business telephone system.

Voice mail is the latest development in telephone-answering machines. When you leave your desk, you simply push a button on your telephone and all incoming calls are recorded and immediately routed to your voice mailbox. Should you leave your office and forget to switch on voice mail, incoming calls are automatically routed to your voice mailbox after a specific number of rings. That means when you need long, uninterrupted periods of time in which to get things done, you don't have to depend on a receptionist, secretary, or assistant to hold, monitor, or take messages from incoming callers. You can then review your messages at a time convenient to you, choose those to which you will respond, and make all callbacks at the same time.

There are only two types of calls in a business environment that require an instant response. The first is a call from your boss, and the second is a call from a customer who is placing an order, but all your calls should be intercepted and screened first to determine which calls can wait and which cannot. If you are fortunate enough to have an assistant or secretary, that person can be used to intercept your calls so that you are not interrupted.

At the Givens Organization we encourage everybody, including supervisors, department managers, directors, and division vice presidents, not to answer the phone directly because of the wasted time involved. Plus, almost every one of our more than four hundred employees who use the telephone as part of their business has voice mail. The number of work hours saved each year is in the tens of thousands.

Success Strategy No. 81: Install fax machines in each department.

One major work interruption we found in our organization, and one that exists in all others, is the time employees spend away from their desks. When we looked at the situation a few years ago, we found that people in most jobs were getting up from their desks and walking to another department to ask questions or deliver memos and papers. The accumulated time wasted was incredible. In addition, every time people traveled from one department to another, they interrupted the people in the other department, and at times there were even lines of people just waiting to interrupt.

Productive time for most people is when they are at their desks. In our executive meeting we asked what is now fondly referred to as the "fannies in seats" question: How can we design a system so that people can communicate effectively with people in other departments without getting up from their desks and without interrupting the people they intend to communicate with?

The answer was the fax machine. A fax machine costs as little as one-fourth the salary of one person for an entire month. With a fax machine in every department in each of our five office buildings in Orlando, communication became easy and effective. If a person needed an answer from someone in another department, he no longer had to get out of his seat and go to the other department. He had only to move as far as the fax machine in his own department. All numbers were preprogrammed on the fax so a simple one-button touch made the call and sent the fax.

The other major advantage of the fax is that you have hard copy—a written record of an exchange between people and departments. We implemented a policy that interdepartmental faxes were to be handwritten to save time, except for those who had PCs and printers on their desks and could type faster than they could write. The answers to any questions, also according to company policy, were to be handwritten on the original fax. Therefore, there is now a paper trail and proof of both how the question was asked and how it was answered.

Another time-saving tool also used at the Givens Organization for those with PCs on their desks is E-mail, a software program that allows one terminal to send messages directly to another terminal. At the Givens Organization we have more than three hundred terminals, all connected through a network and file server. We are able to make very effective use of E-mail as a noninterrupting communications tool, again without the necessity of people leaving their desks or interrupting others.

Letter writing is another activity that can eat up time, or that gets put off to the last minute by those who don't relish the task. I learned to become an effective letter writer out of sheer self-preservation. My first white-collar job, when I was only nineteen, was working at Mueller Company as its sales service correspondent. Literally translated, that meant I was the complaint department. My secretary, Minnie Oliver, and I handled all the customers for this large manufacturer of water and gas pipe fittings. My job was to stay in touch with customers about the status of their orders, all of which were needed "yesterday," and to handle all orders shipped incorrectly.

During the two years I worked at Mueller, I wrote more than seventy-five hundred letters; copies of them were eventually measured in feet. That experience in my first low-level corporate job has served me well; the thousands of letters I have written since then concerning my dozens of companies became a breeze. In the process I've discovered several simple strategies that can improve letter-writing effectiveness.

Success Strategy No. 82:

Write all letters and memos at the same time during your Peak Performance Period.

For most managers, letter writing is a must-do drudgery. It doesn't have to be if you follow just this one procedure for maximizing your letter- and memo-writing skills.

The ability to write meaningful, effective, powerful letters and memos requires a special mind-set. Once you put yourself in that mind-set, it is far more effective to remain there than to switch gears back and forth from letter and memo writing to other business activities. Go through your In box and put in a separate stack all the letters that must be answered and all the memos to which you must respond. Then set aside fifteen to thirty minutes each day during your Peak Performance Period (see Chapter 19) for creating your outgoing correspondence. Write your correspondence at the same time every day, and you can focus your attention and skills on the task at hand and achieve twice as much in half the time. You won't avoid the task by filling your time with lesser priority line-of-least-resistance activities. Don't permit interruptions during this creative period. Intercept all incoming calls with an answering machine or voice mail.

Success Strategy No. 83:

Install select code security locks on departmental doors.

Even after we installed fax machines, E-mail, and new corporate policies, we found there were still dozens of people at the Givens Organization who couldn't shake the habit of getting up from their desks to walk into another department to deliver mail, pass the time of day, or interrupt others in their work environment. Three years ago we decided to make that practice impractical and almost impossible. We installed electronic locks connected to the computer network on each department door; they can be opened only with a credit-sized card "swiped" through the lock. All employees were issued their own identification numbers, and within the magnetic strip on each card was information about which door that particular card would open.

Top executives, of course, have cards that open any locks. Almost all other employees have automatic access only to their own departments. The days of getting up and just walking in to waste time talking to someone in another department were over. Unless an employee needs to enter another department as part of his particular job, his access was restricted. The cost of the system was easily recovered in just a couple of months by increased productivity.

Of course, the security value of this card system is also an advantage, but here we are talking about the "interruption-busting" benefits of such a system. We did have to go one step further, however. When people wanted access to another department with a restricted lock, what do you think they did? They knocked. So as the final step in implementing the system, we were forced to put a sign on each door that said, DO NOT KNOCK!

Employees soon recognized that this system not only helped them become more efficient but also ensured that they would be able to leave promptly and have more personal time for their own activities. We also provide many special activities where they can enjoy the company of their coworkers.

Success Strategy No. 84:

Keep customer service people in their seats by employing special investigators to provide research support.

Because the Givens Organization has a membership of 650,000, customer service is a major part of our business. Each day, just in our Orlando offices, there are more than a hundred people whose sole job it is to interact and communicate with our customers using the telephone. Upon investigation we found that these people were constantly out of their seats to research answers to questions; the information needed could be provided only by paperwork that was stored either in some other department or in central files. When we estimated that 30 to 40 percent of a customer service rep's time might be spent away from the desk, we went back to the same question: How do we keep these people in their seats where they can be the most productive and effective?

Our solution was to assign to each customer service department what we call investigators, about one investigator for every six or seven people who answer the phones. When a telephone rep has a question that requires research into documentation, the request is written up and simply passed on to the investigators who sit in the same telephone room. The investigators do all the research and travel to central files or other departments. The number of calls fielded by each customer service rep went from an average of 80 to over 160 per day. The system had doubled their personal effectiveness. They now concentrate on what they do best: handling people on the telephone.

There seems to be no end to technology. The next obvious question became: How do you research actual copies of documents that are stored in files somewhere else without having people get up from their desks? The first low-tech answer was to have the investigators call once per hour to central files and have a person there pull the files and bring them to the investigator. But a couple of years ago a high-tech answer became available: optical scanning. Each of the permanent files of our members contains an average of ten pieces of paper. That means we have six million documents to which our customer service reps need instant access. Simply entering the data from most of these documents into a computer was not enough. First of all, it would have taken a huge department just to key in the data; and second, handwritten notes, signatures, and other data cannot be keyed in.

Now all documents at the Givens Organization are optically scanned onto disk in a WORM drive, which is a high-density storage unit. In any department that interacts with our members, the actual image of these documents can instantly be pulled up on the computer screen even if the documents were not scanned at the same time. Any authorized person can pull up a member's entire file, document by document, on his terminal. It used to require a huge room with rows and rows of floor-to-ceiling files to store all these documents. That's no longer the case.

Success Strategy No. 85:

If you work in an office, create a controlled open-door policy.

If you have an unlimited open-door policy at your office, it is an open invitation to interruptions. A controlled open-door policy means that people have access to you, but *by appointment only.* No one should be able just to walk into your office for whatever reason, even for something he might think is a crisis or emergency. At the Givens Organization we don't have emergencies. They are not defined or explained in the corporate policy manual. In fact, the manual specifically states that we do not have emergencies, and no one is allowed to treat any situation as an emergency. Therefore, there are no reasons for interruptions. The sun will still come up in the morning, the telephones will still be ringing, and life will go on.

Even though I run many businesses, there is only one person in my entire organization who is allowed to call me directly—my trusted and highly efficient personal assistant, Nita Rawlson. Nobody else, not even the top executives of any of my companies or divisions, can call me directly. And Nita calls me only twice each day. If something important happens after she calls, "it will keep until tomorrow" is the philosophy. My office at home is equipped with a laser-printer fax machine so that Nita can send faxes to me, but she limits herself to about fifteen pages a day. She chooses carefully what she faxes because those faxes include any that are sent by the executives of my other companies. Anybody who has a question that needs an answer has to go through Nita, and the questions must be stated in writing. Nita then distributes them to the appropriate places to get answers, preferably not to me.

Success Strategy No. 86:

To be successful in your own business, hire the best people.

If you own your own business, or ever want to, the most important strategy is to choose the best people available. It doesn't matter what they cost. The best people will make you successful. They will also cut down greatly on the number of times you are interrupted or the number of interruptions you must avoid because they will know how to handle the problem themselves without demanding your time. That is why my business life is devoid of stress and why my personal life is not consumed by business worries.

At this point, systems like the ones I use may seem light-years away for you, but if you have formed a clear picture of your goals and dreams and implement my Super Strategies to achieve them, someday you will live in your own personally designed business and personal worlds. But in the meantime, the sooner you stop the interruptions at home and in the office, the sooner you'll be living life your way.

CHAPTER **17**

Handling Talkers and Dumpers

Nature has given us two ears but only one mouth.
—Benjamin Disraeli

Talkers are those people in your life who measure the value of a conversation by the number of words used. They never seem to run out of inconsequential things to say. Talkers don't listen, they only talk. And they continue to talk, babbling through hours of your valuable time, rendering you totally ineffective during those extended periods of regurgitated verbiage.

Dumpers, on the other hand, are people who use your mind for a trash heap. Life never works for them. Dumpers live from problem to problem, and they love to tell you, time and time again, about how their lives are falling apart and who has "done it to them." Almost all people who consider themselves caring individuals have at least one and often many dumpers in their lives. They attract "dumpers" like flowers attract bees.

Dumpers are drainers.

Dumpers and talkers are usually friends, acquaintances, neighbors, coworkers, or family. They are among the people who are closest to you. You don't want to be rude or impolite, yet talkers and dumpers waste your valuable time and negatively affect your emotions and energy level. Often when confronted by a talker or a dumper, you are involved in something that's important to you. In the process, the talker or dumper diverts your focus and distracts your thoughts. To maintain effectiveness requires that you stop subjecting yourself to unplanned interruptions by a talker or a dumper—or anyone else for that matter.

Here are some strategies to use for lovingly and effectively taking back control of your time.

Success Strategy No. 87:

Screen talkers and dumpers with your telephone-answering machine.

The most common place you encounter talkers and dumpers is on the telephone. If you choose to spend time talking to one or more of them, do it on your schedule, not theirs. The best buffer when you are at home is your answering machine. By allowing the talkers and dumpers in your life to connect only with your answering device and not you directly, you have reduced to zero the level of unplanned negative impact they will have on your life and your time. You then have the power to choose when and if you will call them back. Someone who is in the habit of calling you daily can be corralled into just one conversation with you every few days or whenever you decide to return the call. Your mind and time now have a buffer zone—your answering machine. Over the course of a year, hundreds of hours of chitchat and much energy-draining negativity can be eliminated from your life by following this procedure.

If the talkers and dumpers are part of your work environment, get into the habit of simply but firmly stating that you have work you must get done and just don't have time right at that moment to talk to them. Talkers and dumpers are in the unconscious habit of looking for the line of least resistance, talking to those who will listen as if listening is an admission of the desire to communicate and to sympathize. You must therefore make it politely clear that you do not have time or sympathy to spare.

Success Strategy No. 88:

Immediately set a limit for the time you will spend with a talker.

Let's say that your mom is the talker in your life. How do you handle her lovingly but effectively without compromising control of your time and your life? When your mom calls, you say, "Hi, Mom. I only have two minutes to talk to you right now, but I'm really glad you called." This way your mom feels good because you told her you were glad to hear from her. But at the same time you have limited the conversation to two minutes.

Keep a stopwatch by the phone if necessary—a real one, not a mental one. Click the stopwatch on when you say two minutes, or the conversation can easily turn into an hour. After two minutes politely interrupt with "Mom, thanks for calling. Gotta run. Talk to you soon. Love you. Bye." Then hang up! Never give the talker time to say good-bye or to make another point. If you do, you will have to go through the "good-bye" process again and again until you're pacing the floor and another wasted twenty minutes have elapsed.

I've taught this strategy to thousands of people over the past fifteen years, and I've never had anyone tell me it didn't work. It's that powerful, that simple, and that important. If you have talkers in your life, you may want to talk with them, but if you let them control the conversation, you will lose countless nonrecoverable hours of your valuable time.

Don't get caught in someone else's problems, or they become your problems.

Once there was a man driving across an old bridge that spanned a rushing, rocky river seventy-five feet below. Halfway across the bridge he saw another fellow standing on the railing getting ready to jump, obviously in an effort to end it all. The man in the car slammed on the brakes, leaped out, and yelled with panic, "Young man, young man, wait, wait! Don't jump. Talk to me first." So they sat down to talk, and ten minutes later they both jumped.

Picture this scenario: You've been on the phone for thirty minutes listening to a dumper. At the end of the conversation the dumper says, "I feel so much better now that I've talked to you." Meanwhile, you're falling off the chair from mental, emotional, and physical exhaustion. You've been sucked in. When you become a dumpee, the dumper takes control of your mind. This intense negativity about someone else's problems is like a cancer of the brain, sapping your energy, clouding your perspective, and rending you ineffective. Intense negativity can also make you part of the problem. You wouldn't allow anyone to throw trash on your lawn, so why let anyone throw trash on your mind? Listen to a dumper long enough, and you start thinking negatively too.

But what about being a loving, caring person? Isn't it your obligation to listen to and sympathize with the plight of a dumper? Not at all—at least not in the way you usually do. Here is a three-step strategy for dealing effectively with dumpers that will allow you to remain caring while maintaining your sanity in the process.

Success Strategy No. 89:

Listen, listen to the whole story, listen only once.

- Listen to the dumper's story. Listening is always done with the lips closed and is not conversational.
- Listen to the dumper's whole story. Allow the dumper to finish completely without interjecting your feelings, opinions, or solutions. You simply acknowledge that you are still listening with an occasional "I understand. . . . Yes, I see. . . ."
- Listen to the dumper's whole story only once. When you have heard the story all the way through, your obligation to listen has come to an end. Now it is your responsibility to become part of the solution or at least to avoid becoming part of the problem.

When talking to a dumper, don't get sucked in emotionally. When someone is criticizing or complaining about a spouse, mate, parent, or coworker, don't throw fuel on the fire by agreeing. If you do, you're adding to the problem, not assisting in the solution. Don't make value judgments about the dumper's situation with statements such as "God, that's awful" or "Oh, you poor thing." That, too, adds fuel to the fire. Instead of jumping in with sympathy or suggestions, use this strategy.

Success Strategy No. 90:
Ask the dumper, "What can I do to help?"

Use these six words when the dumper has finished his story and then shut up. You will be surprised to find that most of the time the answer you hear is "Nothing." Often a dumper just wants a listener and is not looking for advice. If that is the case, your solutions are not going to be listened to or received positively, so don't give them. Change the subject or end the conversation. Otherwise, you will be forced to listen to the story all over again.

Only occasionally will a dumper ask, "Well, what do you think I should do?" Then and only then should you offer your suggestions and solutions in a positive, nonjudgmental way. As soon as you hear the first "Yes, but," the conversation is ended. When a dumper replies with the words "Yes, but" or "You don't understand," anything you say past that point is falling on deaf ears. Even when your suggestions are good ones, it makes no difference because the dumper isn't listening. Dumpers often demand nonexistent alternatives instead of workable solutions.

The real test of your own self-discipline comes when the dumper calls or drops by again, eager to give you the latest update or to trudge through the same story once more. However, your responsibility to listen is finished. When a dumper begins to tell you the same story twice, you interrupt with "Excuse me, Jack. I think I really understood what you were going through when you told me the last time. Is there anything I can do to help?" If the answer is "Well, I just want you to listen to me again," you respond, "I care about you, but it won't help either of us to go through the story again. I got it the first time. Is there anything I can do to help?" Always return to these words until the conversation is over or the subject changes.

No matter what the response of the dumper, hold your ground. It is your mind, and only you can protect it. Even when the dumper attempts to push your guilt buttons or calls you unfeeling and uncaring, remain unemotional. Do nothing more than offer your help, and give your advice only if it is wanted. It is not the caring response to listen to the same negative story over and over until you are emotionally drained. You will lose every time.

Talkers and dumpers will more than likely remain a part of your life even though you now know how to handle them. What will change is the amount of time you spend listening to them.

CHAPTER **18**

Cutting the Commute

He worked like hell in the country so he could live in the city, where he worked like hell so he could live in the country.

—DON MARQUIS

Effectiveness by definition requires managing the use of your time—including the time you spend each day getting to and from work. Whether you work for yourself or for someone else, you are not immune to commuting time. The only exception is if your main place of business is in your home. Only then is your commuting time cut to the walking distance between two rooms.

The total number of hours you spend related to your job or career is not limited to the hours you actually work. It also includes the time it takes you to get yourself ready and, usually the big one, the time required to get to your job and back each day. Of these three work-related time elements, the one over which you have the most control, should you choose to exercise it, is your commuting time. To control commuting time you have two options: employing strategies to cut your total commuting time each day, and employing strategies to more effectively use the time you do spend commuting.

Success Strategy No. 91:

Cut your one-way commuting time to twenty minutes or less.

Decatur, Illinois, the small town where I grew up, had a population of only sixty-five thousand, and the possibility of a long commute didn't exist as long as you worked in town. The distance from one side of town to the other was short enough so that when I was in junior high I could ride my bicycle after school to a job at my father's small contracting company on the opposite side of town in only twenty-five minutes. But when I left Decatur in 1963 at age twenty-two to try my fortune in the music business in Nashville, I found myself in a large metropolitan area that required serious commuting time if you worked outside your own neighborhood.

Because I arrived in Nashville with only $400 from an income tax return and everything I owned in a four-by-six trailer, I had to find a job that would produce income while I was getting started in the music business. After trying my hand at insurance company underwriting and then selling advertising for a couple of privately owned newspapers, I got a job in the computer operations department of Genesco. The computer, which was a relatively new concept in the sixties, was my second interest, but nothing to compare with my goal of achieving success in the music business. What I ended up with were two full-time jobs which, without commuting time, took up seventeen hours a day, five days a week. At

Genesco I ran a computer on the midnight shift from midnight to 8 A.M. My wife, Bonnie, had to be at work at Murry-Ohio Manufacturing Company no later than 8:30 A.M. Because we could afford only one car at the time, I had to take the kids to the baby-sitter, drive Bonnie to work, and then continue to my music business office on Record Row, where I wheeled and dealed until five in the evening. Then I picked up Bonnie and the kids, drove home, had supper, and grabbed a couple hours of sleep before I had to report for work at Genesco.

In all, my commuting ate up two hours every day, and it was during this time that I learned the value of controlling commuting time. Every hour I could cut out of my commuting time each week was one extra hour I could have for some much needed sleep. Working this schedule was not a temporary situation. It lasted for seven years, until we left Nashville in 1971.

The solution to the problem was uncomplicated—if I was willing to move. I searched the area around Genesco headquarters and found a two-bedroom rental home that was a ten-minute walk or a three-minute drive from work. That move saved me at least a half-hour of commuting time every day, five days a week, for a total of two and a half hours of extra sleep.

Many of my coworkers at Genesco commuted a half-hour to an hour every day, and I realized that because their commute drained both their time and their energy, it was impossible for them to accomplish what I did in a day even if they wanted to. At that time I decided the maximum commute I would ever allow myself was fifteen minutes when I worked for other people's companies, and eight minutes when I finally owned my own companies. As my companies grew over twenty years and I moved the headquarters from one location to another, within thirty days I always rented or bought a house within a few minutes' drive of the new offices.

I also have made it a point when owning my own companies to avoid having a downtown office. In general there is no such thing as a short commute to the downtown area of a major metropolitan city unless, of course, you choose to live in the downtown area. Today, the Givens Organization occupies a total of five company-owned office buildings in the Orlando, Florida, metropolitan area. All are on the north side of town within a mile or two of each other. My home is on Lake Brantley, just eight minutes from my office.

Long commuting times are just something I have chosen not to deal with in my life. When you reduce your commute, you will be amazed at how much time is freed up to do the things that are really meaningful to your dreams and goals. Often when I am teaching this strategy to an audience in a metropolitan area such as New York, San Francisco, or Boston, someone will invariably say, "I love my job and I love my home, but I despise the two and a half hours that I have to commute every day. What do I do?" The answer is always the same: You either find a desirable home in a desirable neighborhood near where you work or find a similar or better job near where you live. Until faster methods of transportation are available in and around major metropolitan areas, these are the only two real alternatives for freeing up your time and increasing your effectiveness.

There is no right or wrong about which decision you make. The only considerations are what you want to accomplish in your lifetime, how important it is to you, and, if you truly want more available hours in a day to pursue your dreams and goals, what changes you are willing to make to get them.

The amount of commuting time you spend each day is affected by only two major variables: where you work and where you live. Fortunately, both are under your control. They are simply choices you make, but all too often and to your possible detriment they are made independently. If you live and work in a small town such as the one I grew up in, an allowance of fifteen to twenty minutes for one-way commuting time creates no problem. You can probably get between any two points in your town within a reasonable time. But if you live in a larger metropolitan area, your choice of jobs and neighborhoods can easily create a critical time-waste issue. It is not unusual in larger cities for the average commuting time to total thirty minutes to an hour or more each way every day. That's two and a half to five hours spent every week just getting to and from work. What an unnecessary waste of time.

Your objective, plain and simple, is to live close enough to where you work that the one-way commute time is twenty minutes or less. In that way you can preserve your precious time for activities that are far more important to you than driving or riding the train.

Let's say you are currently over the twenty-minute one-way commute limit. Here's how you make your choices. If you value your job more than where you live, move closer to where you work. If you value your home more than your job, however, change jobs. Obviously either decision is a major one involving setting a goal and creating a well-thought-out plan to achieve that goal.

Is the time saved worth making such a major change? You bet it is. Check the Total Commuting Time chart below, and you will quickly see how many days, months, and potentially productive years can be wasted just traveling between the two most important locations in your life.

If you have a spouse who also works outside the home, you may have additional choices to make since a move for the benefit of one of you may negatively affect the commuting time of the other. But a compromise is usually possible, and it is the combination of such choices that will power you toward the level of success you both want to experience.

Planned Television Arts in New York has handled public relations for both me and the Givens Organization for the past ten years. Rick Frischmann, the president and owner, is a personal friend. For the past twenty-five years Rick has traveled one and a half hours on the train from Long Island to his

Total Commuting Time*

One-Way Commuting Time							
Period	**10 min.**	**20 min.**	**30 min.**	**45 min.**	**60 min.**	**90 min.**	**120 min.**
Day	20 min.	40 min.	1 hr.	1.5 hrs.	2 hrs.	3 hrs.	4 hrs.
Week	2 hrs.	3 hrs.	5 hrs.	8 hrs.	10 hrs.	15 hrs.	20 hrs.
Month	7 hrs.	15 hrs.	22 hrs.	33 hrs.	44 hrs.	66 hrs.	88 hrs.
Year	84 hrs. (4 days)	167 hrs. (6 days)	250 hrs. (10 days)	375 hrs. (16 days)	500 hrs. (21 days)	750 hrs. (31 days)	1,000 hrs. (42 days)
10 Years	835 hrs. (35 days)	1,670 hrs. (60 days)	2,500 hrs. (104 days)	3,750 hrs. (156 days)	5,000 hrs. (208 days)	7,500 hrs. (313 days)	10,000 hrs. (417 days)
25 Years	2,088 hrs. (87 days)	4,175 hrs. (174 days)	6,250 hrs. (260 days)	9,375 hrs. (391 days)	12,500 hrs. (521 days)	18,750 hrs. (781 days)	25,000 hrs. (1,042 days)
50 Years	4,175 hrs. (174 days)	8,350 hrs. (348 days)	12,500 hrs. (521 days)	18,750 hrs. (781 days)	25,000 hrs. (1,042 days)	37,500 hrs. (1,563 days)	50,000 hrs. (2,083 days)

*Based on 5 days per week, 50 weeks per year

office in Manhattan and then back again. Out of these twenty-five years of his life he has spent the equivalent of four years sitting on a train. His reasons for commuting: "I love Long Island. I have a beautiful house there. My family is better off on Long Island than in New York City. And I need a Manhattan address for my kind of business, for prestige."

"Great," I said. "But you could live in Phoenix or your condo in Florida and still have a Manhattan address. Your mail could be forwarded to you within twenty-four hours. You could very easily rent a desk in an office owned by someone else, and you could claim a Manhattan address. The point is that you don't have to go through the hassle of commuting to Manhattan every day because 100 percent of your business is done on the phone anyway. Since clients don't normally come to your office, why go through what you do to get there?"

There are alternatives for any commuting situation, depending on how greatly you value your time. I believe there are few, if any, advantages to spending years of your life on either a train or driving to and from work. Your next best alternative is to devise and implement strategies that will make your to-and-from-work travel time more productive.

Success Strategy No. 92:

Use commuting time to increase your knowledge by listening to audiotapes.

With an audiotape player installed in your dash or sitting conveniently beside you on the seat of your car, the possibilities for learning what can benefit you on the job or even personally are limitless. Even if you commute by train or bus, you can listen to audiotapes through earphones without disturbing your fellow passengers.

It has been said that if you listen to tapes on any one subject for only one hour a day, five days a week, for five years, you will end up with the equivalent of a Ph.D. in that subject. If you're like me, you may feel the need to know less than a Ph.D. about a lot of subjects, but the point is that your commuting time can be turned into productive time by using it to increase your knowledge.

When people become members of the Charles J. Givens Organization, the extensive *Financial Library* that comes with the membership is on both audio- and videotapes. It's the same information except that the audiotapes can be played in the car, on the beach, or on an airplane, while the videotapes are generally useful only at home. There are more than eight hours of tape, including three hundred strategies on subjects ranging from insurance to taxes, from investing to estate planning. By listening to the tapes several times over the course of just a few weeks, any person can be well on the way to becoming a financial expert, all during a time that would ordinarily be used for nothing more than complaining about traffic while listening to some music on the radio. And don't forget that if you use your audiotape player for business, tax preparation, investing, or financial planning, the cost of both the player and the tapes is tax deductible.

If you commute by bus or train, you can also use that time to read, do office work, plan your time using your Daily Activities List, or make notes for an upcoming presentation. The possibilities are endless, and the choice is yours. Commuting time is wasted only if you choose to waste it.

Success Strategy No. 93:

Use your commuting time to make necessary phone calls from your car.

By installing a telephone in your car, you can use your commuting time to free up an extra hour or more a day that you would otherwise spend talking on the phone at your office or home. Use your car phone to make necessary callbacks to those people whose calls you want to return, to set up appointments, or to substitute for a brief person to person meeting you might have planned to have when you do get to work.

Before you leave home or your job, be certain to have a list of the calls you intend to make from the car, complete with phone numbers so there is no wasted time or motion once you begin driving.

Success Strategy No. 94:

Keep a mini-cassette recorder in your glove compartment for capturing ideas and dictating letters.

There are two times when I seem to get sudden flashes of insight—ideas that will get lost in the daily shuffle if not immediately captured. Those two times are late at night and, even more frequently, when I am riding in my car. If you've noticed the same pattern in your life, then you will want to be sure to have some medium at hand for writing or recording your brilliant ideas. In your car the best medium is a pocket mini-cassette recorder, which you can buy for as little as $50. The expense is tax deductible, of course, if you use the recorder for business.

Using the recorder while commuting allows you not only to get those good ideas down on tape but also to dictate letters that might otherwise eat up valuable time at home or at the office. If you have your own small business apart from a job in someone else's company, commuting time can be a good time to plan and develop ideas and dictate them into the recorder.

Your overall strategy is clear: Cut your commute to the shortest time possible and then use that time effectively.

CHAPTER **19**

Extending Your Peak Performance Period

Man masters nature not by force but by understanding.
—Jacob Bronowski

Both you and I have a specific time of day when we are most effective. Everyone does. Let's call this time of day your Peak Performance Period. If you ever refer to yourself as a "morning" or a "night" person, you are already aware of your Peak Performance Period. It is that time of day when you have the greatest clarity of thinking, have the most creativity, have the most confidence, and have the most energy. But you may not be aware of how to use these hours to dramatically increase your personal effectiveness.

Success Strategy No. 95:

Determine your hours of peak performance.

Your activities and objectives for each day fall into two categories—those that require maximum brain power and those that require little brain power. Unfortunately, no matter what you wish, your mind and body do not function at peak performance during all your waking hours. Most people find that during the course of a sixteen-hour day, they experience about:

- three hours of peak performance
- five hours of good performance
- six hours of feeling as if they are operating on six cylinders instead of eight, and
- two hours of complete exhaustion

During your Peak Performance Period you are able to produce much more per hour than during off-peak hours. By carefully planning which activities you tackle during these hours of peak performance, you can maximize the results you get from your day. Peak performance hours are the time equivalent of precious gemstones. Great opportunities for maximum effectiveness are lost if these hours are not used correctly. In fact, if you maximized the use of your peak performance hours and did hardly a thing for the rest of the day, you would still feel you had experienced a day full of accomplishment.

To determine your peak performance hours, refer to the chart below. Part A will help you identify the specific hours when your mental energy and capacities are operating at their peak. Part B will help you evaluate how well you currently use these hours. After the chart you will find a list of activities that require peak performance and those that normally do not. This list will help you plan the correct activities to tackle during your peak performance hours. Be certain to follow through with your plan. Get in the habit of using your Peak Performance Periods correctly, and you will immediately notice the increase in your effectiveness.

Determining Your Peak Performance Hours

A. My peak performance hours occur in the:	**and seem to occur during the hours of:**
✓ Check one	
____ Morning	__ A.M. to __ A.M.
____ Afternoon	__ A.M. to __ P.M.
____ Evening	__ P.M. to __ P.M.

B. Check the statement that best describes how you currently use your peak performance hours.

✓ Check one

____ I currently plan my activities and my day around my peak performance hours.

____ I am aware of my peak performance hours but only occasionally schedule my activities around them.

____ I currently do not schedule my activities around my peak performance hours but will begin today.

Scheduling Your Activities Around Peak Performance Hours

Activities that require peak performance:	Activities that can be done in off-peak hours:
Business letter writing	Bill paying
Creative writing	Entertainment
Decision making	Errands
Negotiating	Exercise
Reading (work-related)	Informal discussions
Report writing	Meals
Studying	Meetings
	Personal letter writing
	Phone calls, business and personal
	Quality time with family
	Reading (non-work-related)
	Setting goals and objectives
	Shopping
	Work around the house

Success Strategy No. 96:

Use Peak Performance Periods for activities that require maximum mind power.

Your Peak Performance Periods are those hours during which your brain is functioning at its maximum, your energy level is high, and your attitude says "can do." Therefore, Peak Performance Periods are the best time to:

- Make decisions: Alternatives are clearer, and there is less concern about making the wrong decision.

- Use your creative power: During Peak Performance Periods ideas flow better, more quickly, and more coherently. More powerful words are chosen and placed into well-organized thoughts. Your Peak Performance Period is the time to write reports, plans for a new business, and business letters, or to create new goals and objectives for your business and personal life.
- Negotiate: During this period you will have more confidence when going into any sort of negotiation, from business deals to buying a house or car, or discussing compensation for a new job. You are the most alert. You are the least intimidated.
- Read, study, learn: During Peak Performance Periods your mind absorbs and comprehends more and wanders less. This is the time for work-related reading or study that requires concentration.

My Peak Performance Period is from 7:00 A.M. to 10:30 A.M. These are the hours that are blocked out during my day, seven days a week, for writing or editing my books, articles, and manuals. When I am not working on a project that requires creative writing, the time is used to complete reams of business-related paperwork, study reports, and make the instant decisions required to run my dozens of companies and divisions. I don't attempt to write or do paperwork during the afternoon or evening because I have found through experience that my output is only 40 to 60 percent of what it is during the morning. I also find that my ideas are not as coherent or well organized as they are during my Peak Performance Period. After 10:30 each morning I put down the pen or tape recorder no matter where I am at that point and get on with other activities that don't require a high level of thinking and creativity.

My schedule would not be the most effective for everyone. For instance, Adena doesn't even get up until 9 A.M. But she is often working in her office in our home until midnight.

Adena is just getting going in the afternoon, so she schedules meetings with her divisions during these off-peak hours. After dinner, about 8 P.M., she really hits her stride and uses her Peak Performance Period to do all her creative work, writing, and thinking. Her productivity and effectiveness on this schedule are phenomenal.

Success Strategy No. 97:

Get the best out of your Off-Peak Performance Periods by scheduling them for your routine, noncritical activities.

Running errands, dropping mail off at the post office, and making routine phone calls are examples of tasks that don't take a lot of brain power and can be scheduled during your off-peak hours. Your peak performance hours can occur anytime during your waking day, but they will generally remain the same day after day, including weekends. Your objective is to reserve these hours for your creative activities, thus maximizing your effectiveness. All other activities can just as effectively be scheduled during your off-peak hours.

Success Strategy No. 98:

Avoid negotiating or potentially confrontational meetings during your off-peak hours.

In both your personal life and your business life, negotiation and confrontation are regular occurrences, and whenever they occur, it is important to be at your best. When you are sharp, alert, and confident, you have the best chance of winning or making your point. You may not prevail every time, but your "win" percentage will increase dramatically. That's why, if your Peak Performance Periods are in the morning, you should schedule any negotiations and confrontational meetings during those hours. If your Peak Performance Periods are afternoons or evenings, do your best to schedule accordingly.

The fact that you will not be at your best anytime other than your Peak Performance Periods does not need to become a problem or obstacle, but it is a powerful reason for paying attention to how you schedule your day. When you attempt to force creativity, concentration, and attention to detail during off-peak hours, your reward is often frustration, not accomplishment. You become easily distracted. Obviously the greater the number of your daily peak performance hours, the more effective you can become. Fortunately, there are strategies you can use to extend your high-energy hours of peak performance and reduce the number of hours of poor performance.

Success Strategy No. 99:
Exercise at least every other day.

You can extend your Peak Performance Period by up to two hours each day through exercise alone. The exercise need not be strenuous, like weight lifting, but must be consistent over a period of thirty minutes or more. The best exercise for non–exercise lovers is walking. You can walk a mile in seventeen to eighteen minutes. Thirty minutes to one hour of walking every other day will do wonders to both reduce your stress level and increase the length of your Peak Performance Periods.

Playing tennis or racquetball is a good way to exercise, as is jogging. A planned workout with exercise machines at home or the health club for no less than twenty minutes every other day will also do the trick. But golf (unless you walk), bowling, and bridge, no matter how much fun and how relaxing, do not qualify as Peak Performance Period–extending exercises, although for some they are great stress reducers.

When you begin to exercise, you will notice the difference in your energy levels and the length of peak and near-peak hours after just the first few days. The difference is amazing. You will also notice that you are sleeping up to one hour less per night. In terms of producing results, exercise creates more time than it uses.

Success Strategy No. 100:

Cut down on both the quantity of food and the quantity of fats you eat.

How, when, and what you eat can have a dramatic effect on your performance level and thereby on your continuing effectiveness. Your body must have fat to live, but consuming too much fat will slow you down mentally and physically for up to two hours after every meal. It might surprise you to learn that any big meal high in fats, including fried foods, will demand 40 to 60 percent of your available physical and mental energy over the next two hours just for the digestion process. Load up on hamburgers, fried chicken, other fried foods, or high-fat salad dressing during a quick lunch, and the energy required to digest these foods will cause you to feel exhausted and ineffective all afternoon.

On the other hand, a lunch high in complex carbohydrates, such as salad, vegetables, and fruits, together with a smaller amount of protein, will help keep your energy level high during the afternoon. If you are one who gets tired after lunch, examine your lunchtime eating habits and make changes. The same applies to breakfast for many people.

The other food item that can have a crippling effect on performance is sugar. If at lunchtime you drink sugar-loaded soft drinks, tea, or coffee, the sugar causes your blood-sugar level to shoot up, triggering your insulin response, which reduces the level quickly and often leaves you with that totally fatigued feeling. It might even result in a craving for more sugar or caffeine, which continues the cycle.

Your Peak Performance Periods contain your most important hours. Treat them with respect, and they will return to you rewards that are consistent with greater effectiveness.

No longer will you have the feeling that you worked long and hard but just didn't seem to get much accomplished. Correctly scheduling your Peak Performance Periods is a method of mastering the art of working smarter instead of harder.

CHAPTER **20**

Fighting Fatigue

A winner paces himself; a loser has only two speeds: hysterical and lethargic.

—SYDNEY J. HARRIS

At the opposite end of Peak Performance Periods are those hours in the day when you feel totally fatigued and not much good for anything. Have you ever said to yourself, "I'm just too tired. I'll do it later"? That's an indication you've stepped into total fatigue time. Fatigue seems a natural excuse for inaction; when repeated over time, it leads to a pattern of personal ineffectiveness. Get tired, and you are often stopped in your tracks. But there are powerful strategies you can use to overcome fatigue and reduce the number of totally fatigued hours you experience each day. For maximum effectiveness, all these strategies should be used together.

Success Strategy No. 101: Push past fatigue.

Fatigue does not have to impede your progress toward your objectives and goals. Getting tired is not a signal to quit. Instead, fatigue can be used as a signal that it is time to switch gears from a creative project best done during Peak Performance Periods to a project needing less brain power. There is normally no end to the number of activities on your list from which you can choose, but you will find that when you hit your fatigue time, you can operate more effectively on lower priority projects.

Many people, when tired, mistakenly attempt to continue to work on projects requiring too much concentration and creativity, and only end up becoming stalled by frustration. Others simply quit. The effect of the fatigue-inaction response then becomes cumulative, resulting in the feeling of getting further and further behind. If you get into the habit of quitting a task just because you're feeling tired, your mind begins to play tricks on you. Whenever you face a challenging project that requires intense or creative thought, your mind may then trigger fatigue to create an excuse for not even getting started.

Alertness and fatigue occur in about ninety-minute cycles, just as hunger does. You are likely to feel more tired during twenty of every ninety minutes than during the other seventy minutes. But the bad news is also the good news: When you do feel tired, you will feel that way only during a twenty-minute period during each cycle. If you continue to stay awake and remain active in the face of fatigue, the fatigue will pass, and then once again, for no apparent reason, you will experience alertness. By becoming more aware of your body's responses, you will discover your fatigue cycle and be able to use it to your benefit.

How do you push through the fatigue cycles you will encounter? Just do it. Pushing past fatigue means consciously choosing to stay active through the roughest twenty minutes of the cycle, forcing yourself to concentrate without self-criticism or frustration, aware that the fatigue factor will soon pass without the necessity of sleep or stopping your activity.

During most periods of the day you can expect to experience twenty-minute fatigue cycles, but there is one period when you can expect fatigue to last longer. Even if you are in good to excellent health, you will still typically experience about two hours of ragged-out chronic fatigue each day, a time when you feel totally ineffective and want to stare at walls instead of rush down halls. For many people these fatigue hours occur after lunch or after work. Stress, eating habits, and lack of exercise all contribute to longer, deeper fatigue periods. All are manageable through setting habit-changing goals. Here is a set of strategies I have used for fifteen years that will also help you push past fatigue.

Success Strategy No. 102:
Drink plenty of water.

When you feel fatigue beginning to set in, drink two to three glasses of water and then repeat the process again in fifteen minutes. Loading up the body with water activates the lymphatic system and flushes out toxins, including lactic acid, which is a main physical cause of fatigue. You will feel the effect within five minutes. You will also be running to the rest room more often, of course, but the fatigue-reducing effect is remarkable. One glass of water won't do it, but several glasses will.

Success Strategy No. 103:
Breathe deeply and sit up straight.

Take ten deep breaths. Breathe in deeply and quickly to the count of two, completely filling your lungs. Hold for two seconds, then exhale slowly to the count of four. Do this breathing exercise while sitting up straight or standing. You will increase the supply of oxygen in the blood, which then carries it to your brain, causing you to feel more alert. You will actually feel it happen in an instant. Before I go on stage to lecture, I do this exercise to increase my level of alertness. It is like turning on a light switch.

You should also be aware that fatigue can feed on itself. When you get tired, you tend to slump, and when you slump, you can get much less air into your lungs than when sitting up straight. Decreasing the air capacity in your lungs means less oxygen to the brain, which leads to increased fatigue.

Try it. Slump over with your back rounded. Attempt to take a deep, deep breath, and you will find it is virtually impossible. The lungs just won't hold much air. Now sit up straight and throw your shoulders back. Attempt that deep breath again, slowly breathing in more and more air. Notice that you have at least twice the lung capacity just by changing the way you hold your body. The more fatigued you feel, the more you will tend to slump. Reverse the process by consciously and continuously reminding yourself to straighten up and keep your lungs full of air.

Success Strategy No. 104:
Do some quick exercises.

Do ten push-ups or jog in place for thirty seconds. Exercise will help eliminate fatigue by quickly increasing your heart rate, which slows down dramatically when you become fatigued.

Success Strategy No. 105:
Trigger your adrenal glands.

There is a point in the palm of your hand which, when rubbed for twenty to thirty seconds, will trigger your adrenal glands to pump adrenaline into your system, making you feel more alert and alive. The point lies approximately one inch below the base of the longest finger of each hand, in your upper palm. You will feel a bump, which is part of the bone, at the correct place. Place your thumb on that point and, pressing fairly hard, rub in a circular motion for twenty to thirty seconds. Do the same thing on your other hand, and within a minute you will feel a sense of alertness and renewed energy. Do this whenever you experience fatigue or when you wake up drowsy from a deep sleep or a nap. I use this strategy two or three times every day.

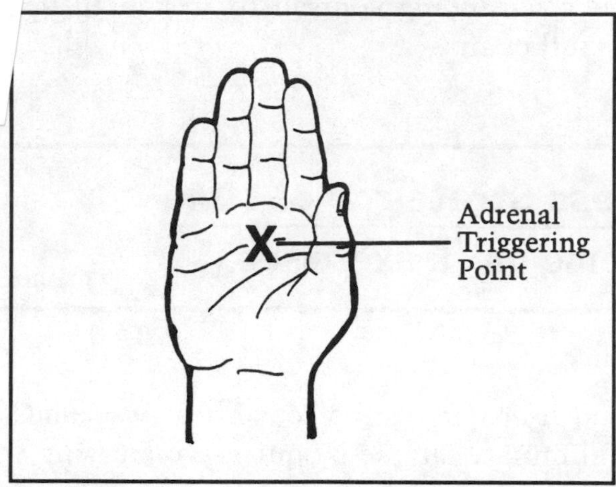

Extreme long-term fatigue used to play a major part in my life. It was triggered daily by a condition known as hypoglycemia, which is abnormally low blood sugar, and although most people are aware of the problem today, according to many physicians in the fifties and sixties, it just didn't exist. When enough sugar, which is carried by the blood, does not reach the brain, thinking becomes unclear and disoriented. If something is not eaten at this point, anyone with hypoglycemia can get dizzy and even pass out.

In my teens and twenties, when I was experiencing extreme fatigue, I was existing on a diet of junk food and at least five six-ounce Cokes a day. Without realizing it, I was continually triggering the hypoglycemic response. The onset of low blood sugar creates a craving for sugar or sweets, and when ingested by itself, sugar causes the blood-sugar level to rise almost instantly. Then within a few minutes insulin is pumped into the bloodstream, which withdraws the sugar and stores it as fat, and the blood-sugar level drops even lower than before. The cycle repeats itself if you eat more sweets or drink more sodas or even drink more coffee, and the feeling is one of continuous short-term highs followed by extreme lows as the body sends off survival alarms that make it crave sugar, coffee, or alcohol—anything for a short-term blood-sugar fix, regardless of the long-term potential damage.

By the time I was twenty, I realized I had a problem. I was pushing and working as hard and as long as I could, coupled with partying at least three nights a week. To stay awake I consumed boxes of No Doz, which is basically concentrated caffeine. Caffeine also triggers the adrenal glands, pumping adrenaline into the system, which is what causes that temporary feeling of alertness and energy. Unfortunately, if you overstimulate the adrenal glands, as heavy coffee drinkers do, adrenal exhaustion is the result. With no more adrenaline to pump into the system, the caffeine then has the opposite effect: It creates extremely short term alertness followed by longer-term fatigue.

The continuous repetition of that cycle had me practically walking into walls, and finally I went to see a doctor. "Let's put you into the hospital for some tests," he said. It was the first time since having my tonsils out at age four that I'd spent any real time in the hospital. I thought: I hope I don't have some strange, unknown, incurable disease. But day after day, test after test, I figured they were getting closer to finding a reason for my extreme exhaustion. On the seventh day the doctor walked into my room, bouncing and bubbly, and announced, "I have good news for you, Mr. Givens. There's absolutely nothing wrong with you."

My lower jaw dropped in amazement. "What are you talking about?" I said. "I live my life so exhausted, I can't stay awake half the time. I fall asleep if I just sit or lie down on the couch after getting home from work. I take No Doz by the handful and drink coffee by the pot just to be able to move, and you're trying to tell me there's nothing wrong with me?"

"Well, all the tests came back negative" was the surprised, defensive reply. "Maybe it's all in your head."

That experience caused me at an early age to become more responsible for my own level of health—long before it was fashionable. I began to watch what I did that preceded the onset of fatigue and also noted anything I did that seemed to eliminate it. I talked to people who had a similar problem to see what they had discovered. I learned to use the strategies that I'm sharing with you in this chapter to prevent the onset of chronic fatigue, whether caused by hypoglycemia or not. At the same time I learned that in order to reach my objectives, no matter how tired I became, I had to move on, pushing past fatigue, accomplishing what I set out to do and finishing on schedule.

It was fifteen years later before I first heard the word *hypoglycemia* and doctors began to admit that there was such a condition. Those with hypoglycemia have learned to eat something containing protein every two to three hours to prevent their blood sugar from dropping. When I began to eat correctly—giving up pumping sugar into my system with Cokes, coffee, and desserts—and then began to take high-potency multiple vitamins and minerals to keep my system balanced, my hypoglycemia actually went away. And so did the chronic fatigue associated with it. My energy level stays high—higher than I could ever have imagined in those early days, a factor that certainly contributes to my level of effectiveness.

If you feel tired and also have steady cravings for sugar, caffeine, and sweets, try my fatigue-busting strategy of cutting these foods out of your diet and eating some protein snack or vegetables every few hours. For the first three days you may actually feel worse, as your body rejects the sugar addiction, but after that, if you stick to this routine, you will notice an increase in your energy level, alertness, emotional balance, and even your ability to sleep soundly at night. In addition, you may prefer to see a nutritionist or a doctor. Learning how to control and balance your blood sugar can have a dramatic impact not only on your effectiveness and your ability to achieve your goals but also on your personal happiness and well-being.

Success Strategy No. 106:
Refocus on your goals and objectives.

A powerful mental antidote to the onset of fatigue is to remind yourself why it is important to stay on track. Since by now you are filling your day with prioritized activities, think about how your current activity is important to your goals. Push yourself through the twenty minutes of down time. If the fatigue you are experiencing is more than just a part of a ninety-minute fatigue cycle, however, consider switching to a less mentally demanding objective or use the time to take a short nap.

Success Strategy No. 107:
Use short naps to overcome fatigue.

The mind and body can actually replenish their abilities and strength with as little as a fifteen-to-twenty-minute nap during the daytime. I have used the napping technique as a fatigue-buster ever since I was a kid and read about Thomas Edison's practice of lying down in his laboratory for frequent naps. This strategy has served me well for thirty-five years.

Of course you're going to get tired if you sleep 6 to 8 hours a night and have a 16-to-18-hour waking stretch in between. Napping for twenty minutes to an hour sometime during your waking hours will ward off fatigue. You will need less sleep at night, thus adding an hour or two of awake time to your day. But more important, you will also add dramatically to the amount of your productive and effective time. Just one extra productive and effective hour per day will give you 360 more effective hours per year, or the equivalent of forty-five extra 8-hour days! That's an extra six and one-half weeks per year of productive time.

Oh, I've heard all the excuses, such as:

"I don't have time to nap."

You have time to do anything you choose once time is under your control.

"I'm not in a work environment that allows me to nap."

Then wait until you get home and take a short, undisturbed nap right before dinner. No phones, no interruptions.

And the big one:

"I don't nap because I am more tired when I wake up."

If that's you, over the years you have just gotten out of the habit of napping. After a week of practice you'll be a pro and have tremendously reduced fatigue and stress.

I usually take a forty-five-minute nap around 4 or 5 P.M. Make taking a brief nap part of your daily routine, and you will find, when you get the hang of it, that you will sleep fewer hours during the night and be far more effective during your waking hours. By applying all the Success Strategies in this chapter when you are experiencing either short-term or long-term fatigue, you will instantly and automatically decrease its depth and frequency, which will speed you on your path toward achieving your objectives and goals.

CHAPTER 21

Flattening Your Fears

You've got to be taught to hate and fear . . . it's got to be drummed in your dear little ear.

—OSCAR HAMMERSTEIN,
SOUTH PACIFIC

Two of the greatest cripplers to effectiveness, achievement, and enjoyment are worry and fear. Both retard your progress and cause inaction just when action is needed the most. Fear is not something you're born with, and worry is not something that's required of you. Fear is learned, and worry is nothing more than an unmanaged thought pattern.

Fear was initially learned from your parents and your early experiences. Your mother may have said to you, as mine did, "Don't run out into the street. You'll get hit by a car!" Taken literally that statement is, of course, untrue. Lots of people run out into the street without getting hit by cars. Part of your mom's loving mission, however, was to instill fear in order, she thought, to protect you so you would think before darting out into the street to chase a ball.

Caution is a mental process; fear is a destructive emotion.

Unfortunately, the more your mom repeated fear-instilling statements, the more they became programmed in your subconscious mind as a reality. A real but unnecessary fear of streets, cars, or even going outdoors at all could have been the result for you, as it has been for countless numbers of people. What your mom meant to say was "When you're approaching a street, be careful. Look both ways so that you and an automobile don't attempt to occupy the same space at the same time because you will be damaged far more than the automobile." Our moms meant to teach us caution as well as good common sense, but instead they inadvertently instilled fear. The results in my case were measurable. Fear of streets, which I had as a kid, caused me to freeze at the curb even when cars were a block away. I repeatedly had dreams of crossing a street with a car bearing down on me and my not being able to run to get out of the way. The car was moving at regular speed while I was moving in slow motion.

The experience of an event you don't quite understand as a child is the second way fear is programmed into your mind. If, as a child, you reach up and grab a hot pan on a gas stove, you will immediately jerk your hand away. No thinking required. However, that experience may cause you to become unnecessarily fearful of fire or anything that appears hot. No real danger is inherent in the fire or the hot pan, but only in how you interact with them. It is natural to be cautious with things that are hot and could injure you if you touched them, but it is unnatural to be afraid of them. After a trauma-producing event like grabbing a hot pan, each time you reach for a pan you may feel a trembling in your hand and a queasiness in your stomach for no reason other than that the association between pans and pain has been programmed in your mind.

The depth of fear programmed in your mind is controlled by two elements:

- the depth of emotion you experience during or after any single traumatic event
- the number of repetitions of a fear-producing experience

When you have experienced a traumatic event—being stung by a bee or bitten by a dog, for example, or feeling claustrophobic and helpless in a small elevator that jerks as if the cable is about to break, or being laughed at in school for a presentation that you gave in front of the class—it triggers unpleasant or negative emotions. The depth of your fear of bees, dogs, elevators, or speaking in front of a group is a function of the depth of emotions you first felt, and if fear-producing events are repeated, your fear of those events intensifies.

When you say to yourself or to someone else, "I'm afraid of that," what you are really saying is that you don't like the intense emotions you experience when confronted by what you fear. The emotions are not dangerous, only unpleasant. Yet you begin to avoid more and more experiences, even opportunities, in order not to trigger those feelings. Bees, dogs, elevators, public speaking, and almost anything else you normally encounter in life have no real danger associated with them. Yet because of the fear programmed in your mind, confronting these objects or events causes your survival systems to react. Even with your desire to avoid fear-triggering circumstances, it is a safe bet you won't always be able to. Each time the emotions of fear are triggered and you experience the intense desire to run from a situation, the fear becomes more deeply ingrained. In other words, fear, an emotion you want to rid yourself of, feeds on itself.

Remember when you were young and fearless, doing things you wouldn't dream of doing now? The reason is that as you have gotten older, you have become more and more fearful as each fear became self-perpetuating. The process can and must be reversed. Otherwise, your life may be lived in a box that becomes smaller and smaller as each fear takes on greater importance. From the time you were born until now, you may have subconsciously taken on dozens of fears, some of which occasionally cause severe negative reactions, and others that are present but hardly noticed. Some you have overcome without thinking about it, others are still with you and affecting your life.

You may wonder what other people fear. Here is a list of the most common fears based on the percentage of people who experience them.

Top 12 Fears		Scientific Name
1. Speaking before a group	(40%)	Topophobia
2. Heights	(30%)	Acrophobia
3. Insects and bugs	(20%)	Entomophobia
4. Financial problems	(20%)	Atephobia
5. Deep water	(20%)	Bathophobia
6. Disease	(20%)	Pathophobia
7. Death	(20%)	Thanatophobia
8. Flying	(20%)	Aerophobia
9. Loneliness	(15%)	Monophobia
10. Dogs	(10%)	Cynophobia
11. Driving/riding in a car	(10%)	Ochophobia
12. Dark	(10%)	Nyctophobia

Fear causes the reaction of avoidance or inaction.

Fear can be dangerous to your health, wealth, and happiness, as well as your peace of mind. You've probably come to believe, as I once did, that fear is healthy and natural because it cautions you about potentially dangerous situations. It is not. Fear is unhealthy and unnatural, and one of the goals on your Goals List should be to get rid of fear's hold on you. Operating at maximum effectiveness depends on it. Fear creates a brick wall between you and your destinations. To achieve your dreams and goals there is no doubt that you will continuously face the things you fear. The only alternative is to give up on your dreams and goals, and settle for mediocrity. You'll have a lot of company, but the experience will not be rewarding.

To accomplish what you want in life, you will constantly be sailing uncharted waters, doing things you have not done before. That is not to say it is impossible to accomplish what you want and still hang on to fear, but you will find yourself making time-consuming detours and taking longer paths just to avoid what you fear. Remember, effectiveness is the process of producing maximum results in minimum time. The detours caused by fear create minimum results while expanding the required time to reach your goals.

There is an important difference between fear and worry: Fear is event-related and worry is mentally created. For instance, seeing a car go out of control and suddenly head your way as you walk down an unprotected sidewalk could certainly produce event-related fear. In this instance you are truly in danger. Fear can and should trigger the adrenaline response in your body and give you the strength to move yourself quickly from the path of the oncoming car.

However, if while walking down the same sidewalk you create only a mental picture of passing cars going out of control and heading your way for a potential disaster, you are generating worry which has little to do with reality.

Worry is an accumulation of thoughts about future, potentially negative outcomes.

Worry involves imagined events that have not yet occurred. For instance, you can be driving to work and begin worrying about a potentially negative outcome of a meeting at which you have not yet arrived. In fact, the worry could pertain to a meeting that isn't even scheduled to occur for a week or more. In this case the worry has nothing to do with your present activity—driving the car.

Worry is mental, worry is negative, and therefore worry is wasted, destructive thought energy. Worry is a projection of your focus or consciousness into some time in the future. Since your only point of power is in the present, worry renders you mentally powerless. Worry is inaction, not action. Only action produces results. Inaction doesn't produce, create, or change a thing.

Worry comes in many shapes and sizes, but regardless of the object or subject, it is always about potential negative outcomes. Here are just a few examples:

- Worry that something you have done will be found out.
- Worry that something you desire or feel you need won't come about.
- Worry about family members or friends and how they will turn out.
- Worry that you won't finish a project before time runs out.
- Worry that you will lose your job and about the income you'll be without.
- Worry that your health or life will give out.
- Worry that before your bills are paid your money won't hold out.
- Worry that a plan you have made won't work out.

Fear, unlike worry, is an event-triggered emotion. Fear happens only when you are faced with a set of circumstances in which you are both directly and currently involved. A fear of snakes, for instance, occurs only when you are in the presence of a snake or you have reason to believe there is a real chance that you might soon encounter one. If you have a fear of public speaking and are in a group where several members are being chosen to get up and talk in front of the rest of the crowd, you will more than likely experience fear. Fear does not occur unless you are in the proximity of the circumstances you fear.

Could you worry about public speaking? Of course. Maybe you have been asked to give a talk at your service club meeting in two weeks. The more you think about it, the more you begin to see yourself flubbing it. You think, What if they're not interested? What if I say the wrong thing? What if . . . ? What if . . . ? That's worry.

Worry is the process of mentally creating potential negative outcomes.

Worry generally involves some type of loss, such as loss of life, health, love, money, your job, or a hundred other possibilities. Worry and fear are two different sides of the same coin. Worry includes negative thoughts and emotions about what might happen, while fear is your body's and mind's reaction to what is happening. Both are unnatural and destructive.

Worry can and will:

- keep you awake at night, rendering you less effective the next day.
- slow you down by distracting you from the important tasks at hand.

- cause ulcers and other stress-related diseases.
- cause you to lose the ability to differentiate what's real from what's only imagined.
- cause you to unnecessarily lose trust and confidence in yourself and others.
- render you ineffective.

The more you worry, the more of these negative outcomes you will experience. I have never discovered anything positive about worry. Worry creates nothing, decides nothing, and accomplishes nothing. Therefore, worry is one process on your path to greater effectiveness that you want to eliminate.

Success Strategy No. 108:

Eliminate worry by refocusing your thoughts on the present.

Since worry is nothing more than a combination of negative thoughts, the amount of time you spend worrying and the effect of that worry can be brought under your total control.

Worry is crippling because it projects your mind into an imagined negative future, which then incapacitates you and renders you ineffective in the present. In addition, because of the power of your mind to bring into your life whatever you visualize, constant worrying only increases your chances of creating the very experiences you seek to avoid. To the extent you spend time worrying, your mental focus is on the future while your only point of power and accomplishment remains in the present.

Worry is what I call a default mental process, meaning that you don't have to consciously do a thing to make worry happen. It will happen by default. On the other hand, to make worry go away and to get out of the habit of worrying, you must consciously take action. To eliminate worry, refocus your attention on something in the present moment. Anytime you find yourself in worry mode, no matter what the subject or object of that worry, you can use this strategy to get rid of the worry. Clear your mind of the worrying thoughts by thinking about something else—something positive going on right now. Your mind cannot hold a positive and a negative thought at the same time. When you focus on something positive in the present, there is no room left in your mind for worry or any other negativity.

Fear is an even stronger emotion than worry, and potentially more crippling. As a kid I was afraid of everything, and quite often my intended actions were crippled by fear. Like many youngsters I picked up my fears from my mother, who seemed to be afraid of everything and was dramatically vocal about it, including her fear of bugs, mice, and snakes. Believe it or not, I was even afraid to fish. As a kid I couldn't go fishing because I was terrified of having to touch a live fish. It didn't become a problem, however, because I was also afraid of worms, which prevented me from going fishing in the first place. I was also afraid of spiders, dogs, snakes, and anything else that moved. My fear of rejection and saying the wrong thing caused me to become withdrawn around adults. I was so afraid of loud noises that the Fourth of July was traumatic for me. Fear, therefore, was a dominant force in how I ran my life. In fact, here is my original fear list. I was afraid of:

- auto accidents
- being yelled at
- dogs and cats
- embarrassment
- fish
- heights
- swimming in the ocean
- high bridges
- horses
- loud noises
- negotiating
- pain
- snakes
- talking on the telephone

- rejection
- failure
- sharks
- being startled
- bugs
- electricity
- farm animals
- having my arms held down
- lightning
- missing an opportunity
- older, wealthier, smarter people
- spiders
- walking barefoot in the grass
- worms

My fear of snakes was one of the few fears for which I could trace the source. When I was nine years old, we had a maid named Mrs. Kachinski who came to work every day from her farm outside Decatur, Illinois. I'd never been to a farm, so my parents thought it might be a good idea for me to spend the day with her and her children. Everything was new to me, from the iron water-pump handle in the kitchen to the unpasteurized cream-filled milk.

Country boys just love to play jokes on city kids, so after breakfast one of the Kachinski boys said with a snicker, "Let's go down to the river." It sounded great to me, and we walked through the fields until we came to a stream that was about twenty feet wide. The kids maneuvered me under a tall tree. Then, suddenly, one of the boys with panic on his face yelled, "Look out!" and pointed directly above my head. My eyes shot skyward, and hanging from a branch and staring me straight in the eyes was a huge black snake, a water moccasin. It was already dead, but how was I to know? The kids had put it there just for my benefit. Its head was a mere foot away from my face.

My knees started to buckle, and a chill ran down my spine. I felt as if I was about to faint. I jumped away, gasping for breath, and the kids couldn't stop laughing for fifteen minutes. Not only was I terrified by the snake, but I felt like an absolute fool and was as embarrassed as I could be. Every kid wants to appear brave.

A year later I was at a construction site on Glencoe Avenue, not far from my home, where a new house was being built. I was in short pants sitting on the ground, watching the construction workers finish off the basement about eight feet below. Before I got there, they had killed a four-foot rattlesnake they found while digging and had placed it on a board. I didn't see it until one of the workers yelled, "Here, kid, catch!" and threw the snake up and out of the hole. It landed right at my feet. I rolled back from that spot, heart pounding and not taking my eyes off the snake, which, of course, didn't move. Panic went through me as I was again being laughed at. For the next several years I was so afraid of snakes that I wouldn't walk in the woods or take a walk after dark. If I did, I was always looking down at my feet, terrified that a snake was going to jump out and "get me." I checked under my bed and in the closet before I turned out the lights each night, in case there was a snake lurking somewhere in the room.

In the eighth grade I thought to myself, This is silly. All snakes aren't dangerous. So I got the "S" volume of the encyclopedia off the shelf and turned to "Snakes." I found a full-page colored illustration of all different kinds of snakes, and I decided to simply run my finger down the page, touching each of the pictures. I couldn't do it. My fear of snakes was so deeply ingrained by then that my mind would not allow my finger even to touch the page. I froze.

My fear of snakes was so intense that it began, in many ways, to control my life—where I went, what I did, and where my attention was focused. When playing golf as a teenager I lost countless golf balls, because when a ball went into the rough I refused to follow. Even at age thirty when I was selling mountain real estate, I refused to leave the road to show a lot to a prospective buyer. Instead, I would tell my clients, "It's a beautiful lot. Go up there, walk around, and have a great time." That procedure didn't do much to enhance my sales.

But even the deepest fears can be conquered on your own. Today, I've handled dozens of snakes all over the world with absolutely no fear. I've conducted private expeditions for weeks at a time into some of the wildest and most remote jungles and rain forests of the world, something that was once beyond my imagination. So many of my most incredible life experiences would never have occurred if I had not made it a priority to deprogram the fears that were causing continuous ineffectiveness in my life. You can do the same. The strategies that I used and that you can also use will squelch your ingrained fears and transform you into a fearless SuperSelf full of determination and courage.

Success Strategy No. 109: Constantly confront the things you fear.

My fears were limiting both my enjoyment of life and my ability to achieve my dreams, to say nothing of my level of effectiveness. I decided the best way to get over my fears was to face each one head-on, until the experience or even the anticipation of the experience no longer slowed me down. One by one I confronted the things I feared the most, again and again if necessary until they no longer maintained a grip on my life and actions. I began by making a list of every fear I had ever experienced. Then I shut my eyes and pointed to the list. I opened my eyes, and whatever I was touching, I told myself, was what I would tackle first. My finger rested on the fear of heights. I had had the courage to make a list and to make a mental commitment to face my fears, and now I had to carry through with that commitment.

I figured that my fear of heights could be overcome only by experiencing heights over and over until the fear went away. Now, you cannot get much higher than in an airplane, so I decided that the most promising way to face my fear of heights was to take flying lessons or jump out of a plane.

The following Saturday I drove outside of town toward the small Decatur Municipal Airport—two small buildings in the middle of what was once a cornfield. I had the intention of signing up for flying lessons. As I pulled into the small parking lot, I saw six guys next to the single narrow runway, packing parachutes. Here's my opportunity, I thought, my chance to get over my fear of heights once and for all. Just strap on a parachute, go up in a plane, and jump out. All I had to do was force myself into and out of the plane; the rest would take care of itself. After all, I was not exactly a stranger to the new sport of skydiving. I had read a library book on the subject not two months before. I had even practiced landings in the backyard, jumping backward off a stepladder, but I had made it only to the fifth step before my fear of heights took over.

I walked over to the skydivers and said nervously, "Is there a chance I could jump with you today?"

"Sure, if you've had some experience," one of them replied.

"Well, not much," I said truthfully, and then I added not so truthfully, "But I have jumped a couple of times with the club up in Lincoln." I figured that Lincoln was just far enough away so that he wouldn't know if I had jumped there or not.

They gave me a bright red zippered jumpsuit and an old leather football helmet with tape over the ear holes—there were no sports helmets in those days. The jumpmaster told me I could go up in the next plane. He gave me a parachute, and I watched the other jumpers strap themselves into their chutes, then followed the same procedure.

Well, I thought, this can't be too difficult. They jump from a four-seater Cessna 172 single-engine plane, so I'll do what the guy in front of me does. Guess who they put in the front seat? The new guy—me!

My second fear then took over—fear of rejection—which at the time seemed to exceed the fear of killing myself. I was not about to tell them that I didn't know what I was doing. I was terrified. Not only did I have no experience in jumping, I'd never even been up in an airplane except for a short flight as a Cub Scout in the sixth grade.

When I strapped myself into the right front seat of the plane, I noticed there was no door. As we took off, I watched bug-eyed as the ground got farther and farther away. The jumpmaster, who was sitting behind me, tapped me on the shoulder and asked, "How high do you think we are? We're jumping at thirty-five hundred feet." I answered, "Thirty-five hundred feet!" He laughed. "We're only at about four hundred feet."

We got higher and higher, and everything below became smaller and smaller. I remembered from the library book that when you get to jumping altitude, the pilot idles the engine and the jumpmaster taps your helmet, which is the signal for you to step, not jump, outside the plane. You put your right foot on the tire, the left on the metal step under the doorway, and you hang on to the strut under the wing with both hands. Then on cue you jump. What in the world am I doing here? I kept thinking. I've made a big mistake. But I was too embarrassed to admit it to anyone.

The jumpmaster tapped my helmet. I didn't even want to unfasten my seat belt, but there was no other way out. I kept telling myself not to look down, to keep looking at the sky. I turned and with my left foot felt for the step. Then grabbing the diagonal strut, I moved my other foot to the tire. My heart was thumping as the wind ripped by at 80 mph. The jumpmaster leaned out and slapped me on the helmet. That meant let go. Instead I froze. All I wanted to do was get back in the plane, but I knew that was impossible. I had read in the book about two plane crashes caused by first-time skydivers panicking under the wing and climbing back into the plane, only to have their spring-loaded parachutes burst open, filling the cockpit with cloth and blinding the pilot. Jumpmasters were now trained to force the panicking parachutist to jump, no matter what the method. The next time the jumpmaster slapped me on the helmet so hard it made my ears ring. He was beginning to suspect what was going on.

I took a restricted deep breath and let go, thinking about arching my back and spreading my arms and legs like in the pictures. It didn't work. Instead I folded in the middle, flipped over on my back, and when I opened my eyes, all I could see was the sky. I was dropping like a dead weight, upside down, instead of floating in a spread-eagle position and taking advantage of the fall-slowing air resistance.

My chute was set to open automatically since I was still a novice skydiver—more novice than they suspected. The chute is packed in a long cylindrical sleeve and then rolled into a canvas bag. The small spring-loaded pilot chute pops out when the rip cord is pulled, which pulls out the sleeve from which the chute then deploys. Or at least that's what is supposed to happen. But because I was falling with my back to the ground, when the pilot chute popped out, the sleeve and parachute came out underneath me, ran up between my legs, and in an instant wrapped and tangled around my right leg. I was not only falling at 175 mph, I was tangled in my parachute, which wouldn't open.

At that moment I had an unwanted but revealing lesson in the mechanics of fear. Up to that point I had worried about "What if . . . ? What if . . . ?" Now suddenly everything I had worried might happen *was* happening. I was seconds away from the big splash with no one to get me out of the potentially fatal predicament except me, and I had no more time for worry. My mentally created worry had been instantly transformed into an event-related fear. But instead of panic, a calmer sense of urgency coupled with clarity of thinking took over. I pulled my knees up to my chest and began unwrapping the chute from around my leg one turn at a time.

The chute suddenly flew free of my body, and when it came open, the jerk was so severe that I figured I had either broken something on me or the chute. Still stunned, I looked up to see if everything was in order with the parachute, but how would I know since I'd never been that close to an open parachute before? "I'm alive," I screamed out loud, and I actually started singing as my body, slowed to 17 mph, edged its way to earth. Then I noticed that the landing zone at the airport was nowhere near where I was. I was headed for the middle of a cornfield, and suddenly another fear took over. Oh my God, snakes! I thought.

Relief turned to terror as I hit the ground hard, not knowing quite how to land. It took me less than thirty seconds to roll that chute into a pile and stand on it so that the snakes couldn't get me. My mind had created pictures of groups of snakes attacking me from every direction. It took the jumpmaster and a crew fifteen minutes to find me after the plane landed. Driving around and yelling, they told me which way to walk to get out of the seven-foot-tall corn. When the jumpmaster finally spotted me, he was shaking his head. He said somewhat angrily, "Chuck, you owe me two dollars and ninety-five cents." "For what?" I asked. "For cleaning my jumpsuit because of what happened to me when I saw what happened to you!"

The jumpmaster told me that at the point my chute finally did open, I had only about four seconds before I hit the ground. Did I jump again? You bet I did. Not that day, but the next week and on through the summer. I knew if I didn't do it again, my fear could be worse than ever. However, I did agree to do some training first.

Facing my fear head-on had worked. My fear of heights was reduced by at least 80 percent. I still got uneasy and sometimes queasy feelings in my stomach, but there was no doubt that I could both jump and handle the fear. In the last fifteen years my fear of heights has totally left me. It was completely deprogrammed. I've walked ledges only three feet wide with a thousand-foot drop on each side, climbed a rope eight stories into the air, and scaled sheer cliffs with ropes and rope ladders hanging off pinions hammered into the rocks. You, too, will find that the experience of conquering your fears is so freeing and such a confidence builder that every fear-busting experience is worth it.

I had been right. If I was willing to accept the challenge, no matter how badly it scared me, I could conquer my fears. One by one and year after year I tackled fear after fear on my list until fear was no longer a factor in my life. The same will be true for you. No, I am not recommending that you jump out of an airplane without training. But I am telling you that if you are willing to confront things you fear, no matter how rough it feels inside, you will have the aliveness-producing experience of breaking through your limits. You will even find as I did that all of your fears are interrelated. As you deprogram one, other unrelated fears seem to release their hold on you at the same time and in the same process.

What you fear controls your life. What you control has no power over your life. Conquering fear can be an exciting experience when it is accomplished in a spirit of challenge and fun. To make that kind of excitement part of your own experience, include on your Dreams List and your Goals List all that you desire to conquer, including your fears.

I believe that my total lack of fear is one of the major reasons I've been so successful both in business and in my personal life. People are reluctant to challenge a fearless person because that is a person who cannot be upset, intimidated, or manipulated. A fearless person is like a Sherman tank rolling through a forest of small trees—unstoppable. Supreme self-confidence comes from knowing that you are totally capable of handling anything that comes up in your life. It is the true experience of your SuperSelf.

Success Strategy No. 110:

Act even in the face of fear.

Somewhere along the path of growing up and older, we came to believe that fear was an acceptable excuse for inaction and avoidance. It is not. True, you can still live your life avoiding almost everything you fear or that upsets you, but it will not be the same life. Opportunities will slip by unnoticed. Great potential experiences will be missed, and at the extreme, life will become mundane instead of magnificent.

Yet you still have the choice of facing your fears, and getting beyond fear requires choice after choice of acting even in the face of fear. You must believe that it is okay to be afraid and still proceed. If you fear speaking in public, for example, just do it, positively and forcefully, regardless of what emotions are triggered underneath. Separate in your mind the emotions from the event. The emotions are generally related to past events and have little to do with your current circumstances. To successfully conquer fear, you must be committed to action in the face of fear.

Success Strategy No. 111:

Visualize a positive outcome for every fear-triggering situation you face.

When you are confronted by a fear-triggering situation, you can become caught up in it and actually add to your fear instead of eliminating it. Which direction you go depends on your mental attitude and perspective. React positively, not negatively, to the situation. Remind yourself that you are a totally capable person. Think to yourself that it is okay to be afraid and still proceed. See yourself successfully handling the situation, whether it is a growling dog or a speech you are about to give. Don't act and think like a victim, and you won't become one. Test the waters slowly and cautiously when possible, but with determination. Stay positive.

To succeed in reaching your dreams and goals in the shortest time, you must be willing to constantly and consistently confront the things you fear. By confronting what you fear, fear begins to lose its control over you.

The first step in confronting fears is to identify what you fear.

Take a look at the checklist on the next page. Follow the directions to make a personal checklist that identifies the things you fear the most.

Identifying Your Fears

The following is a list of the things, events, and actions that most commonly trigger fear. Rate each from 0 to 3 based on its effect on you when you encounter it.

0 = No effect
1 = Makes me twinge
2 = Serious; makes me withdraw and try to avoid it at all costs
3 = Terrifies me

0 1 2 3 Snakes
0 1 2 3 Insects/spiders
0 1 2 3 Dogs
0 1 2 3 Sharks/eels
0 1 2 3 Other animals (list)
____
____
0 1 2 3 Pain
0 1 2 3 The dark
0 1 2 3 Loud noises
0 1 2 3 Deep water
0 1 2 3 Elevators/escalators
0 1 2 3 Dirt/germs
0 1 2 3 Successful people
0 1 2 3 Tests/exams
0 1 2 3 Being hurt emotionally
0 1 2 3 Being mugged/raped
0 1 2 3 Being hurt physically
0 1 2 3 Disappointment
0 1 2 3 Being yelled at
0 1 2 3 Sex

0 1 2 3 Financial problems
0 1 2 3 Old age
0 1 2 3 Sickness
0 1 2 3 Death
0 1 2 3 Driving/riding in a car
0 1 2 3 Loneliness
0 1 2 3 Flying
0 1 2 3 Elevators/closed spaces
0 1 2 3 Falling/heights
0 1 2 3 Failure
0 1 2 3 Speaking up
0 1 2 3 Commitment
0 1 2 3 Embarrassment
0 1 2 3 Saying the wrong thing
0 1 2 3 Speaking before a group
0 1 2 3 Swimming

Others
0 1 2 3 ______________
0 1 2 3 ______________
0 1 2 3 ______________
0 1 2 3 ______________

Now that you have identified the things and situations you fear the most, make it your goal to overcome those fears. Add that goal to your Goals List and look for or create opportunities to confront what you fear. Work the hardest on those you marked 2 and 3. These are the fears that are getting in your way of experiencing maximum effectiveness.

From this point it's up to you. I can only stress the importance of facing and dealing with what you fear. You must be the one to accept the challenge. Confronting your fear of heights could mean going to the fifth floor of a building and standing next to a floor-to-ceiling window for five minutes, then repeating this process once a week for the next few weeks until you realize that you are totally capable of standing near a drop-off without fear of falling. Then you can move on to the tenth floor or to the observation deck of a tall building, or on to another fear entirely. It's your choice. Your objective is to meet what you fear at an ever greater level of intensity until you have conquered that fear. Be daring—you already have it within you.

My son Rob recently took a group of twenty-five Givens Organization employees, both men and women, to a bungee-jumping site in Florida. Bungee jumping consists of leaping off a 150-foot (fifteen-story) tower with strong rubber cords tied securely to your ankles. You stop just short of the water and bounce back up 50 feet because of the elasticity of the cords. Most of the participants frankly admitted they were terrified at the thought of jumping and went only to watch, but by day's end Rob had all of them jumping. The energy and feeling of accomplishment arming the group was overwhelming. They had overcome their own fears and had encouraged one another to attain success. Unfortunately, in life you will more often find yourself around people who criticize rather than encourage you. Stop listening to people who tell you "you can't" and spend more time with those few who tell you "you can."

When confronting what you fear, you will quickly discover

that the actual experience is nothing like the negative event you imagined. Confront a fear of flying (actually a fear of falling) by getting on a plane, and you will find that the plane does not fall out of the sky—no matter how many times you fly or how deeply you fear it. Confront your fear of snakes, and you will find that snakes are not slimy, vicious, or evil. They are dry to the touch, lazy, and unusually passive. Confront your fear of public speaking, and you will find you won't faint, freeze up, or make a fool of yourself. You can do it.

After successfully confronting and challenging any fear, you'll also find that the big deals in your everyday life become smaller deals. You will overreact less and stay more in control. You will have the confidence to make quicker, positive decisions, and you will find yourself more willing to take on greater challenges, which will lead you closer to your dreams and goals.

Success Strategy No. 112:

Create a mind-movie to experience the event you fear in a nonthreatening environment.

A second method of overcoming fear is to confront what you fear in your mind instead of in your environment. Your fears are in your mind, so use your mind to overcome them with what I call a "mind-movie," the experience of a real event that occurs in your imagination only. Mind-movies are an extremely effective fear-busting technique and are about 50 percent as effective in deprogramming fears as facing the actual fear-triggering event. To create a mind-movie, find a quiet place to sit and close your eyes. Envision yourself going through the fear-triggering situation over and over. See yourself handling the situation successfully. Years ago I used this process anytime I was going into a situation that required negotiation, sales skills, or public speaking. I always saw myself as the victor, the winner, and more often than not I was.

Subconsciously, you generally avoid what you fear as well as any environment in which the fear might be triggered. If you fear snakes and bugs, for example, you will avoid walking in the woods, running barefoot through your yard, camping, hiking, and many other positive, potentially beautiful experiences. By consciously and unconsciously avoiding all situations or environments in which your fear may be triggered, you set limits for all of your experiences. Limited potential experiences inhibit your alternatives and build unscalable walls around your opportunities. If you're willing to accept the challenge of facing what you fear, you will find your fears will back down. You can even expand the limits of your experience to the point where nothing in life—not things, events, circumstances, other people, or even you yourself—can hold you back or render you ineffective.

CHAPTER **22**

Handling Stress

When everything seems to be going against you, remember that the airplane takes off against the wind, not with it.

—Henry Ford

The normal state of the human mind and body is the state of total health and relaxation. That is the normal state, not the abnormal state. It is healthy and stress-free people who are normal, not those constantly operating in a state of tension and anxiety.

Continuing stress, which is caused by worry, negative thoughts, and negative emotions, often results in ulcers, arthritis, cancer, and many other diseases that are often avoidable. Stress literally causes the body to deteriorate. Disease is the result, not the cause, of stress. Stress is self-created and self-perpetuated. The bad news is that eighty-two million people in the United States suffer from acute tension and anxiety. They have taken the first major step toward ill health through the misuse of their minds and emotions. But the good news is that stress can be corralled and controlled.

A hundred years ago people began to believe that medical science was the answer to the quality of life. Develop a list of medicines and cures, and everyone will be living a life of push-button health. It didn't happen. As the level of medical technology increased, so did the level of stress, and as stress levels increased, new stress-related diseases were created as fast as the new medicines eliminated the old diseases. As the medicines got better, the diseases caused by stress, tension, and modern living only got worse.

Stress is a mental and physical condition about which there seems to be little that is positive, productive, or desirable. Stress is a condition that seems to creep into life uninvited and unwanted, and is often unnoticed for a time. Check any medical reference, and you will find the following symptoms typical of stress:

- apprehension
- anxiety
- strain
- tension
- distress
- frustration
- worry

You can add to this list anger, jealousy, hurt, and a dozen other negative emotions. How many of them have you experienced in the past week? Not one of these mental and physical experiences would you consciously choose if you knew you had a choice. You *do* have the choice of how often and to what extent you experience these symptoms of stress, but it is a safe bet that no one has shown you why or how.

Stress is created by the body's natural defense system, which is attempting to protect itself from perceived possible destruction. Stress and its related symptoms are created when your mind begins to run wild with negativity or thoughts of potential negative outcomes. Most stress is perception-related and has little to do with any real life-threatening danger from your environment, yet your body reacts as if your very life were at risk.

That reaction began with your ancestors millions of years ago, and you haven't gotten over it yet. It's called the flight-or-fight response. All humans are born with this instinctive reaction, and we are not alone. Animals also have a preprogrammed flight-or-fight response and, in general, will either flee or attack in a threatening situation. Acceptable human behavior doesn't allow such simple choices, however. The purpose of this reaction is survival, and it is supposed to be triggered only in the face of imminent real danger, such as a life-threatening situation. Obviously, this is a condition that occurs only rarely in most of our lives.

Here's how your flight-or-fight response was meant to work in life-threatening situations. Let's say you're stopped at a stop light and forgot to lock your car door. A man jumps in on the passenger side, wielding a twelve-inch knife. Your flight-or-fight alternatives are clear. Open the car door and run, or be brave (and/or stupid) and attempt to take the knife away from this menacing stranger. Your flight-or-fight response helps you achieve either action by triggering the following measurable changes in your body:

- Your blood pressure rises, and your heart starts pumping faster to carry more blood and oxygen throughout your body to increase your alertness.
- Your adrenal glands are triggered, releasing adrenaline and other hormones into your system to give you increased energy and strength.
- You start sweating to cool your body and dissipate the heat generated by your increased body activity.
- Your muscles tense to prepare you for either fleeing or fighting.
- Your senses become more acute.
- You begin to breathe almost in gasps to draw more oxygen into your lungs.

When the danger is over and you've survived, you're either two blocks away in a safe haven, or the police have arrived after you've disarmed your visitor. Your mind says danger is no longer imminent, and your entire system begins to slow down.

In this example, the danger was indeed real and may even have been life-threatening. But there are dozens of daily non-life-threatening occurrences that trigger the same reactions. For instance:

- Worry about not completing a project on time.
- A scary movie you are watching that is specifically designed to terrify you.
- A first date with someone.
- Worry about overdue bills.
- Anger about your car breaking down.
- A near miss on the highway.
- Concern about getting yelled at by the boss because of work that is due but not done.
- The fear of being mugged or raped as you find yourself walking from a building to your car in the middle of a parking lot late at night.
- The fear of snakes as you walk through the woods.

You can also trigger the flight-or-fight response just from the unknowns involved in otherwise positive events, such as:

- holidays
- your vacation
- a dinner party you are giving
- a television or newspaper interview
- applying for a job
- going back to school for the first time in years
- playing golf with people you respect or perceive as intimidating

Externally produced physical damage or injuries that can cause stress include:

- burning yourself
- stubbing your toe
- bumping your head
- extreme hunger

Ill health can also cause stress, including:

- nausea
- headache
- flu/colds
- sinusitis
- arthritis

In fact, any semi-intense worry, fear, pain, or illness can push the button on your flight-or-fight response, triggering the accompanying reactions and keeping you under a continuous level of stress.

It sometimes seems that life was simpler long ago, and it was far easier to separate real danger from danger that was only perceived. Today, with sensory overload coming from a fast-paced life, your flight-or-fight response can be triggered as many as a dozen times a day by stress-producing but certainly not life-threatening situations. The changes that occur in your body when the flight-or-fight response is triggered give you increased strength and stamina in the short run. But in the long run, the price you pay if this response is triggered over and over again is tremendous physical and emotional damage to your system, including a number of stress-related diseases.

The flight-or-fight response is aptly named because these two words describe your choices as your subconscious mind sees them. You can use the extra energy and stamina generated by the response to run or flee, or to stand your ground and fight the source of the problem. Continual stress is created because neither of these responses is usually an acceptable alternative for the situations in which you normally find yourself. For instance, let's say your boss is yelling at you because of something he or she thinks you didn't accomplish or didn't do correctly. You don't relish being yelled at, so your flight-or-fight response is triggered. You want to either run out of the office or punch your boss on the nose.

But what may have been acceptable behavior a hundred thousand years ago will not work in an office environment. If you choose either of these alternatives, you will probably find yourself out of a job. There is often no place to flee or no reasonable way you can win by fighting. So you stifle your flight-or-fight response, bite your lip to keep from saying what is on your mind, and for the rest of the day, as you continue to replay the events in your mind, your body and your mind remain in a state of excess unregulated, unvented energy and stress.

Stress, tension, and anxiety are cumulative, and if they are not dissipated, they produce ever-increasing levels of stress and tension. By continuously triggering stress-producing reactions, your body begins to wear itself down as if it were eating itself from the inside out. You are probably familiar with some of the direct results of high levels of continuing stress:

- emotional outbursts and explosions
- migraine headaches
- high blood pressure
- ulcers
- skin rashes
- insomnia
- depression
- lack of energy, fatigue
- tension headaches
- heart attacks
- nervous twitches
- fear, worry, and apprehension
- clumsiness

But the effects go even beyond the obvious. Continual stress reactions tear down the body's immune system until almost any disease has the opportunity to destroy your health.

Worry, fear, anxiety, tension, and stress are all effects of the way you use your mind and body. Clearly, they are a major obstacle to your personal effectiveness, and they are conditions you want to get rid of. Changing these reactions and your level of stress requires changing the way you use your mind and body. Handled correctly, stress and stress-related symptoms will disappear in direct correlation to the number and frequency of positive changes you make in your life.

Yes, there is also positive stress. For example, when your muscles tense while you're playing tennis or other sports, the temporary tension is positive and under your control, as opposed to the flight-or-fight response, which is an instinct. Even eating a meal puts temporary but minor stress on your body. It is positive in that the increased energy is required to digest the food, unless you overeat. Eating is not normally life-threatening, nor does it trigger the flight-or-fight response, but overeating can burn up to 60 percent of your available energy for up to two hours and can cause a number of stress-related symptoms. In fact, overeating itself is stress-related.

Some say they work better under pressure. Pressure is often caused by worry about not completing a project on time—worry that triggers the flight-or-fight response, providing extra energy to put the system into high gear. But if you anticipate a negative outcome, pressure produces stress. If you anticipate a positive outcome, pressure becomes a form of self-motivation, one of the keys to long-term achievement.

Think of your physical system as a great potential storehouse of energy, like a huge battery storing electricity. Stress is negative energy that, if not properly controlled, can destroy the entire system. Over the years I've used a number of both physical and mental stress-busting strategies. They are simple and practical, and used on a continuing basis, they will keep your system in tip-top shape.

Success Strategy No. 113:

Exercise for twenty minutes to one hour every other day to help drain accumulated stress.

Exercise, real exercise, is the process of inducing your muscles to go through alternating cycles of tension and relaxation. Both muscle tension and fatigue are stress-related symptoms that can affect the entire body. Forcing your muscles from an abnormal state of tension into a more normal state of relaxation helps alleviate the stress. Exercise is a stress buster because your muscles are operating as they were designed to operate, not as a repository for stress. Because it stimulates your entire system and reduces built-up stress, exercise creates far more energy than it uses.

Success Strategy No. 114:

Eliminate negativity from your life.

In 1978 I was teaching a SuperSelf program in Lynchburg, Virginia, and we were discussing negativity as a cause of stress and physical problems. A woman told the group, "I get violently ill every night, and I have for the last ten years. I get sick to my stomach, and I end up vomiting. Night after night, it's always the same."

"All effects have preceding causes," I said. "Let's see if we can make the connection. Tell me exactly what you do from the moment you get home until the time you go to bed, since your illness occurs only during that one period of time."

"Well," she said, "every day I come home from work, feed the cat, put dinner on, and then sit down and watch the news on TV."

"Do you ever miss a broadcast?" I asked her.

"Oh, no," she replied. "I just have to watch the news because I feel so sorry for those people who are starving or in auto accidents, but I thank my lucky stars that it's not me."

"You may be getting mentally and emotionally involved in the events shown on the screen," I told her. "When there's a wreck, you're feeling and experiencing the wreck as if you were there. You're thinking about what might happen to you and how you might suffer, or how your family would feel if you weren't around anymore."

"That's right," she said. "The things that happen to people are just awful."

I asked her to do an experiment. For one week she was not to watch or listen to the news—no matter what was happening or how badly she wanted to. She agreed, and the following week when she returned to class, she said, "I didn't watch the news for a whole week, and you won't believe what happened. No problems. The nausea went away, the upset and the sickness, and for the first time in ten years I experienced positive productive evenings!"

This true story illustrates the immense immediate impact of negativity from any source on your life. Even if negativity does not cause you to throw up or feel noticeably ill, it is eating away at you like an undetected cancer. Negativity causes intense stress. Events in your own life and in the lives of others, if you get sucked into them, affect you for as long as your mind dwells on them, producing emotional and physical stress reactions. Not only can reactions to events affect your life, but they can even control it. That's why you must become aware of and begin to eliminate the negative events, thoughts, emotions, and even the negative people in your life.

Success Strategy No. 115:
Continuously affirm to yourself, "It's just an event."

Your life each day can be viewed as a stream of connected events—some positive and some not so positive. The not-so-positive or negative events can cause great stress, but they have only the stress-producing power over you that you assign to them. Separate your perceptions, opinions, and value judgments of a negative event *from* the event. Affirm to yourself, "It's just an event," and you will avoid triggering stress reactions.

Because time proceeds in one direction only, you do not have the power or the option to change the outcome of an event. But you have total power to choose how or whether you will respond or react to the event, thereby influencing succeeding events and outcomes. It is likely that, because of different beliefs, values, and opinions, four people who see exactly the same event will relate and react to it totally differently. But beliefs, values, and opinions are always in the mind, not in the event. Use that knowledge to separate your emotions from the events that occur in your life.

Probably 80 percent of the stress you experience during your life is created solely by how you use your mind. Learn to use your mind correctly, and your stress level will be automatically reduced. Use your mind as you always have and as those around you do, and your stress level will continue to build up until your body breaks down. Therefore, your goal is to stop reacting mentally and emotionally to what is going on around you, to perceive each new situation as just a neutral event. Then you can choose unemotionally what response to make. Your life stays under your control.

Daily life in the nineties is full of potentially stress-triggering events. The more active you are in your life, the busier you get, the more challenges you accept, and the more goals you set, the greater your potential for stress. Yet your stress level is something over which you can exercise almost total control, should you choose to.

Success Strategy No. 116:

To reduce stress, don't make value judgments about people or events.

A value judgment occurs when you inject strong opinions, beliefs, or feelings into or about an event. Value judgments include: good or bad, just or unjust, right or wrong, pleasant or sickening. None of these value judgments exists in the event itself, but only in how your mind chooses to perceive the event. The moment you begin to inject negative opinions, feelings, or beliefs into the event, you automatically stir up negative stress-producing emotions. Make a negative value judgment about the outcome of an event, an experience, or even another person and you end up upset and full of stress.

Stress can be measured in a biofeedback laboratory with a device called an electromyograph. One interesting stress-intensity test is to ask a subject connected to the electromyograph to put a finger in an empty light socket that is not plugged in. Consciously, the subject knows that there is absolutely no danger. But there's a program in the subconscious mind that associates light sockets with electricity and the placing of a finger in the socket with a very unpleasant shock, even when the socket is not plugged in! The moment the subject puts a finger in that light socket, the needles of the electromyograph go off the scale—total stress. It will take five or ten minutes for the needle to go back down. It is cause and effect. When you make a value judgment about an event, that value judgment will cause undetected stress just as surely as the predictable light socket experiment. Avoid making value judgments about events and you will be able to respond appropriately to any situation—without stress.

Success Strategy No. 117:

To cut stress, disconnect your emotions from the outcome of events.

Another easy way to guarantee stress is to tie your emotions to the outcome of an event. Let's say that for more than a year your goal has been to buy your dream home. You finally find the house, and you apply for a loan for 80 percent of the value. This house means a lot to you, and as a result you begin to hang your emotions on the outcome of your loan application. How? By saying to yourself, "If I get this loan, then I'll really be happy. If I get this loan, then I'll really feel good about myself and my life." If-then statements such as these set up a dependency program in your mind. When you state, "If I get this loan, then I'll really be happy," you have also programmed your mind to believe, "If I don't get the loan, I will be miserable, self-critical, disappointed, and upset." You have set yourself up for a potential onslaught of negative emotions. In truth, it wasn't your intention to put any program into your mind, but that's not how the mind works.

The if-then connection also causes another emotional reaction. During the period until the event period is thirty minutes, thirty days, preprogrammed yourself to experien When you say to yourself, "If the ev happy," you have automatically said to you allow myself to be happy until the event occurs."

Remember, the event itself is neutral. The outcome example will take one of two forms. The loan officer either will or will not grant you the loan. But either way, your emotions have been programmed to react to the loan officer's decision. You have tied yourself emotionally into the outcome of an event over which you have no control. You have taken a neutral event and made it into a big emotional deal.

In reality, it's just an event. But as soon as you hang your emotions on the outcome of an event, you have given that event power to control your emotions from the present moment to the outcome and even beyond. You have eliminated from your experience the potential of a positive, stress-free state of mind while you are patiently waiting for the result. Moreover, you have put yourself in a no-win situation. Why? Because you can get only one of two possible answers from the loan officer. If the answer is yes, all your stress and negative emotions have been a total waste of your time and energy, and that will certainly diminish whatever positive emotions and reactions you may have. If it is no, your level of stress and negative emotions will certainly increase, and you will probably be reluctant to subject yourself to such a stressful situation again.

On the other hand, disconnecting your emotions from the outcome of an event creates a win-win situation. If the outcome is positive, your emotional reactions will be positive, undiminished by any residue of stress or negativity. You have taken one more step in the direction of your dreams and goals and are ready to take the next step. If the outcome is negative, it may be a temporary setback, but you will have an undiminished store of energy, self-confidence, and positive emotions

[t]hat will propel you to find or create opportunities and experi[en]ces that will turn out in your favor and take you in the direction you want to go.

Success Strategy No. 118:

To disconnect your emotions from the outcome of events, state preferences instead of expectations or demands.

It's all in the way you use your mind. The winning mindset is "I prefer to get the loan, but if the answer is no, no big deal. I'll choose another alternative." Simply thinking and using the word "prefer" allows you to drop the if-then emotional connection to the outcome of events. It is a powerful stress buster and the best way to keep your emotions in balance. You have said to your mind, "My first choice would be to get the loan, but if I don't, no problem. I will simply assess my alternatives and without emotion, disappointment, or self-criticism choose another. I will not be denied."

You can begin at this moment to monitor your thoughts for potentially damaging and stressful emotional connections to the outcome of events. Remember, all events themselves are neutral. The potential emotional damage is done solely by how you view and react to each event in your mind. In the loan example, the loan officer is neutral and unemotional about the outcome of your application; the officer doesn't get mad if you don't qualify or think you're a hero if you do. You're just a number. There is no emotion in the event or process. Therefore, you are totally responsible for your emotions and emotional balance, not the loan officer, the mortgage company, or your unlucky past.

All emotion, including stress, is produced by your mind's perception, and in this case the if-then outcome connection. From now on when you catch yourself thinking or saying, "I will be happy if . . . ," "I will be happy when . . . ," "He'd better . . . ," "She'd better . . . ," "They'd better . . . ," or "They'd better not . . . ," run up a red flag on your mental flagpole as a signal that danger is lurking. Then simply change the thoughts in your mind from demands or expectations to preferences. Like events themselves, preferences are neutral and do not trigger negative emotions even when unmet. Unmet demands and expectations trigger stress and negative emotions. Unmet preferences trigger unemotional desire to find alternatives.

If you have created a demand or ultimatum in your mind and the answer you get is "no," you become angry at others and critical of yourself, feeling that you are an unworthy person. You take the "no" personally instead of using it as feedback and taking corrective action to achieve your goals and objectives. Self-doubt and frustration produce inaction, a condition your life's plan cannot afford. When you demand a "yes" and the answer is "no," there is also greater potential for disappointment, another of the great stress producers. Disappointment is the product of unmet expectations or demands. The fear of disappointment can also lead to increased inaction.

Remember the last time you placed such great importance on the outcome of an event that you even avoided calling to find out the outcome in order to avoid potential disappointment? At least as long as I don't know whether I got the home loan (the car loan, the date, the job, or the special airfare I need for my vacation), you thought, I'm still in the ball game. However, until you got the answer, you inadvertently placed yourself under increased stress and stopped your life in its tracks. Your mind was focused on the potential outcome of an event or decision that had already occurred or had been made, but of which you were unaware. If you demand a "yes," you are setting yourself up for disappointment. If you expect to be disappointed, you almost certainly will be.

When the outcome of an event is set up as a preference instead of a requirement, you won't experience the fear of disappointment and will have the strength and will to check the outcome immediately. Your emotions won't be riding on the answer. The answer therefore influences only the next step you choose to take. Remember the successful salesman's creed: "I view every no as simply one step closer to a yes." In truth, nothing is a big deal. It's only an event. On the day when the decision about the loan is supposed to be made, call at your earliest opportunity and not at your latest. You will avoid disappointment, you will avoid worry and stress, and you will have the answer you need that will enable you to plan your next step: Call the movers or call another loan company.

Stress is actually an unnatural condition to the human system. The natural state is one of relaxation. Therefore, stress is a condition you must cause, and it is caused by the way you use your mind and body. Pick up a rubber band. Put it around your fingers but apply no pressure (see drawing on next page). Notice that the rubber band is in a state of balance or equilibrium. However, if you pull your fingers apart using the force of your muscles, you stretch the rubber band. It is under stress and no longer in equilibrium. But the rubber band is also pulling against your fingers, exerting pressure and keeping the muscles in your hands and arms tense.

Your mind and body work like a rubber band. In their normal state of equilibrium, there is a lack of stress and tension. In order to create stress and tension, you must not only pull your mind/body system away from its normal state of equilibrium, you must also continue to apply pressure to hold it there. Stress is not a permanent condition. Unwanted, prolonged stress is the result of the continual misuse and misunderstanding of your mind/body system. Therefore, getting rid of stress is as much a process of what you stop doing as it is

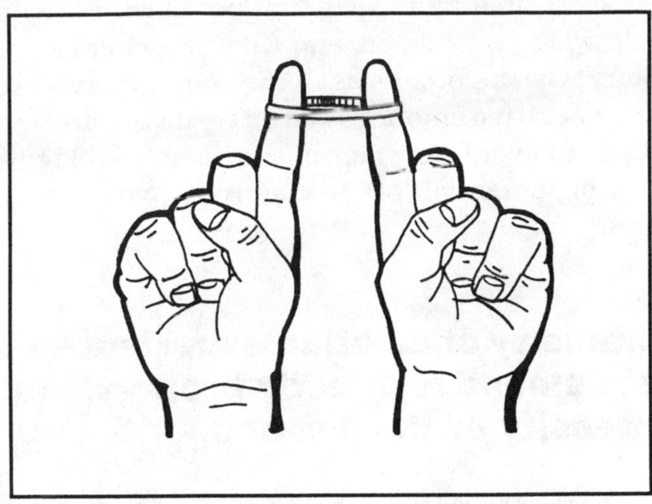

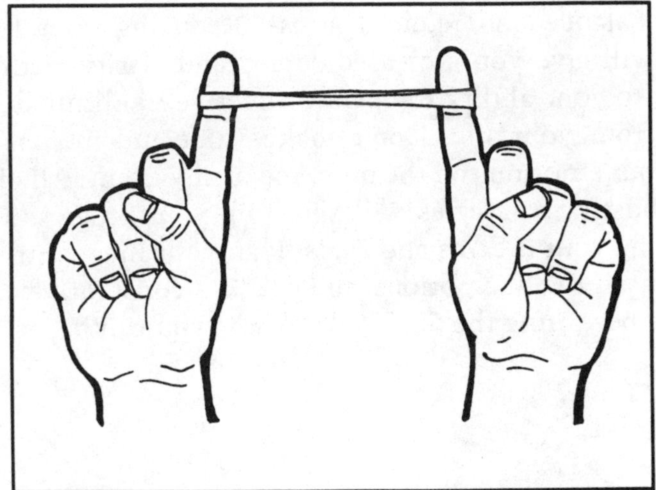

what you begin to do. Without thoughts and actions that continually produce stress in your mind and body, the system will automatically move toward balance.

There is an additional downside to attaching expectations to outcomes. Even if the outcome is positive, the thrill is gone. If you've hung your emotions on the outcome of an event, any satisfaction to be derived from a positive outcome has been dissipated by the expectation. Even if the outcome is exactly what you wanted, you won't experience a thrill in the victory. On the other side of the coin, however, you will experience negative emotions and stress if the outcome is one you sought to avoid. As you can see, there's no big win, but there is a big potential loss in connecting your emotions to outcomes.

The intensity of emotion experienced by an unmet demand is directly proportional to the intensity of the demand.

Preference is your magic word. It opens the doors to emotional balance and reduced stress. Reducing your level of stress will give you increased energy and clarity of thought, adding to your ability to operate effectively. Eliminate negativity from your life. Don't make value judgments. Don't hang your emotions on the outcome of any event. All of these stress-busting strategies will speed up your progress toward achieving your dreams and goals. Plan your life, control your time, master your emotions, and you will constantly be in the state of becoming the SuperSelf I know you can be.

Epilogue

There you have it—a complete system for getting your life, your time, and your emotions under your control. Since every hour of your time is important, every strategy you have learned is important to implement and practice in the exciting, rewarding experience of becoming your SuperSelf.

As your SuperSelf you will be a living, breathing powerhouse of accomplishment and achievement. You will create a new way of life and living. You will not look back. You will keep all of your attention focused on your life's blueprint, moving forward day by day, step by step toward the goals you have set for yourself and the realization of your dreams. You will use the Success Strategies you have learned in the pages of this book time and time again until they become habits. You will take what appears to be failure in stride, using it as feedback and as a reminder of where you have been and where you are going. You will be self-confident, not self-critical. Make my Success Strategies an integral part of your daily life, and you will double your personal effectiveness. They are the operations manual for your life. They put you in control of your time, your emotions, and the events and experiences that occur all around you. With your SuperSelf in the driver's seat and these strategies as your guide, your life will reach the only destination possible—success.

About the Author

CHARLES J. GIVENS, the famous entrepreneur, media personality, bestselling author, and self-made multimillionaire, created the largest and most successful financial planning and educational organization in the world, the Charles J. Givens Organization, with 650,000 members. In his personal life, he has already made most of his dreams a reality—including 180 of the 188 dreams on his original Dreams List; and, most important, living happily with his wife and family in central Florida.

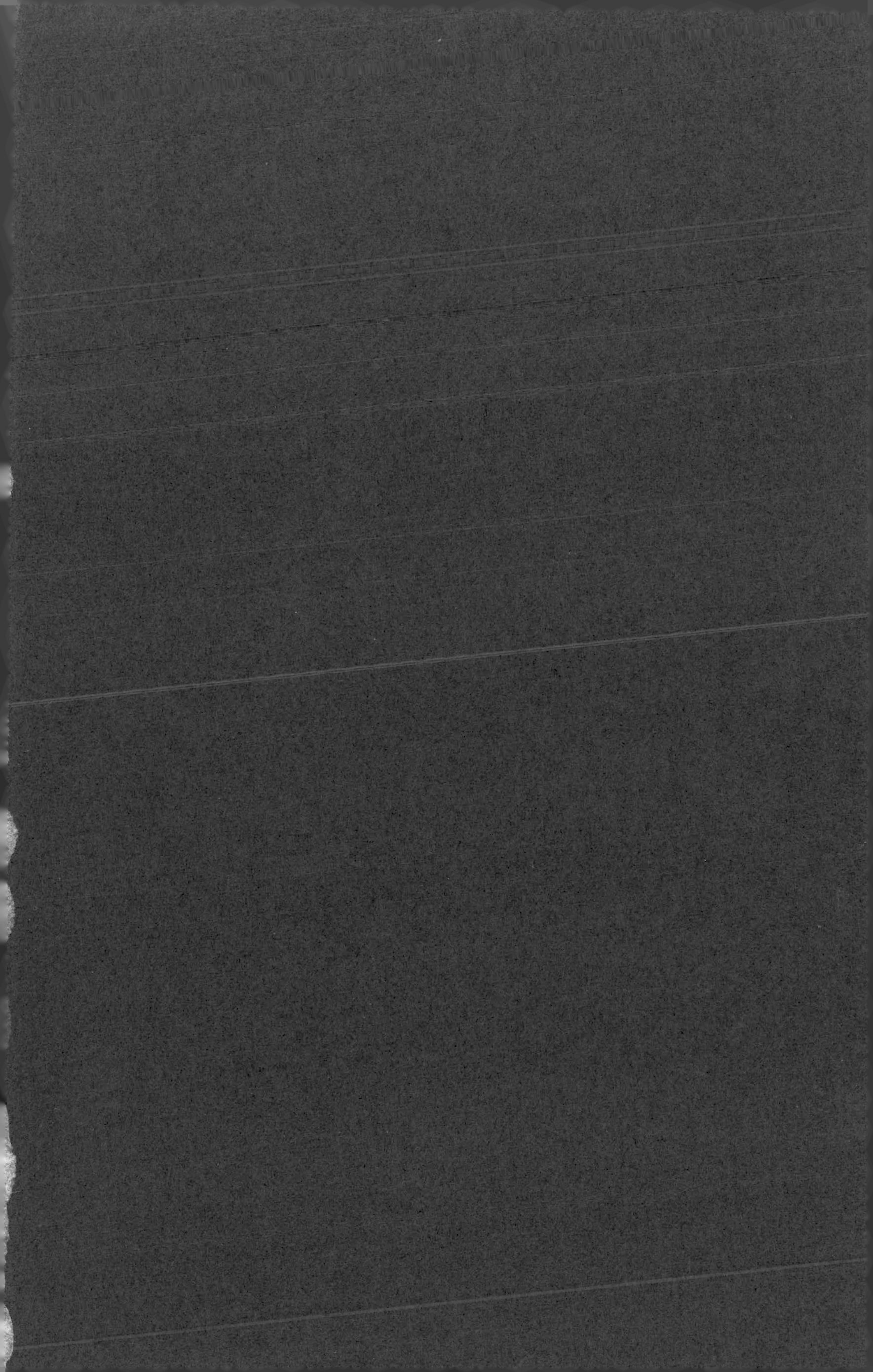